Jane Irwin
Storyteller

Jane Irwin and Jeff Berndt
Co-Creators

 Published by Fiery Studios, PO Box 131133, Ann Arbor, Michigan 48113-1133. fierystudios@hotmail.com http://www.vogelein.com
Second Printing, February 2004. Printed in Canada by Quebecor Lebonfon. ISBN 0-9743110-0-6

Vögelein

CLOCKWORK FAERIE

Jane Irwin
with
Jeff Berndt

Foreward by
Jennifer M. Contino

Fiery Studios

For Mom --

*Who taught me
what it means to
be strong.*

Foreward

When you're little, it's easy to believe in fairy tales and happily ever afters -- those imaginative escapes are encouraged by everyone around you. However, as you mature, the fairy dust and pixie tales are replaced by more realistic offerings and the world of make-believe becomes harder and harder to access. People look at you funny when you're walking around with stuffed animals in one hand and a purse in the other. It's not universally acceptable to have imaginary friends once you start meeting "real" people.

Somewhere along the way everyone grows up and looks for something different. Magic beanstalks, fat men in red suits hanging around with elves, bunnies delivering eggs: as you grow and learn more about the world, those concepts become harder and harder to grasp. But still, a part of us misses childhood, misses imaginary stories, misses believing in the impossible, and yearns for a fanciful tale that appeals to the best of both worlds -- our adult sensibilities and the elements of childhood a lot of us miss.

Jane Irwin's Vögelein is one such creature! It's a delightful series that combines elements of fantasy with legend and lore, set in a modern time with a likable cast, magical beings, and lots of intrigue -- and contains all the right ingredients for a powerful story that bridges the gap between children and adults. Vögelein slowly unfolds and allows readers the chance to experience a tale that quickly becomes more than just beautifully painted images on a page.

Much like her creator, Vögelein is a lot more than meets the eye.

-- Jennifer M. Contino

- Chapter One -

Wanderers Nachtlied

Über allen Gipfeln
Ist Ruh,
In allen Wipfeln
Spürest du
Kaum einen Hauch;
Die Vögelein Schweigen im Walde.
Warte nur, balde
Ruhest du auch.

Wanderer's Nocturne

Over all the mountain peaks
is quiet,
in all the tree tops
you sense hardly a breath;
The little birds are silent in the woods.
Only wait, soon you will also be silent.

--Goethe
--Translation by
Dr. Amanda Eubanks - Winkler

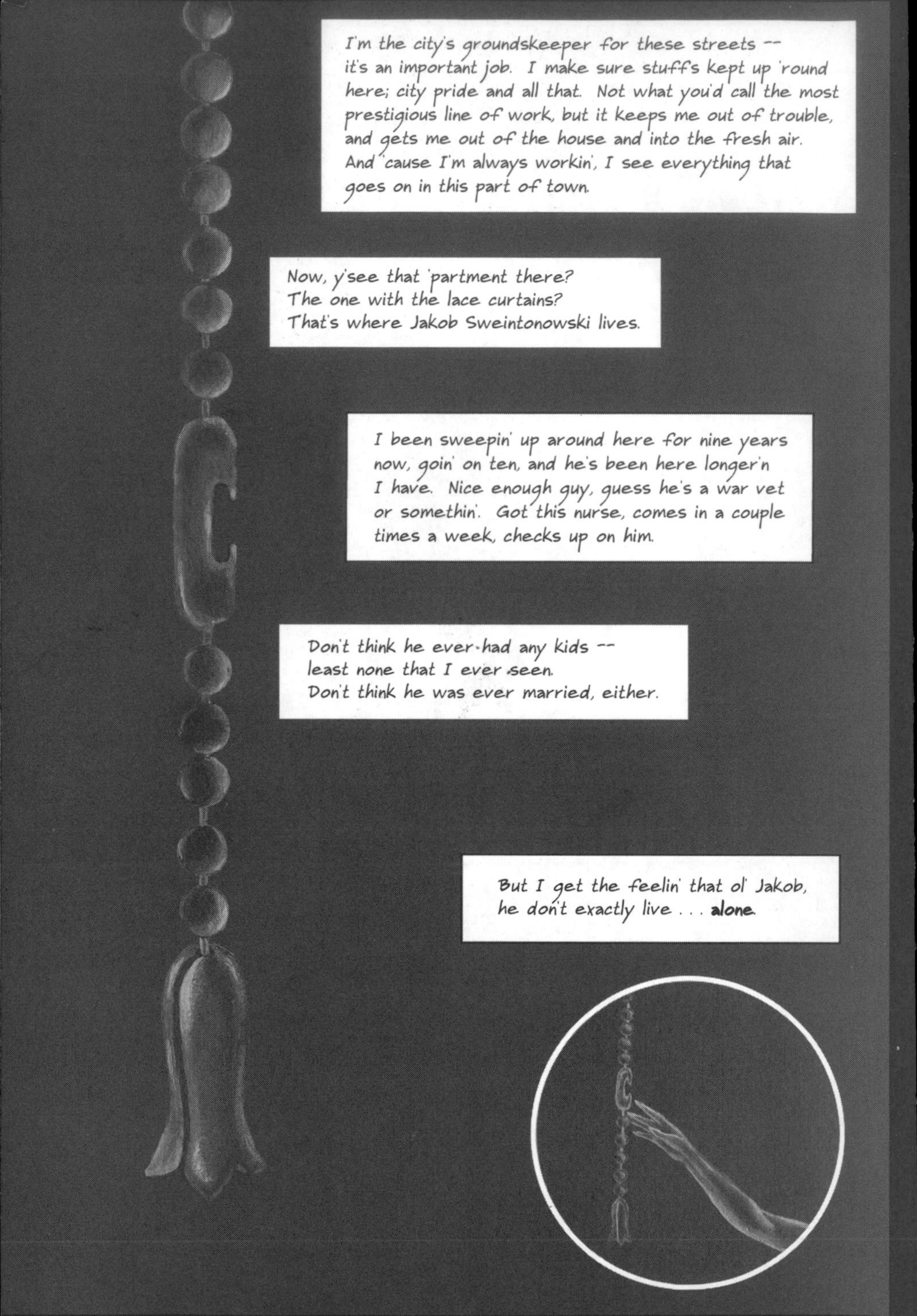
I'm the city's groundskeeper for these streets -- it's an important job. I make sure stuff's kept up 'round here; city pride and all that. Not what you'd call the most prestigious line of work, but it keeps me out of trouble, and gets me out of the house and into the fresh air. And 'cause I'm always workin', I see everything that goes on in this part of town.
Now, y'see that 'partment there? The one with the lace curtains? That's where Jakob Sweintonowski lives.
I been sweepin' up around here for nine years now, goin' on ten, and he's been here longer'n I have. Nice enough guy, guess he's a war vet or somethin'. Got this nurse, comes in a couple times a week, checks up on him.
Don't think he ever had any kids -- least none that I ever seen. Don't think he was ever married, either.
But I get the feelin' that ol' Jakob, he don't exactly live . . . **alone**.

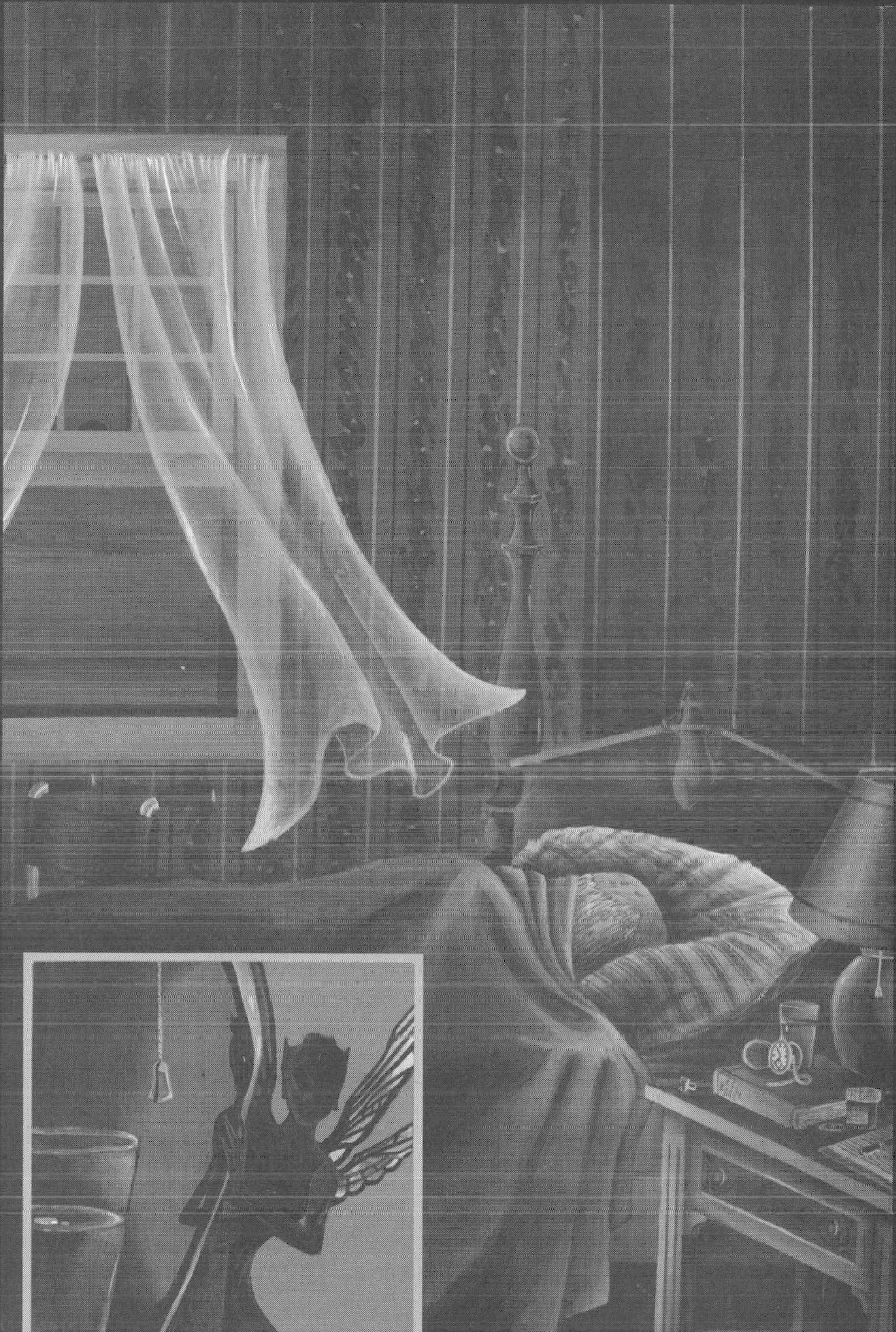

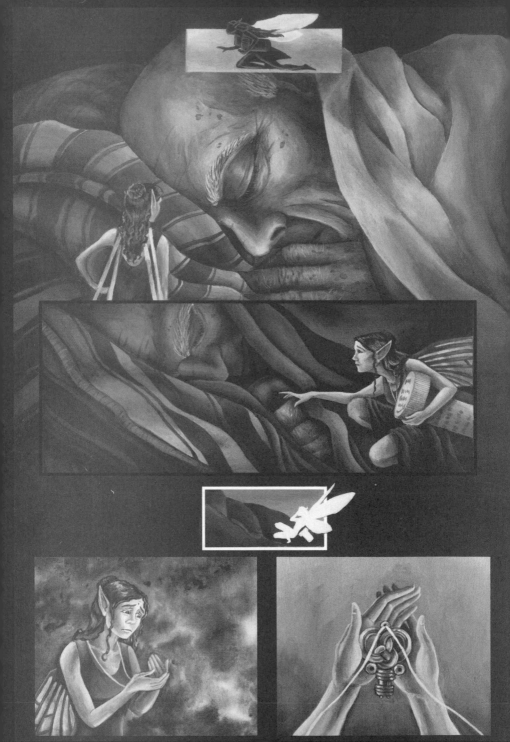

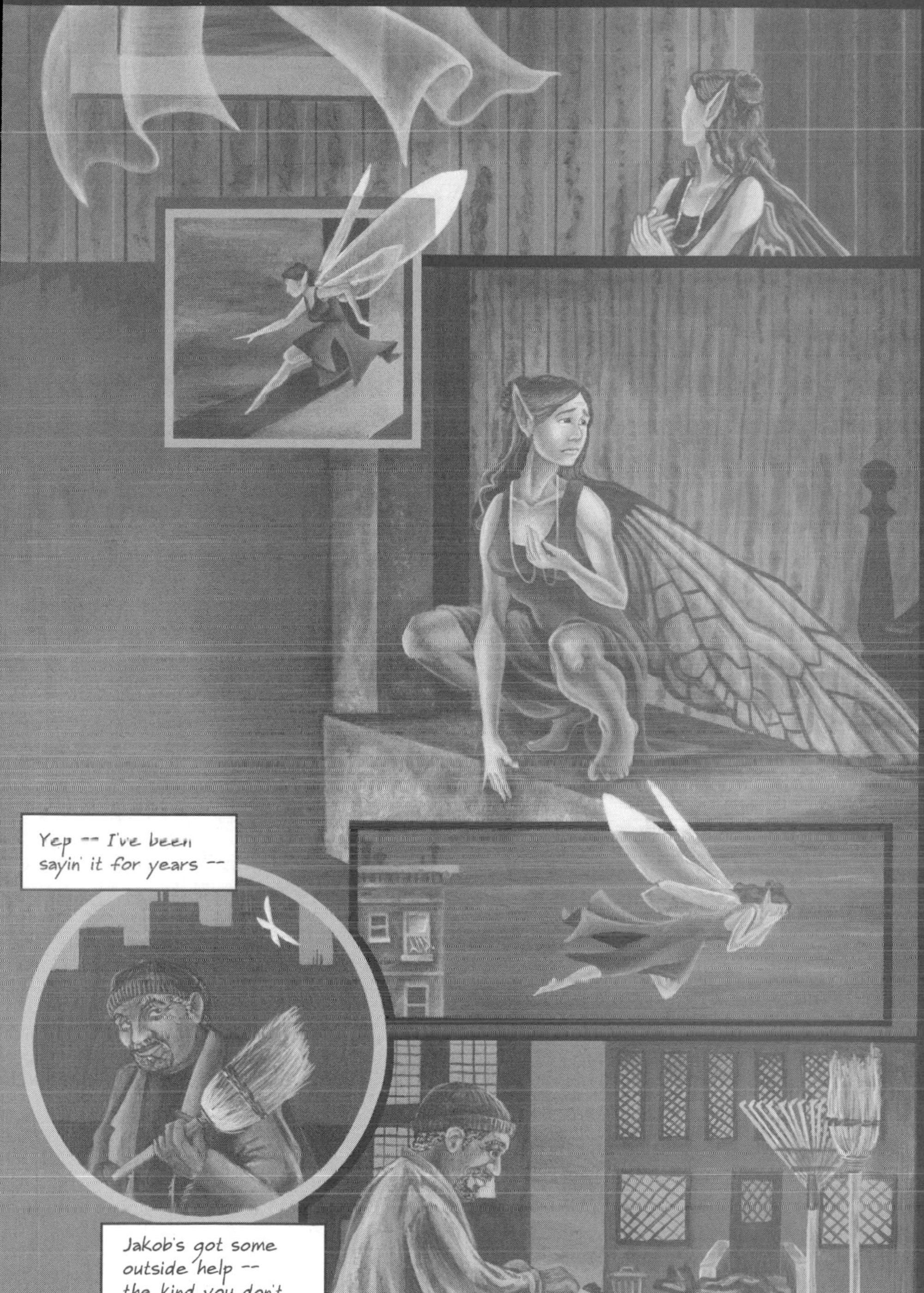
Yep -- I've been sayin' it for years --
Jakob's got some outside help -- the kind you don't come by every day.

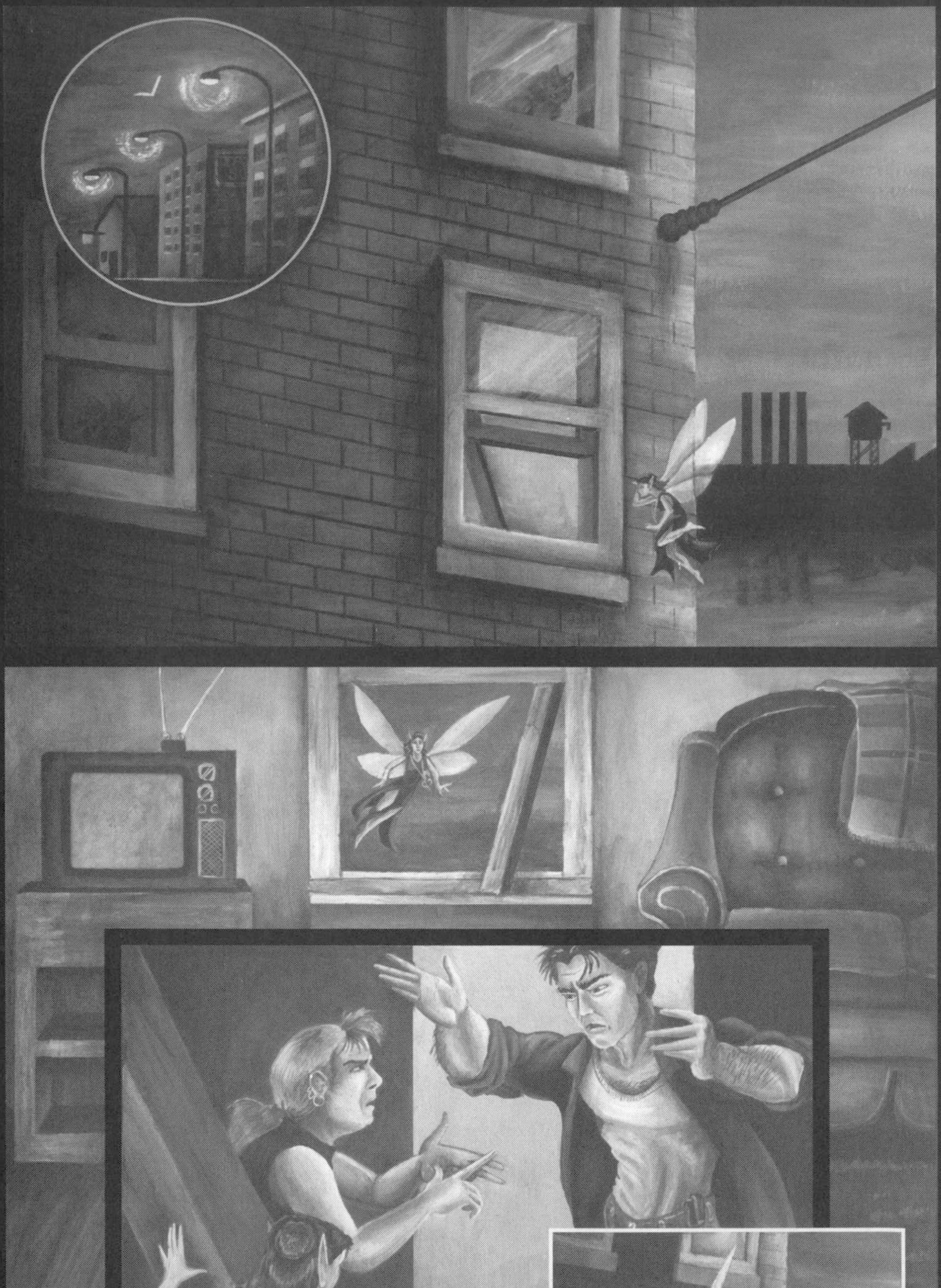

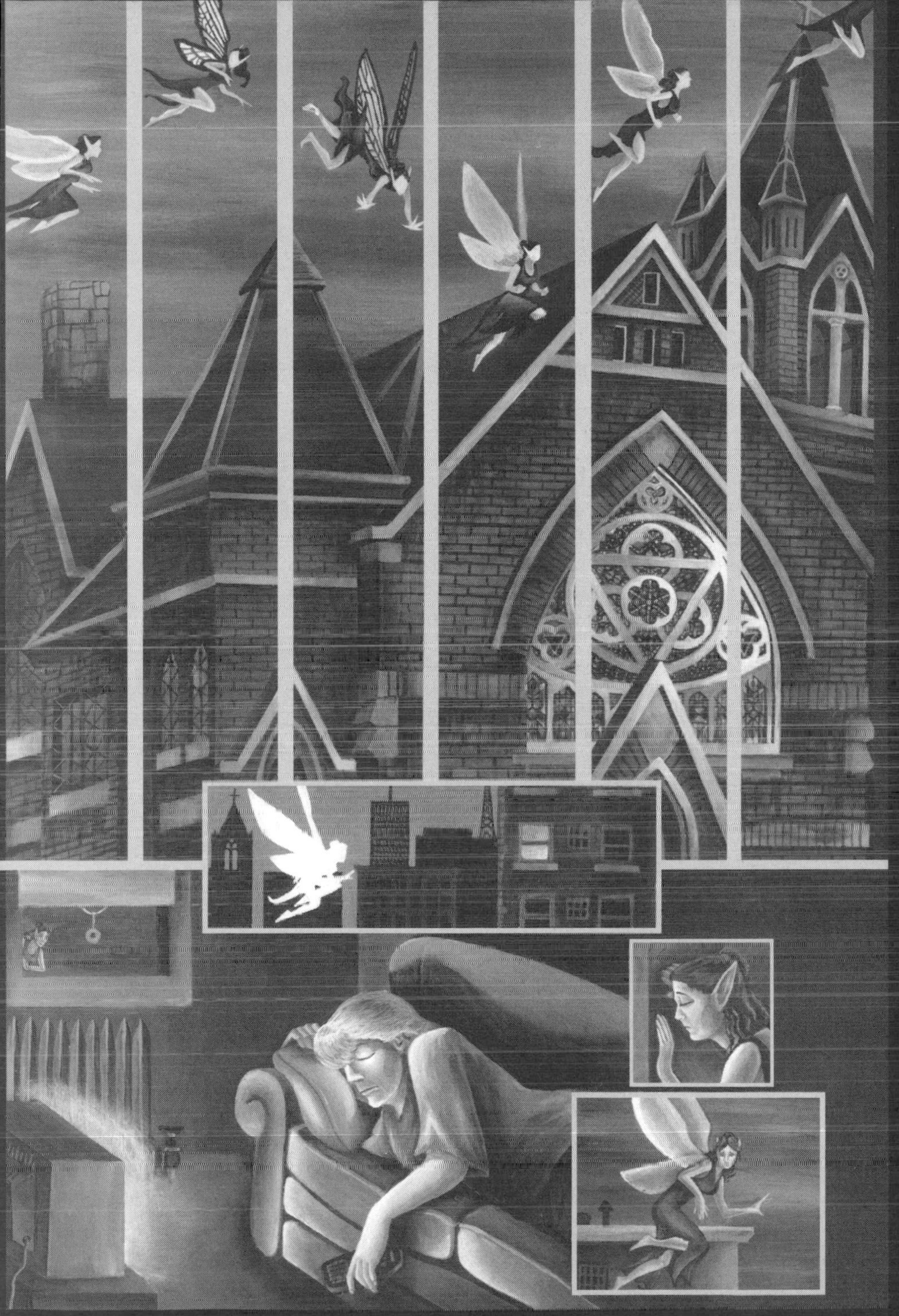

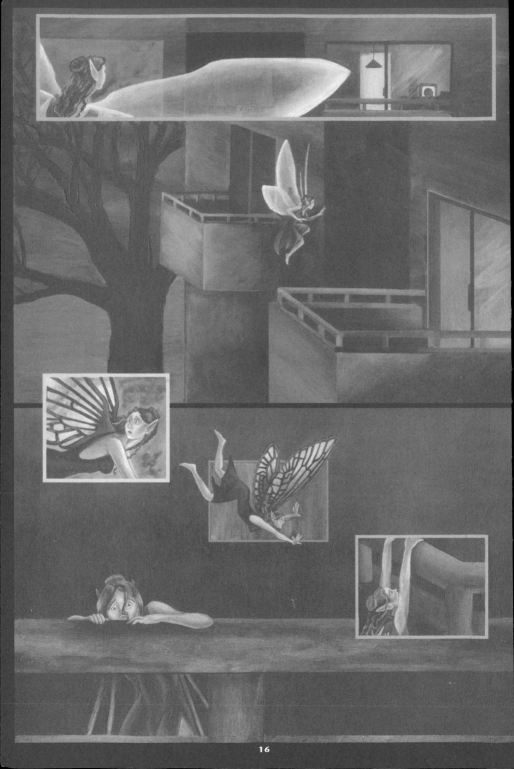

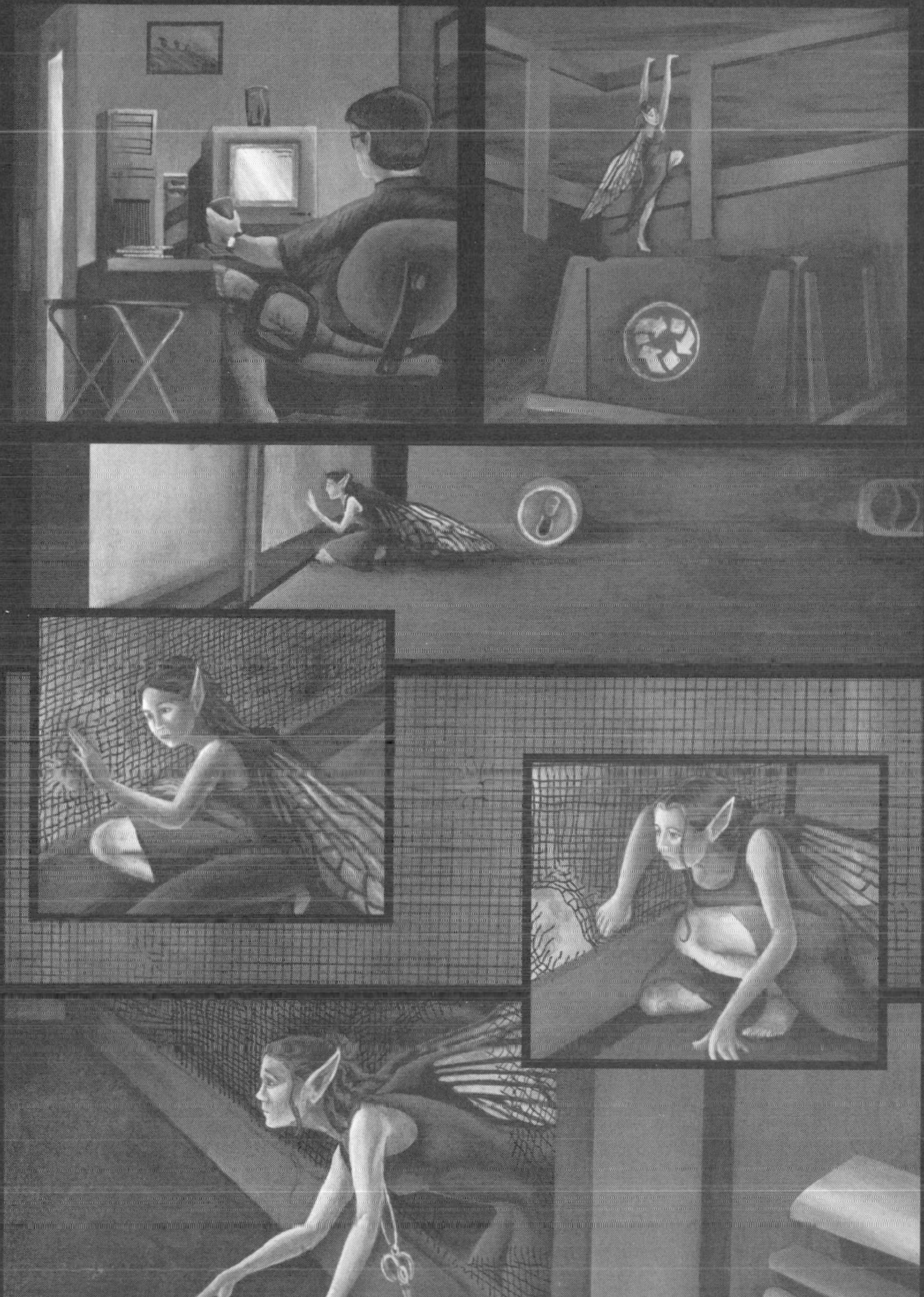

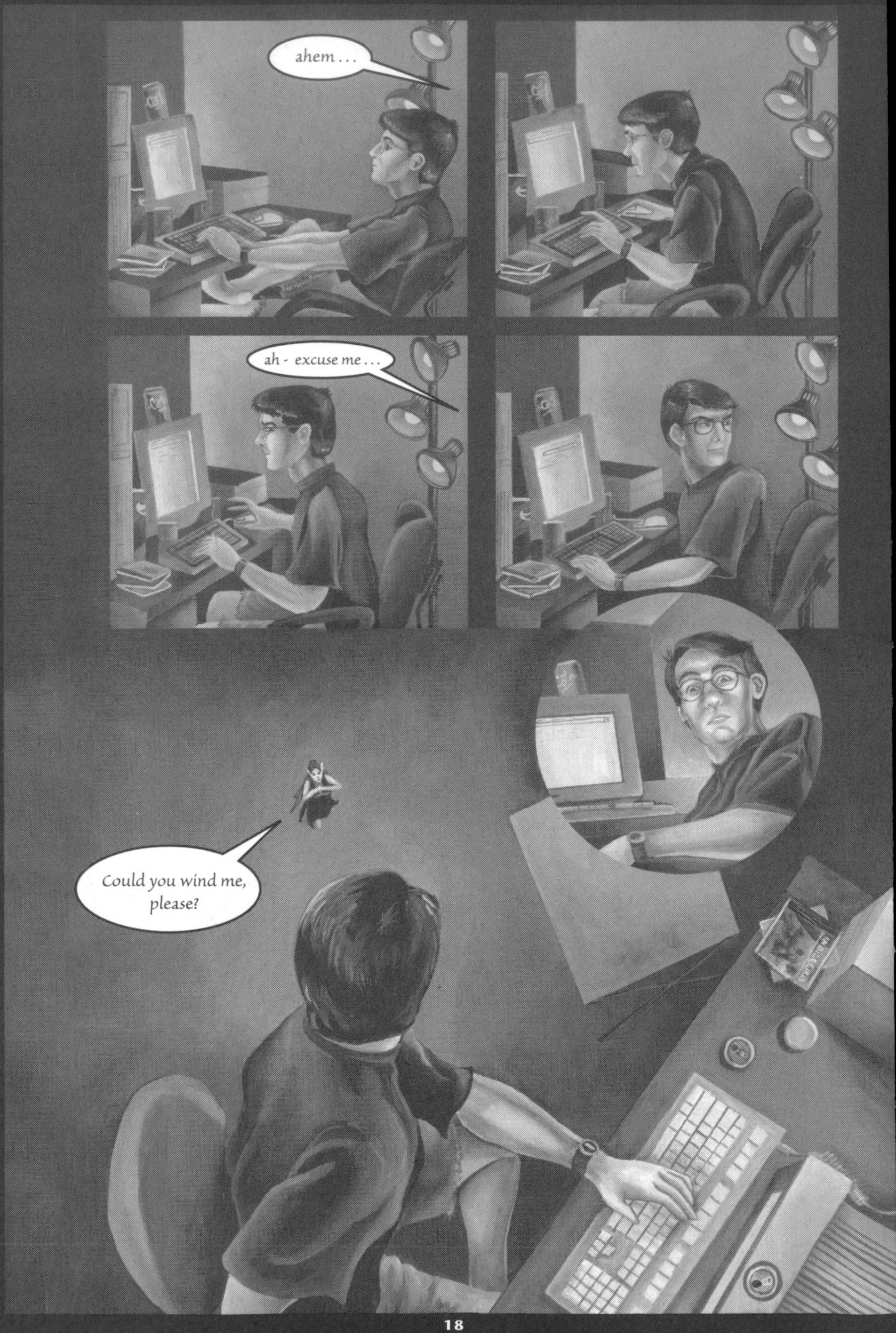
ahem . . .
ah - excuse me . . .
Could you wind me, please?

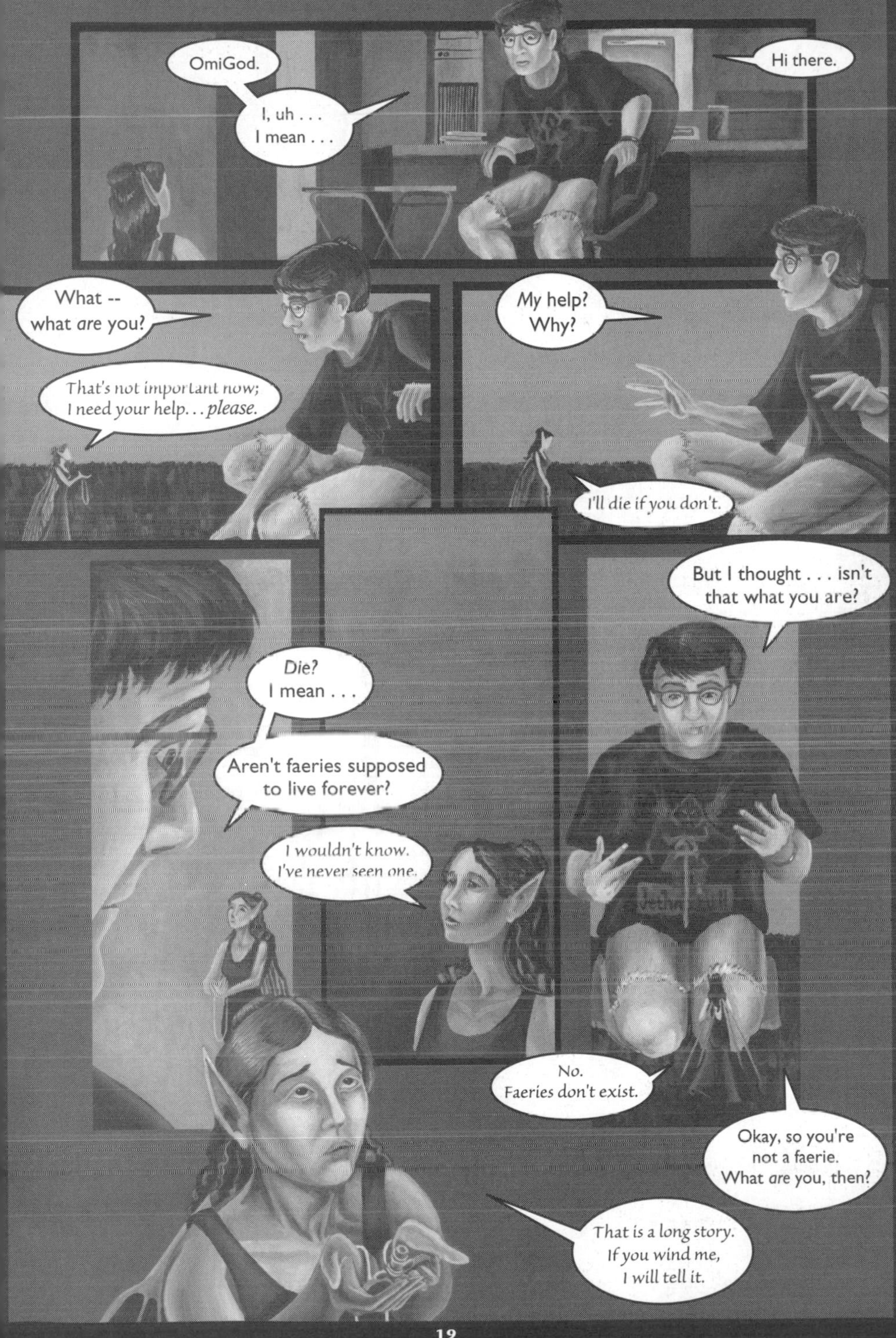
OmiGod.
I, uh . . . I mean . . .
Hi there.
What -- what *are* you?
That's not important now; I need your help. . . *please.*
My help? Why?
I'll die if you don't.
Die? I mean . . .
Aren't faeries supposed to live forever?
I wouldn't know. I've never seen one.
But I thought . . . isn't that what you are?
No. Faeries don't exist.
Okay, so you're not a faerie. What *are* you, then?
That is a long story. If you wind me, I will tell it.

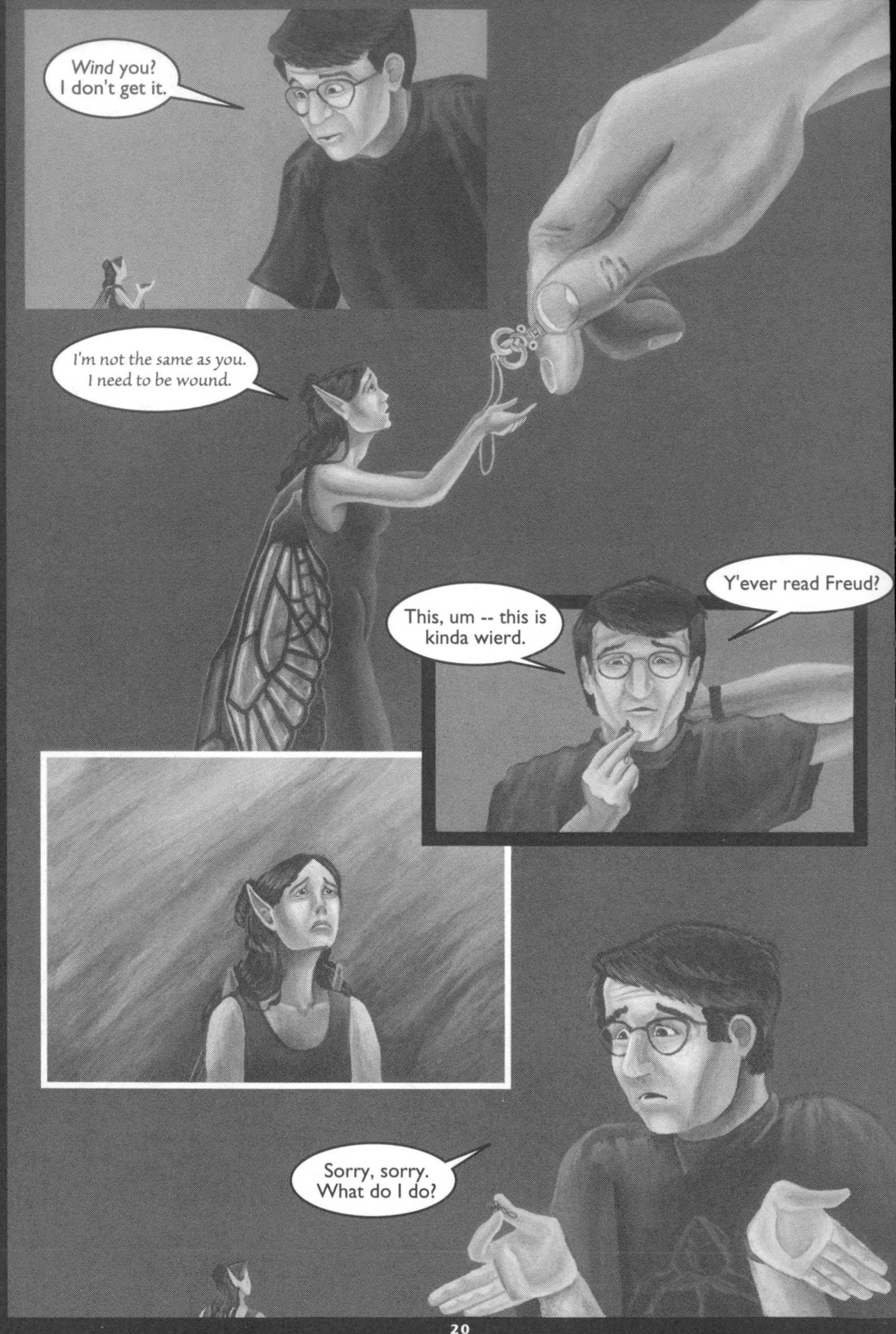
Wind you?
I don't get it.
I'm not the same as you.
I need to be wound.
This, um -- this is kinda wierd.
Y'ever read Freud?
Sorry, sorry.
What do I do?

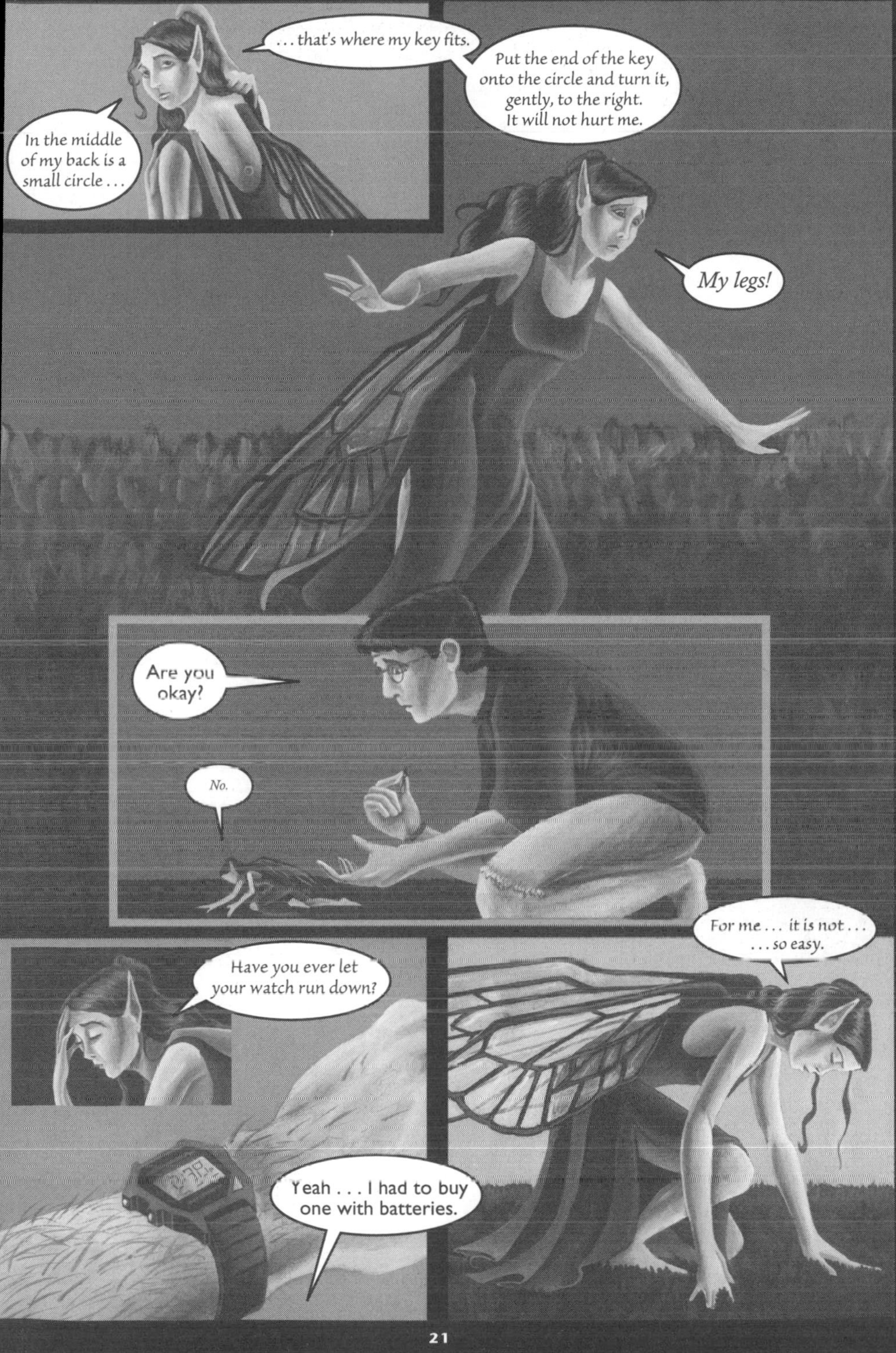
In the middle of my back is a small circle . . .
. . . that's where my key fits.
Put the end of the key onto the circle and turn it, gently, to the right. It will not hurt me.
My legs!
Are you okay?
No.
Have you ever let your watch run down?
Yeah . . . I had to buy one with batteries.
For me . . . it is not . . . . . . so easy.

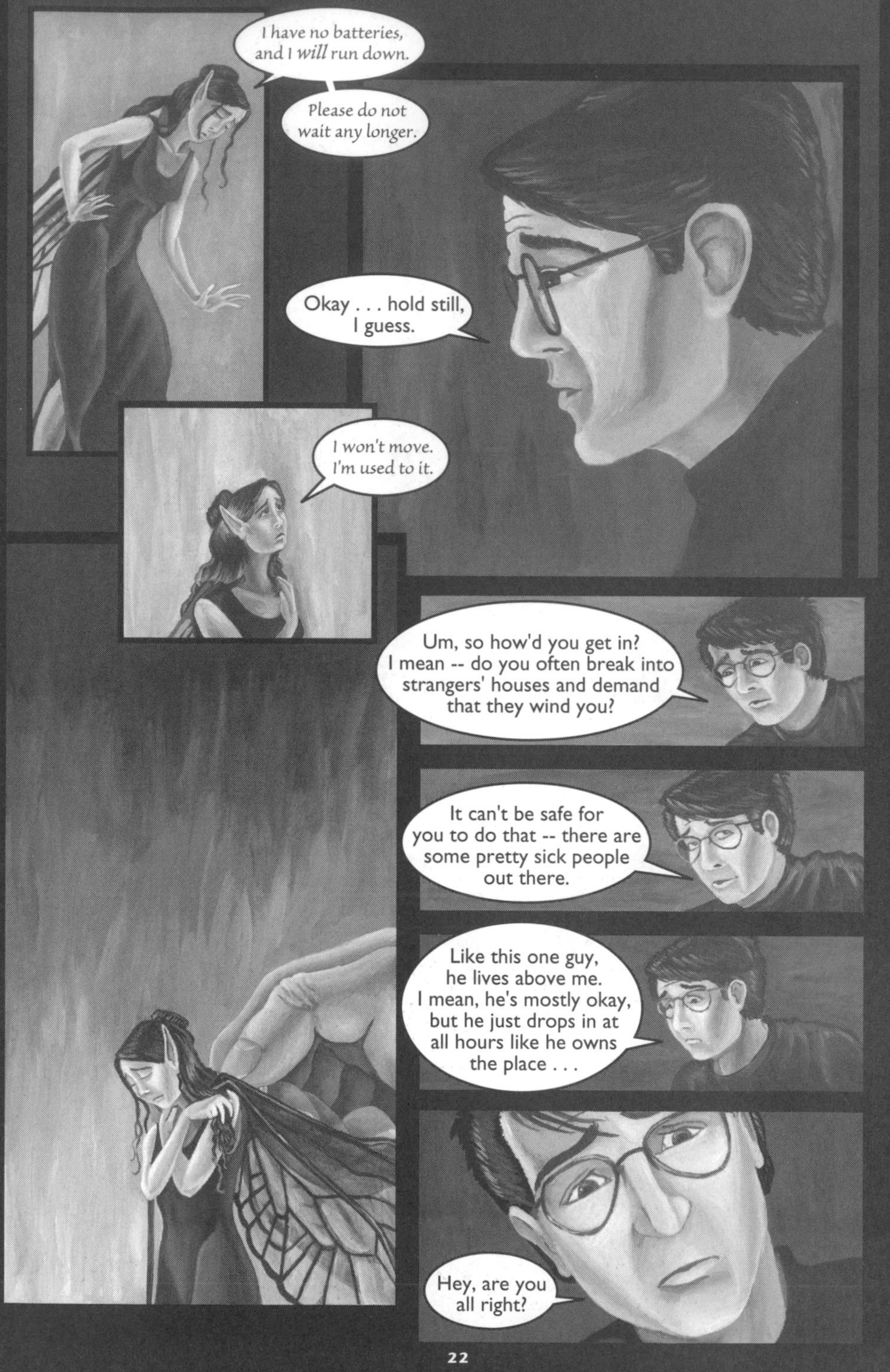
I have no batteries, and I *will* run down.
Please do not wait any longer.
Okay . . . hold still, I guess.
I won't move. I'm used to it.
Um, so how'd you get in? I mean -- do you often break into strangers' houses and demand that they wind you?
It can't be safe for you to do that -- there are some pretty sick people out there.
Like this one guy, he lives above me. I mean, he's mostly okay, but he just drops in at all hours like he owns the place . . .
Hey, are you all right?

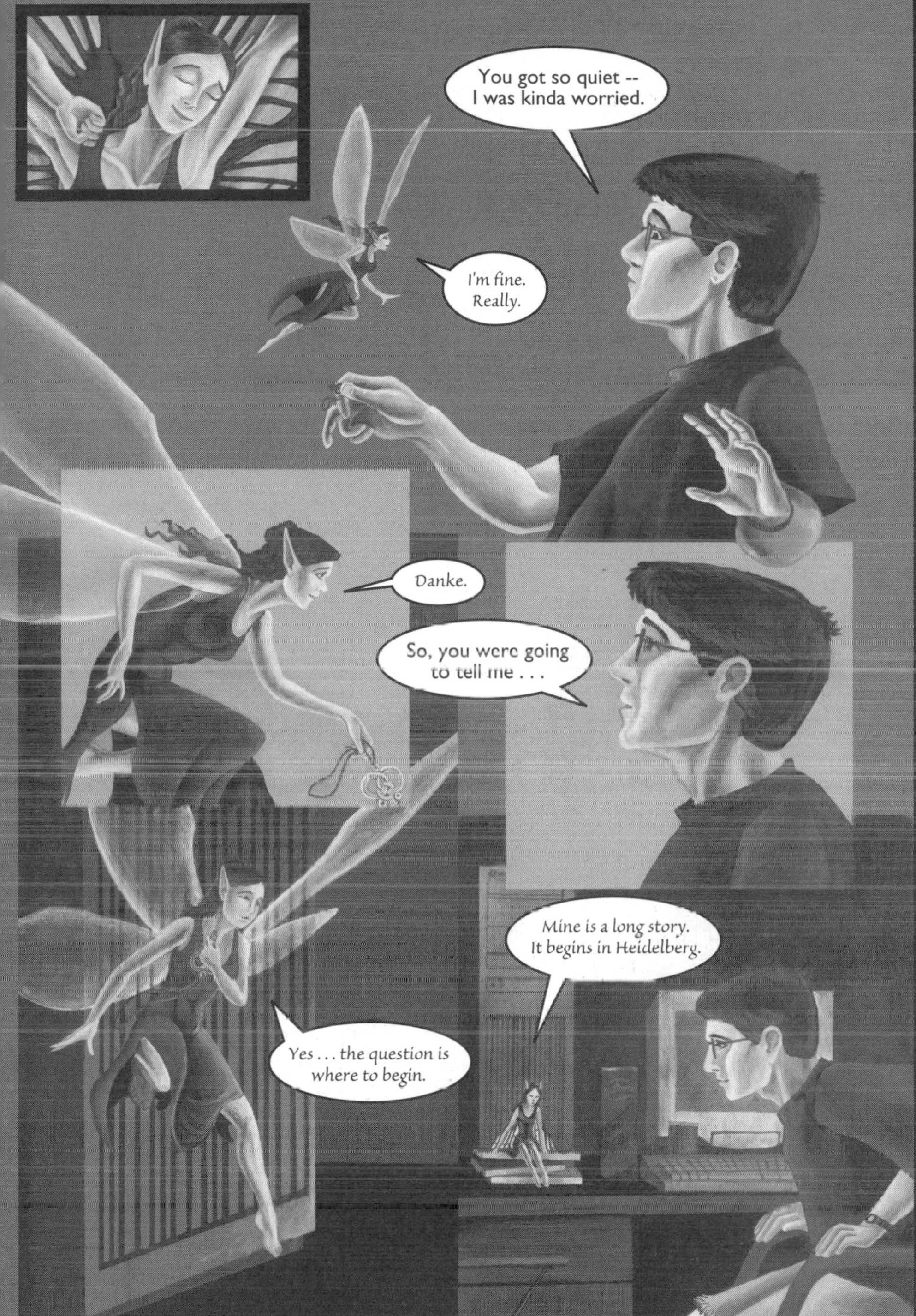
You got so quiet -- I was kinda worried.
I'm fine. Really.
Danke.
So, you were going to tell me . . .
Yes . . . the question is where to begin.
Mine is a long story. It begins in Heidelberg.

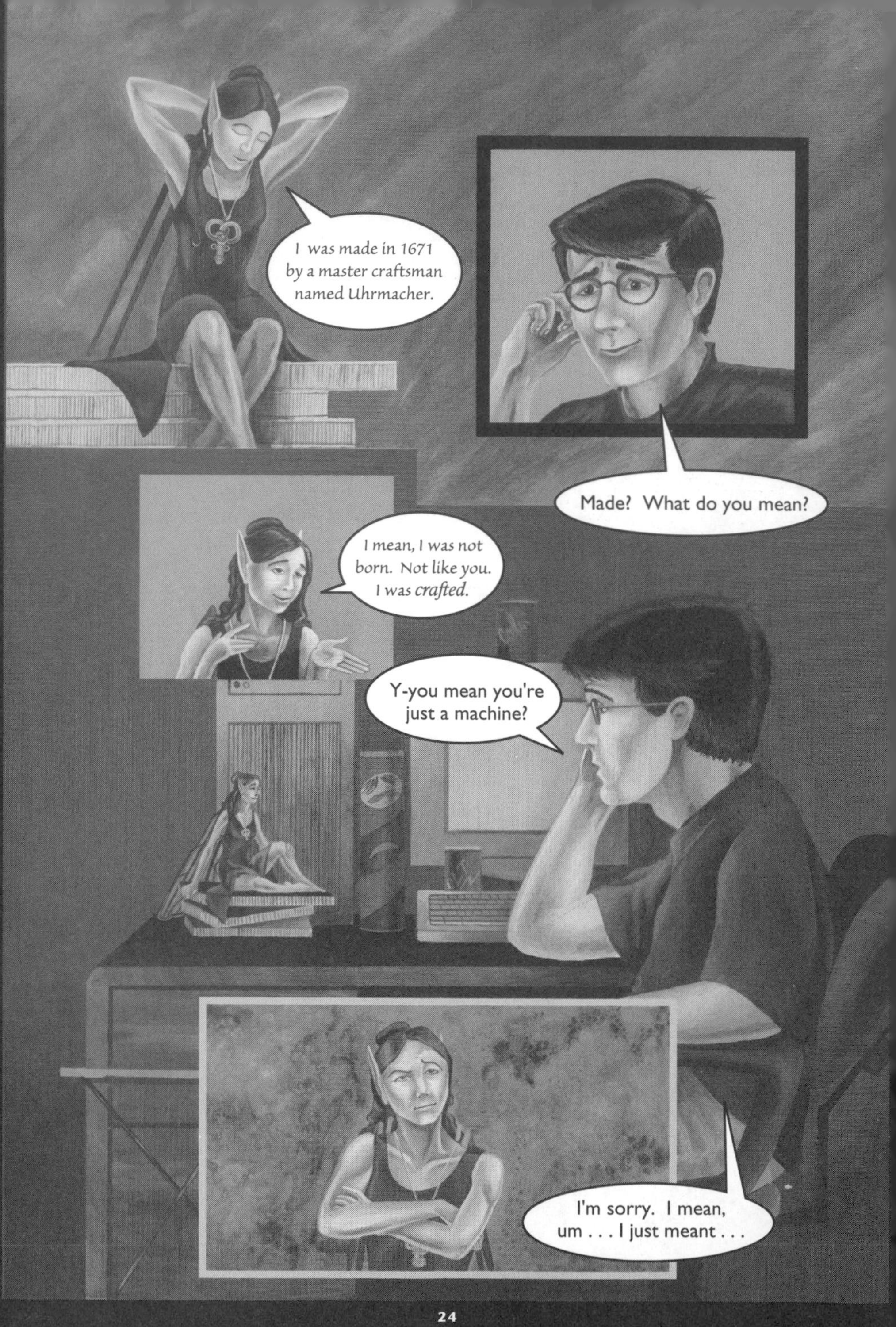
I was made in 1671 by a master craftsman named Uhrmacher.
Made? What do you mean?
I mean, I was not born. Not like you. I was *crafted*.
Y-you mean you're just a machine?
I'm sorry. I mean, um . . . I just meant . . .

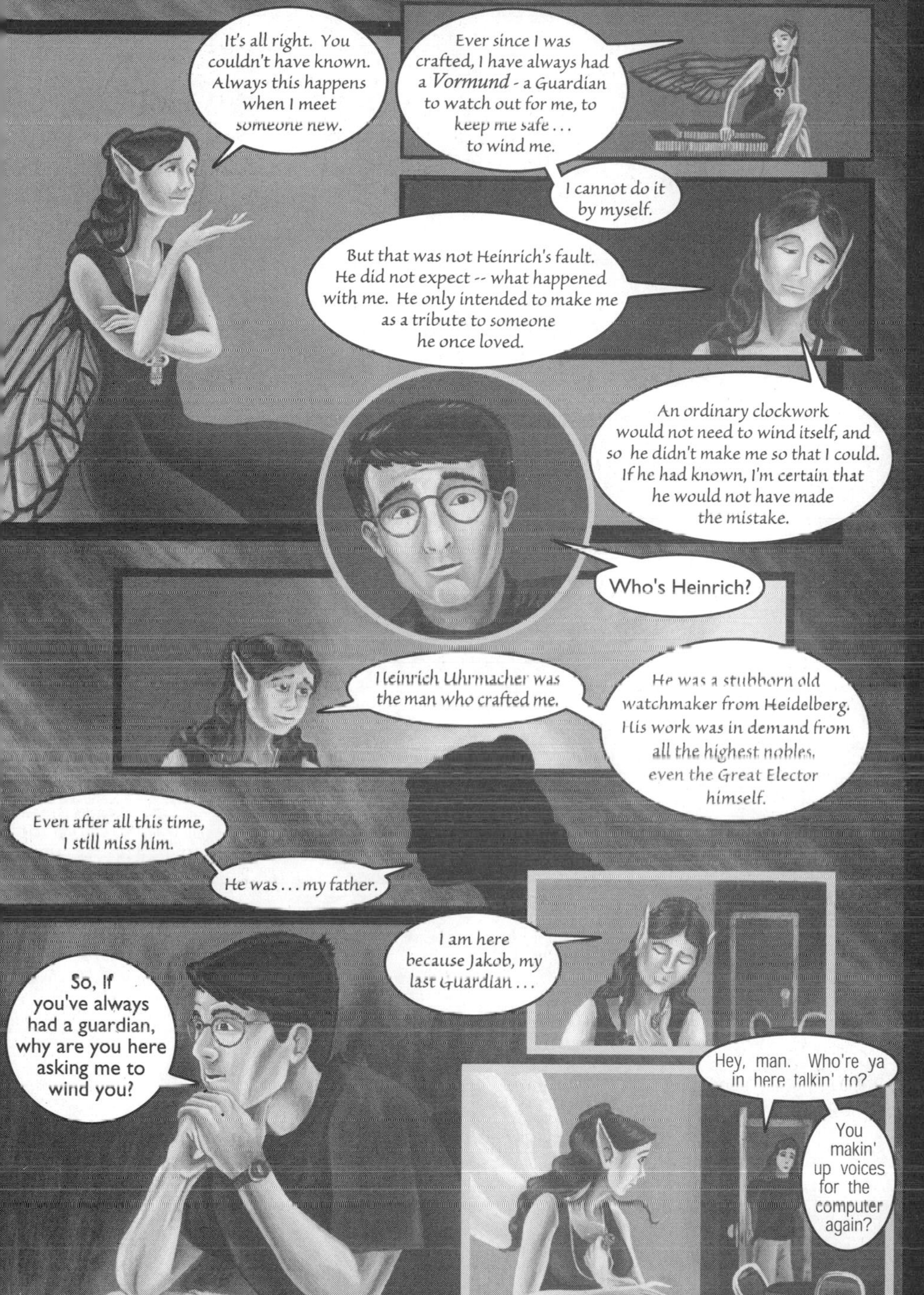
It's all right. You couldn't have known. Always this happens when I meet someone new.
Ever since I was crafted, I have always had a *Vormund* - a Guardian to watch out for me, to keep me safe . . . to wind me.
I cannot do it by myself.
But that was not Heinrich's fault. He did not expect -- what happened with me. He only intended to make me as a tribute to someone he once loved.
An ordinary clockwork would not need to wind itself, and so he didn't make me so that I could. If he had known, I'm certain that he would not have made the mistake.
Who's Heinrich?
Heinrich Uhrmacher was the man who crafted me.
He was a stubborn old watchmaker from Heidelberg. His work was in demand from all the highest nobles, even the Great Elector himself.
Even after all this time, I still miss him.
He was . . . my father.
So, If you've always had a guardian, why are you here asking me to wind you?
I am here because Jakob, my last Guardian . . .
Hey, man. Who're ya in here talkin' to?
You makin' up voices for the computer again?

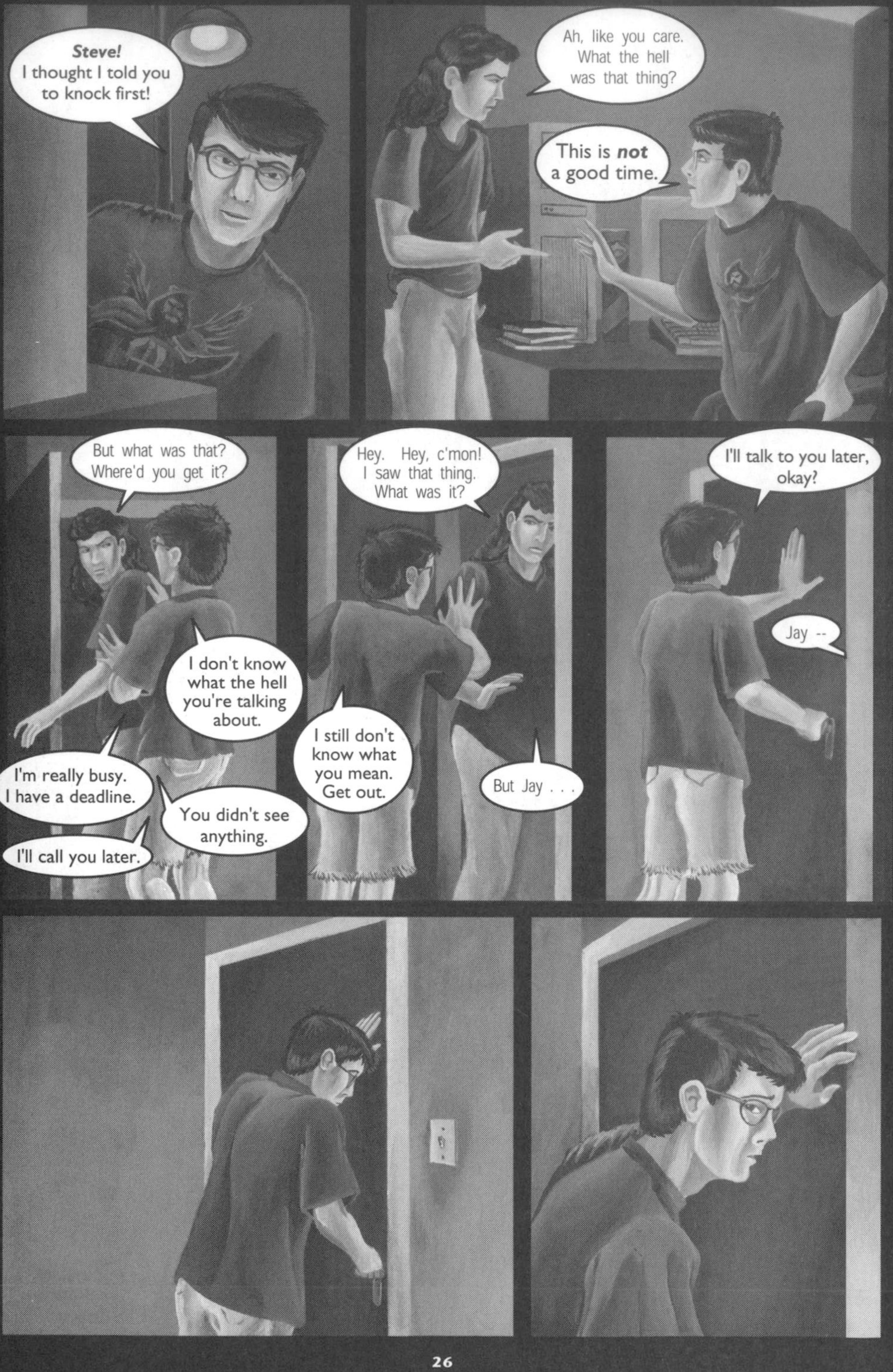

Steve! I thought I told you to knock first!
Ah, like you care. What the hell was that thing?
This is ***not*** a good time.
But what was that? Where'd you get it?
I don't know what the hell you're talking about.
I'm really busy. I have a deadline.
You didn't see anything.
I'll call you later.
Hey. Hey, c'mon! I saw that thing. What was it?
I still don't know what you mean. Get out.
But Jay . . .
I'll talk to you later, okay?
Jay --

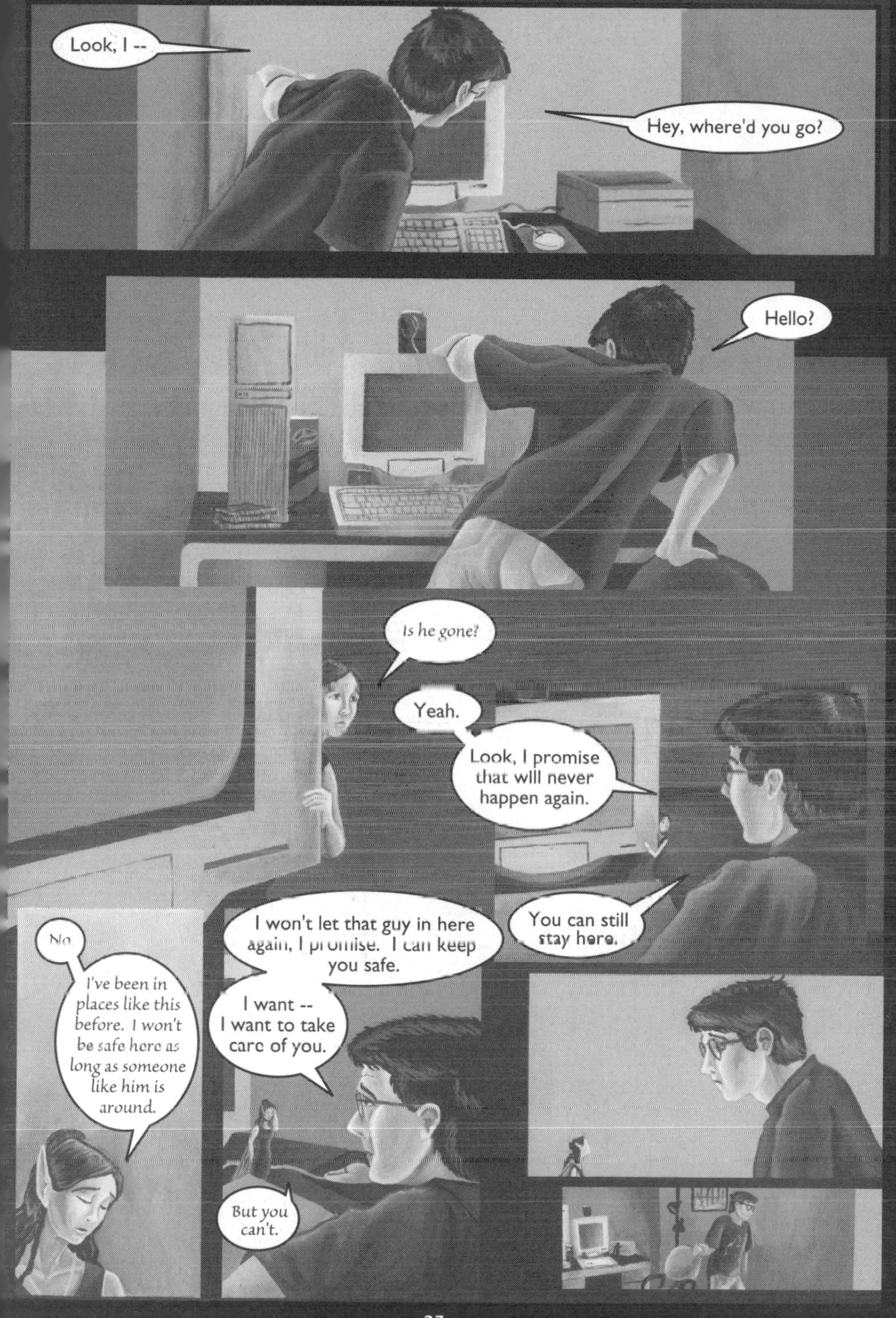
Look, I --
Hey, where'd you go?
Hello?
Is he gone?
Yeah.
Look, I promise that will never happen again.
You can still stay here.
I won't let that guy in here again, I promise. I can keep you safe.
No.
I've been in places like this before. I won't be safe here as long as someone like him is around.
I want -- I want to take care of you.
But you can't.

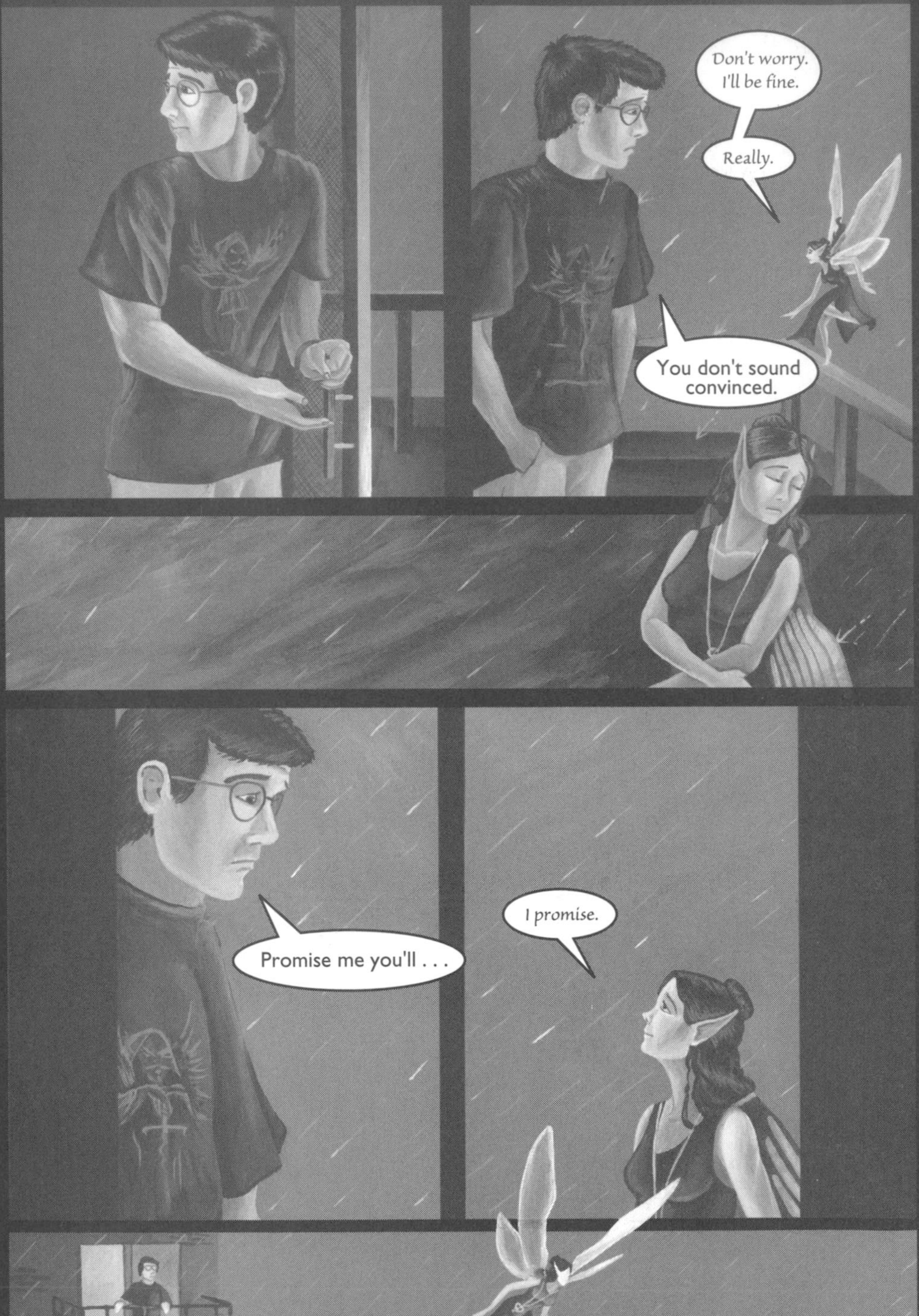
Don't worry. I'll be fine.
Really.
You don't sound convinced.
Promise me you'll . . .
I promise.

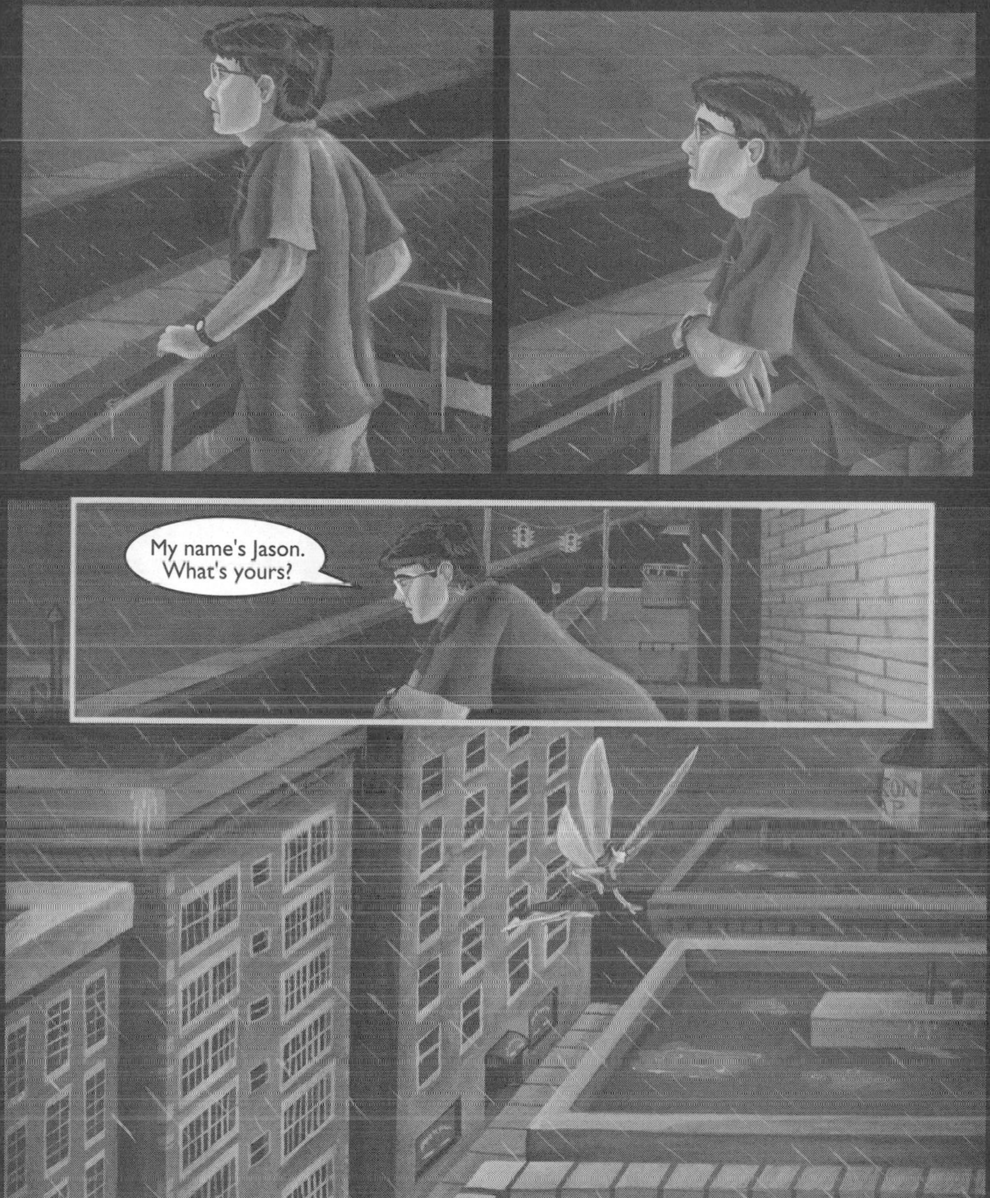

My name's Jason. What's yours?
I feel just terrible, Heinrich! My wings move so slowly -- and my arms, too! I have never felt like this before. Why does it hurt so?
You are feeling sad. I was afraid this might happen.
What do you mean? What is wrong with me?

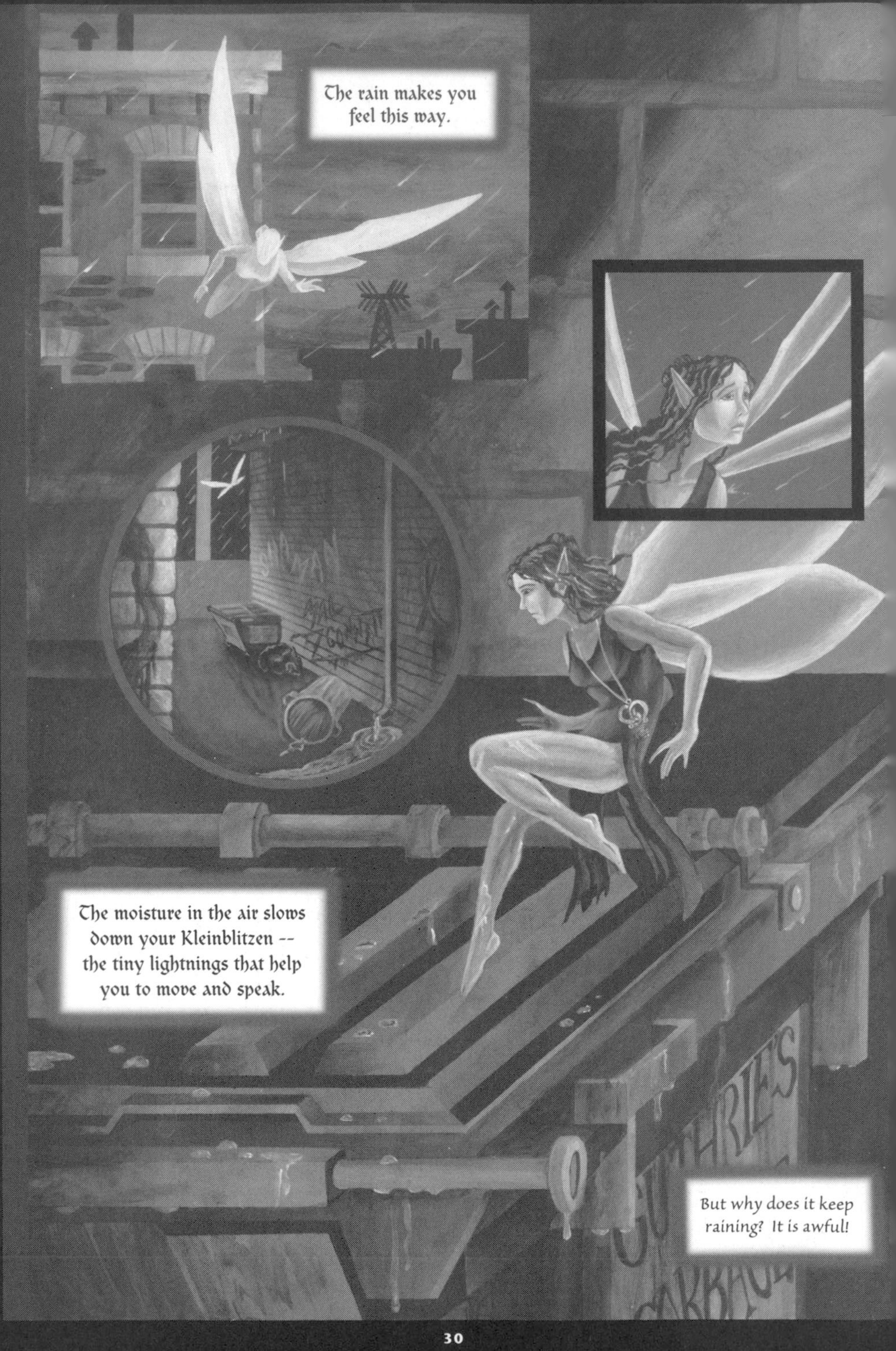
The rain makes you feel this way.
The moisture in the air slows down your Kleinblitzen -- the tiny lightnings that help you to move and speak.
But why does it keep raining? It is awful!

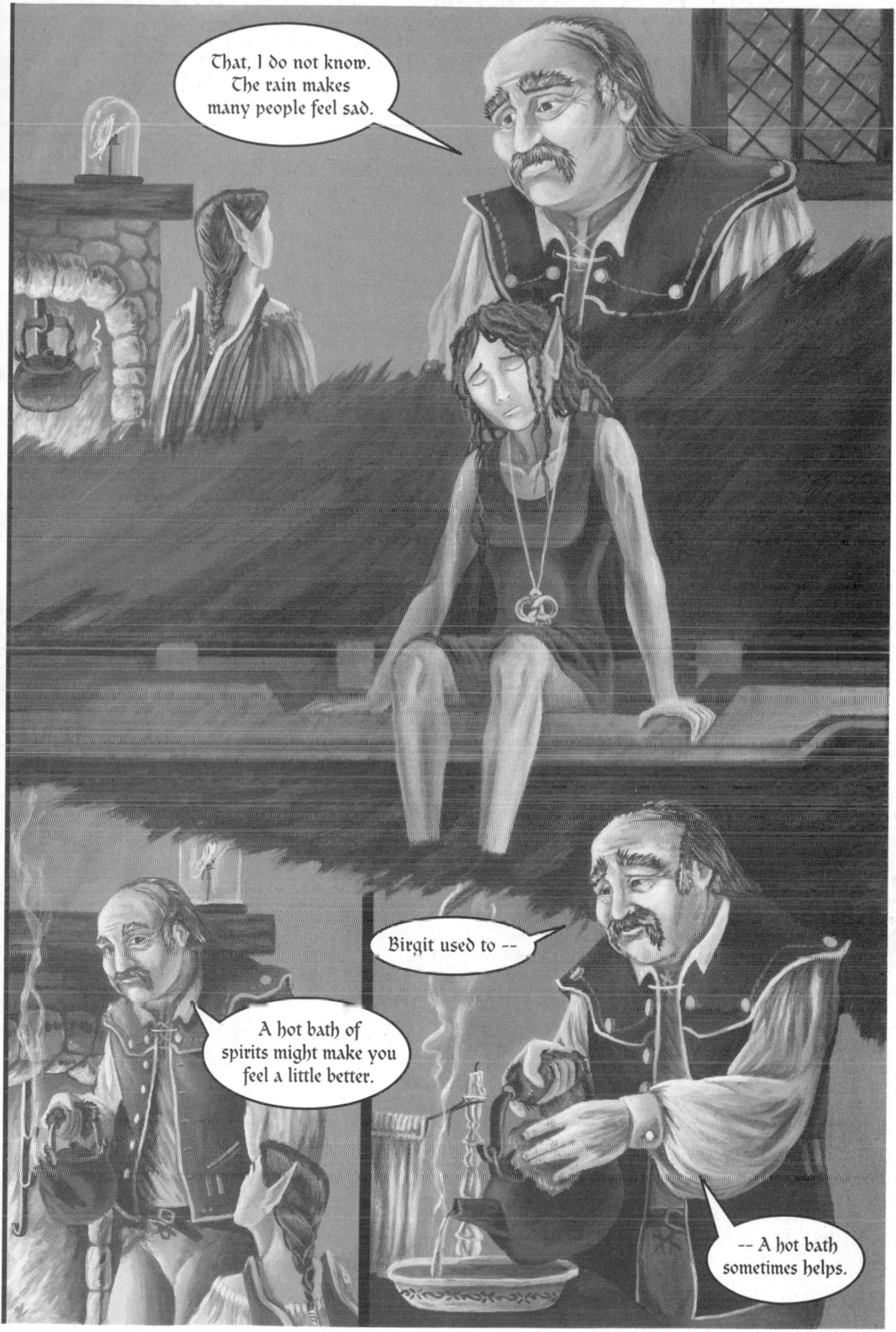
That, I do not know. The rain makes many people feel sad.
A hot bath of spirits might make you feel a little better.
Birgit used to --
-- A hot bath sometimes helps.

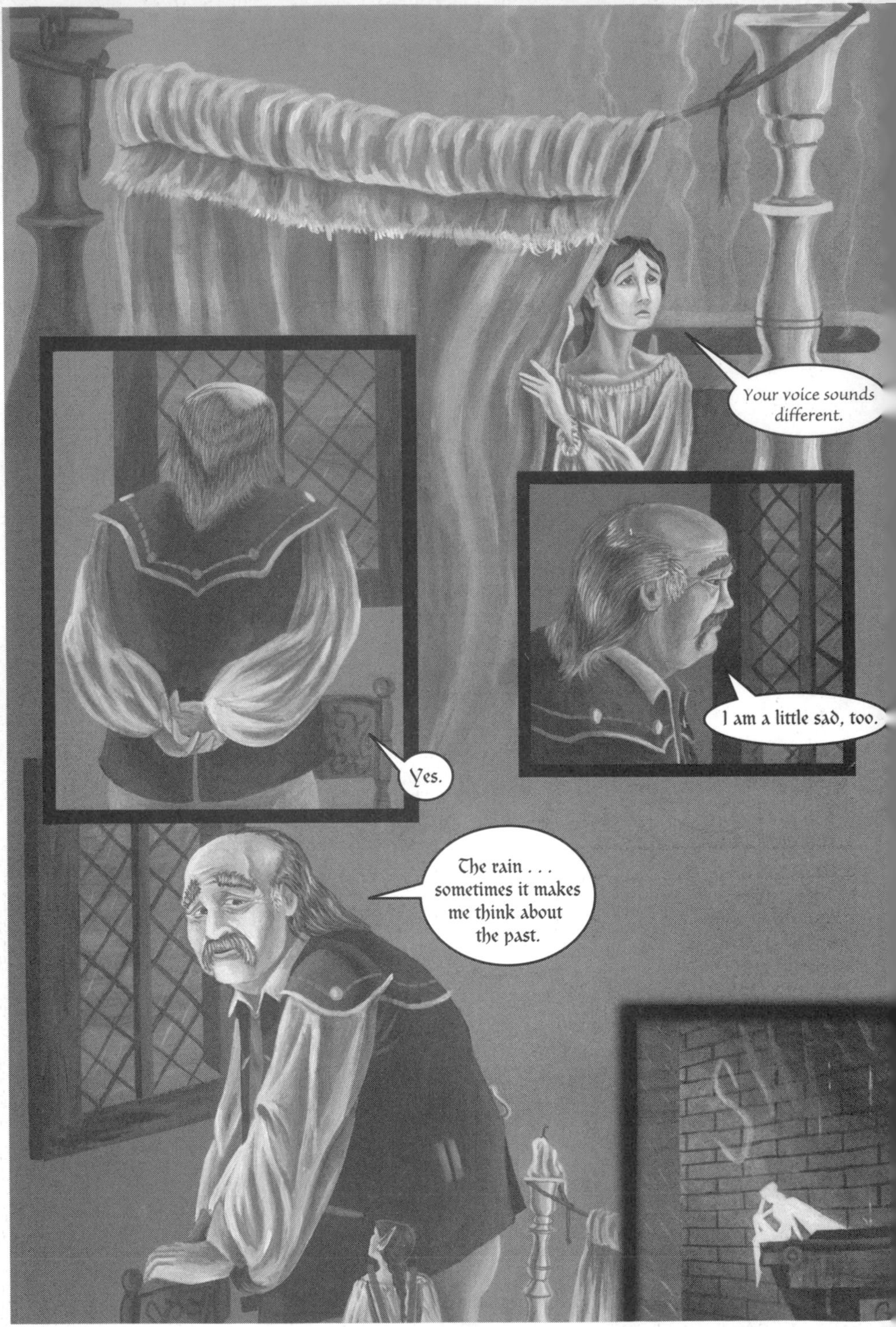
Your voice sounds different.
Yes.
I am a little sad, too.
The rain . . . sometimes it makes me think about the past.

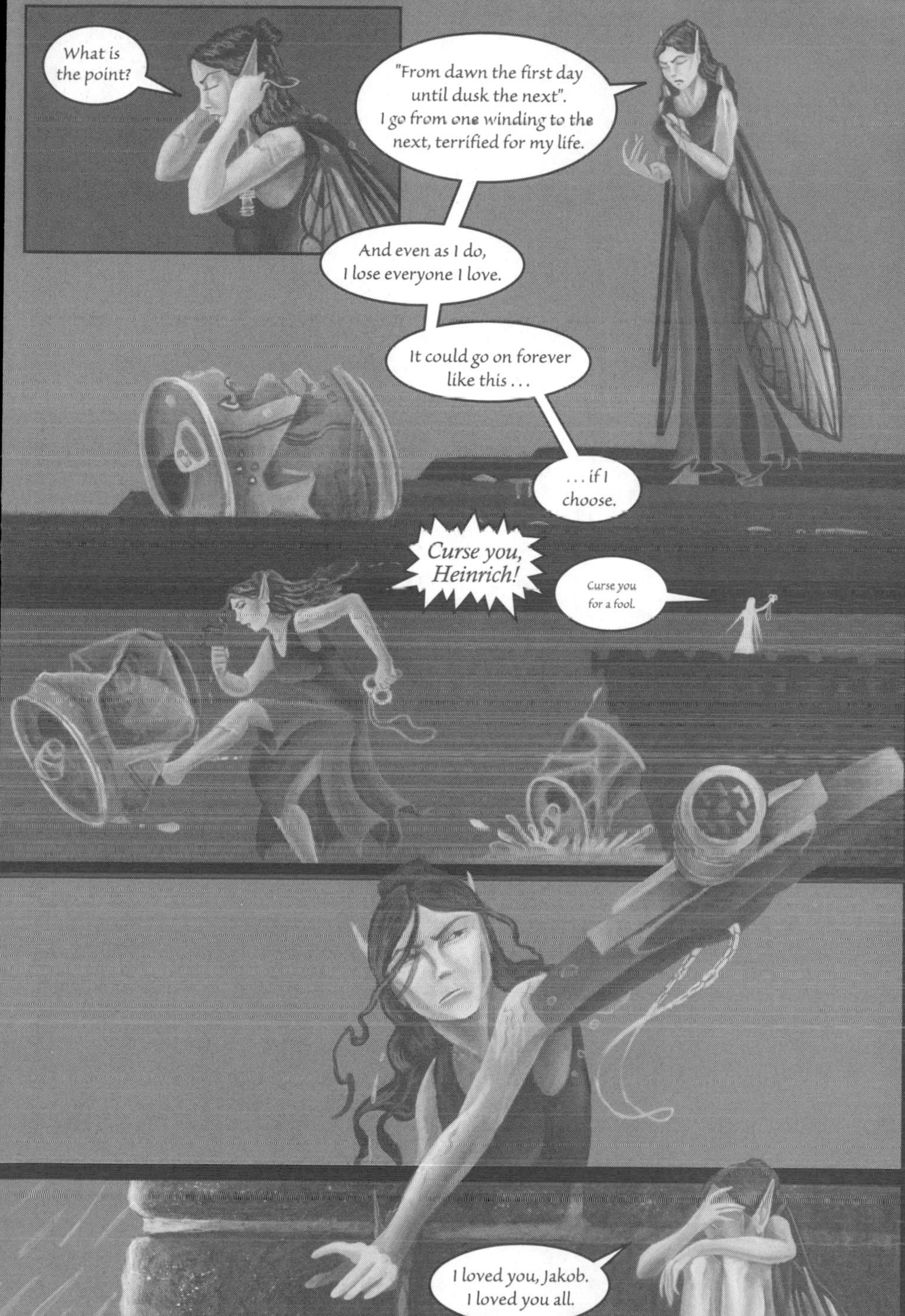
What is the point?
"From dawn the first day until dusk the next". I go from one winding to the next, terrified for my life.
And even as I do, I lose everyone I love.
It could go on forever like this . . .
. . . if I choose.
Curse you, Heinrich!
Curse you for a fool.
I loved you, Jakob. I loved you all.

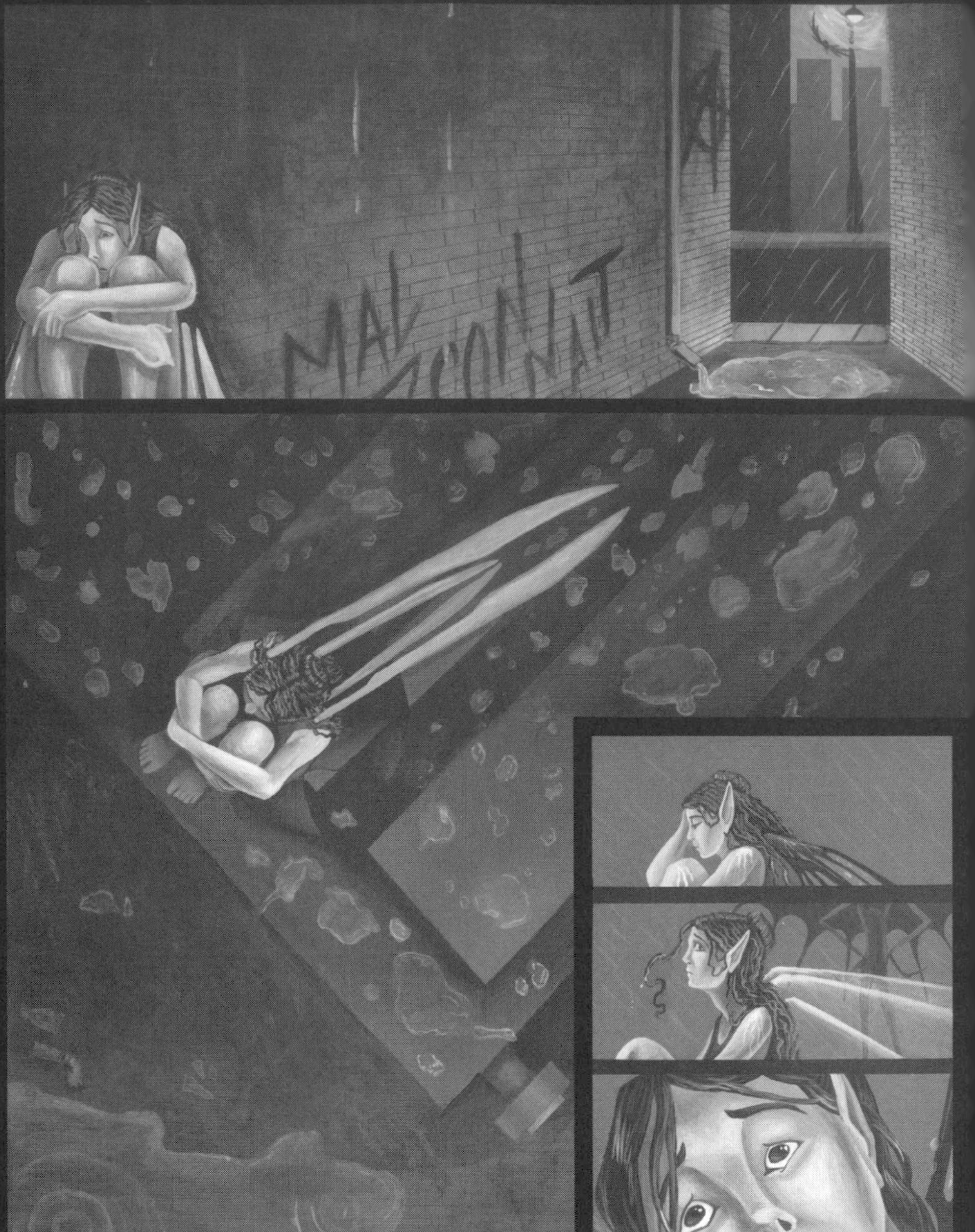

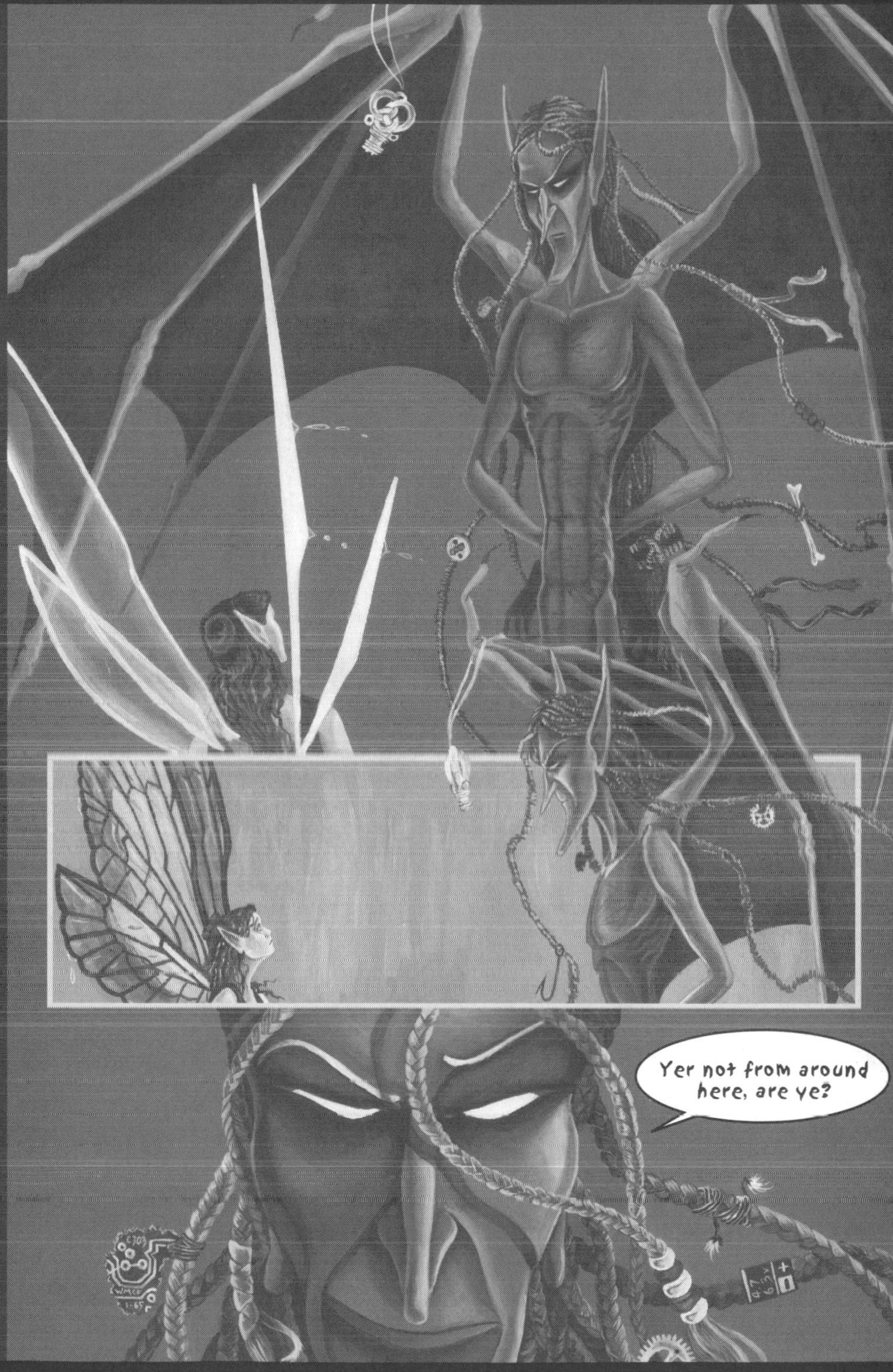
Yer not from around here, are ye?

- Chapter Two -

Wild Creatures

The Highscrapers climb to
    darken the land
Sun only leaks through in the
    heighth of the day
And steamrollered pavement
    levels the land
And the Megapolis Transit
    Authority sends trains to
    scream through the earth
And we forget.

But bear in mind, that eyes still
    shine in the shadows
Bear in mind, that claws still
    curl in the dark
Bear in mind, there are still
    wild creatures
And they are not so frightened of us
    as once they were.
                  -- J. K. Berndt

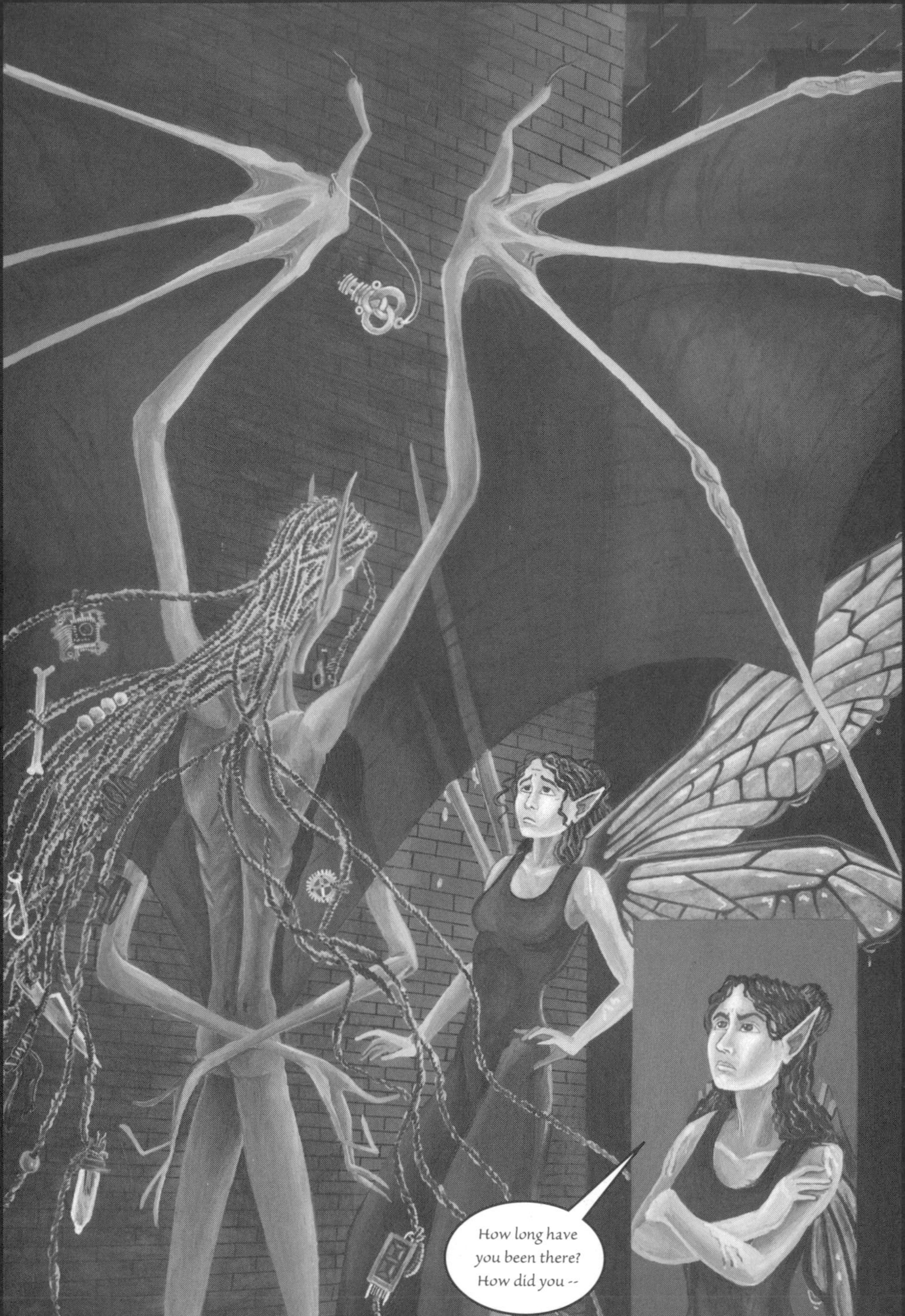
How long have you been there? How did you --

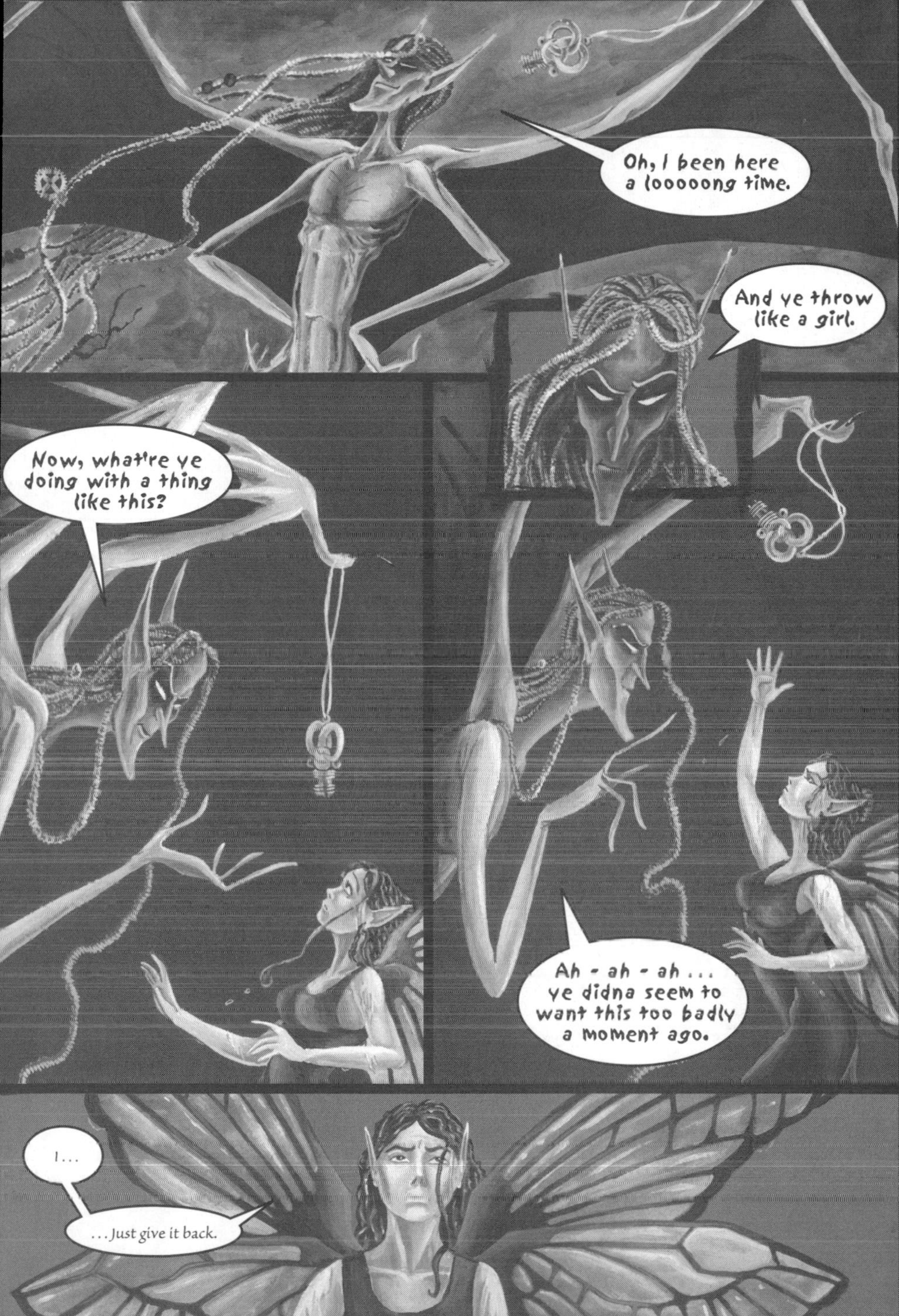
Oh, I been here a looooong time.
And ye throw like a girl.
Now, what're ye doing with a thing like this?
Ah - ah - ah . . . ye didna seem to want this too badly a moment ago.
I . . .
. . . Just give it back.

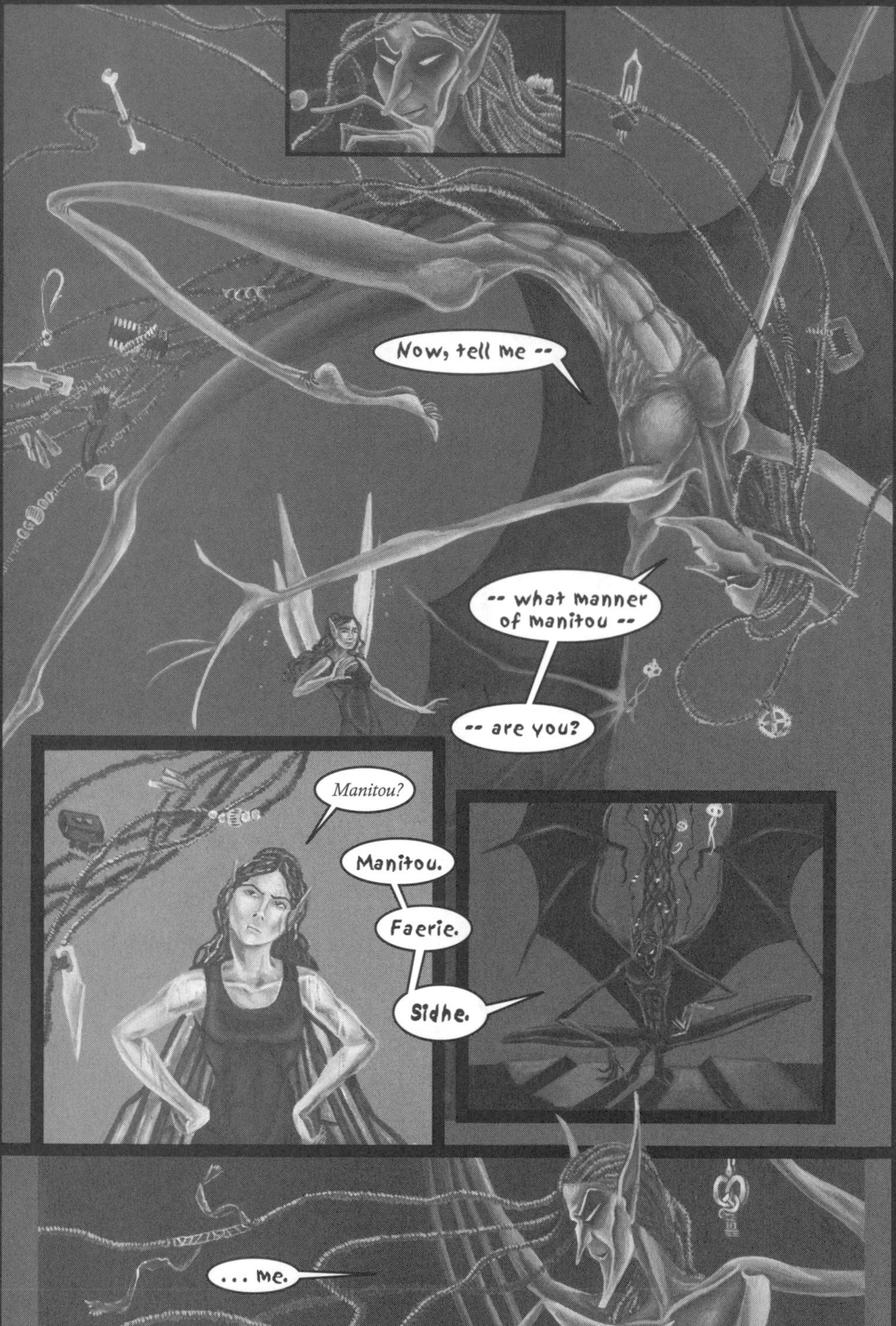
Now, tell me --
-- what manner of manitou --
-- are you?
Manitou?
Manitou.
Faerie.
Sidhe.
. . . me.

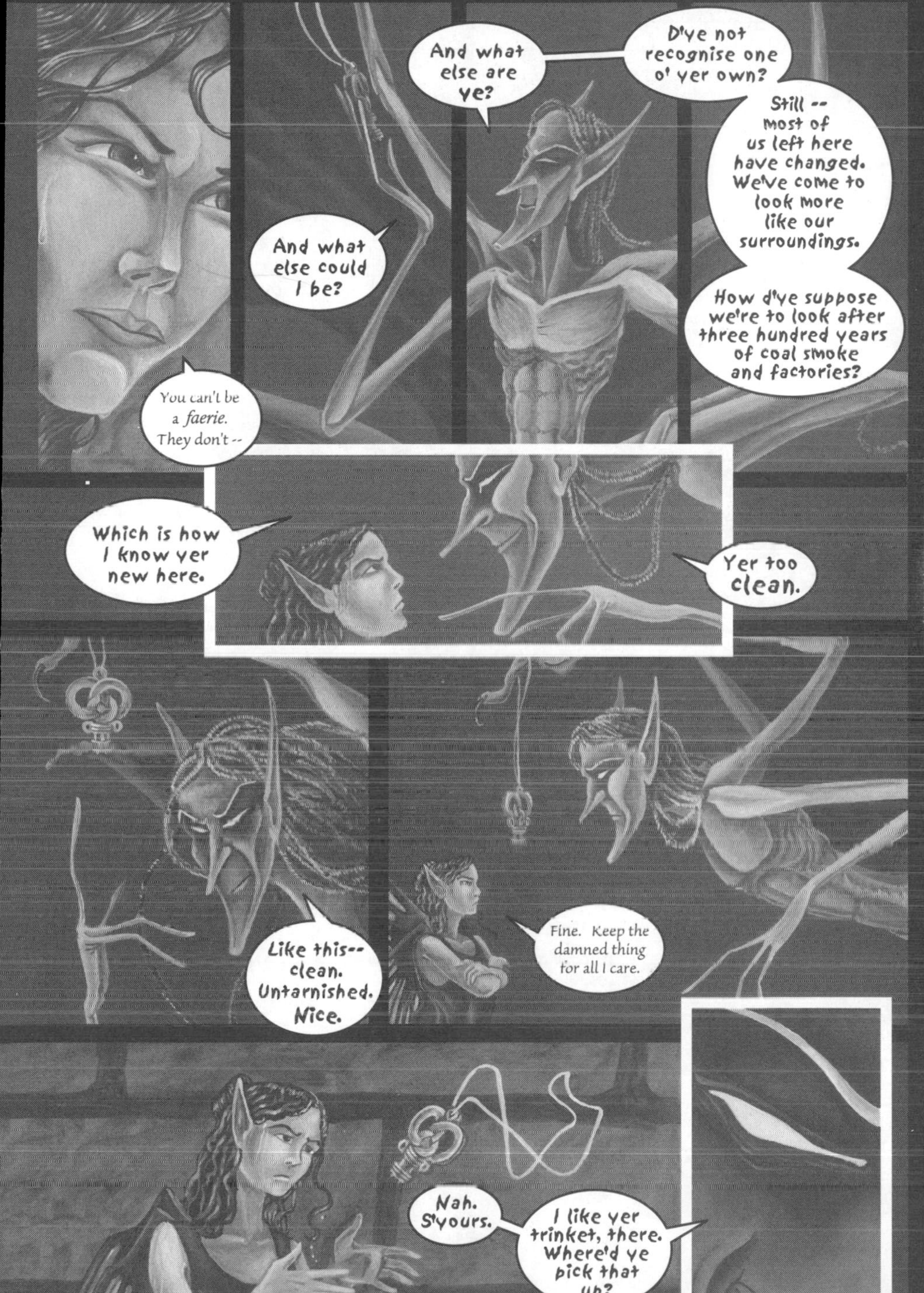
And what else are ye?
D'ye not recognise one o' yer own?
You can't be a *faerie*. They don't --
And what else could I be?
Still -- most of us left here have changed. We've come to look more like our surroundings.
How d'ye suppose we're to look after three hundred years of coal smoke and factories?
Which is how I know yer new here.
Yer too clean.
Like this-- clean. Untarnished. Nice.
Fine. Keep the damned thing for all I care.
I like yer trinket, there. Where'd ye pick that up?
Nah. S'yours.

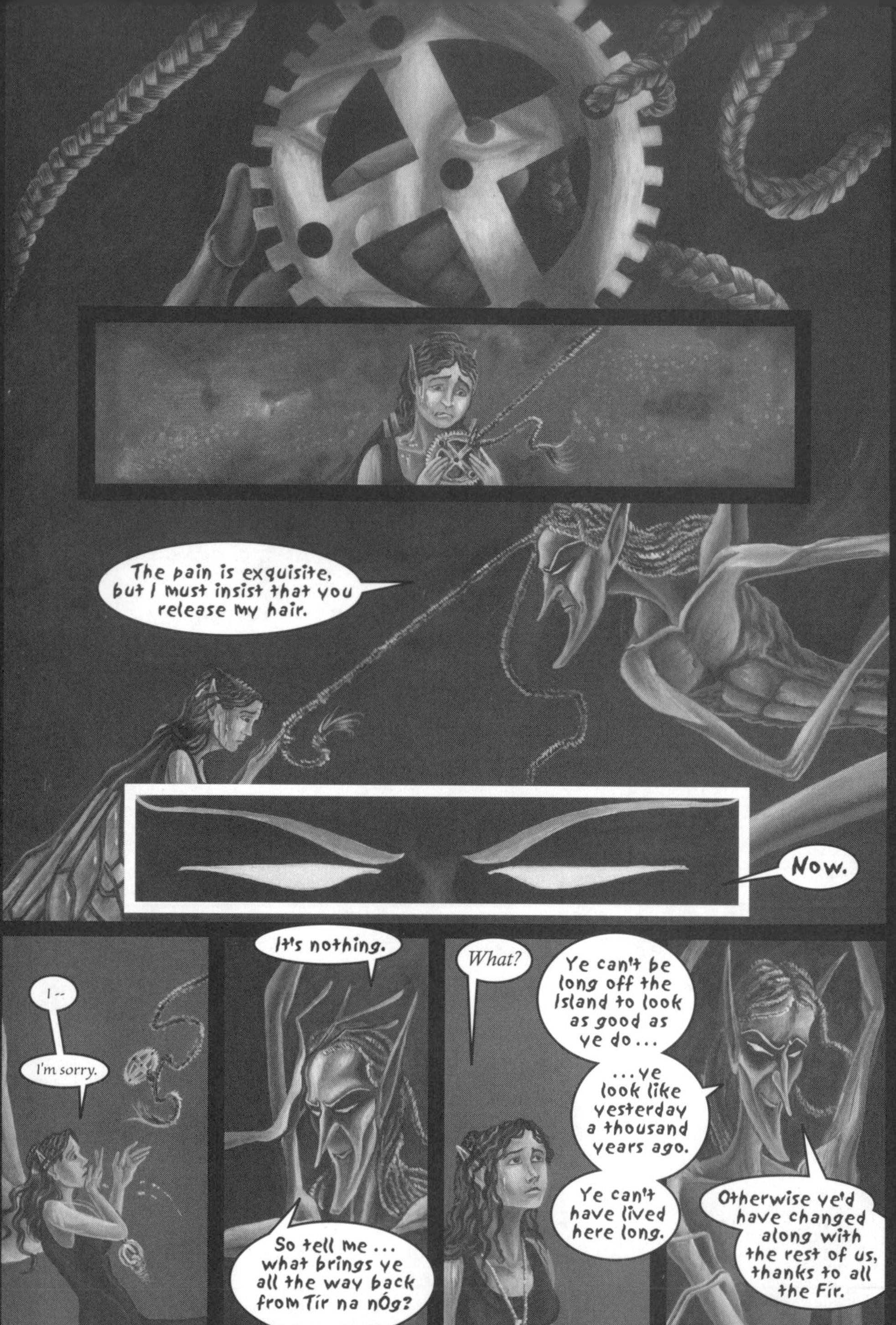

The pain is exquisite, but I must insist that you release my hair.
Now.
I --
I'm sorry.
It's nothing.
So tell me ... what brings ye all the way back from Tír na nÓg?
What?
Ye can't be long off the Island to look as good as ye do...
...ye look like yesterday a thousand years ago.
Ye can't have lived here long.
Otherwise ye'd have changed along with the rest of us, thanks to all the Fír.

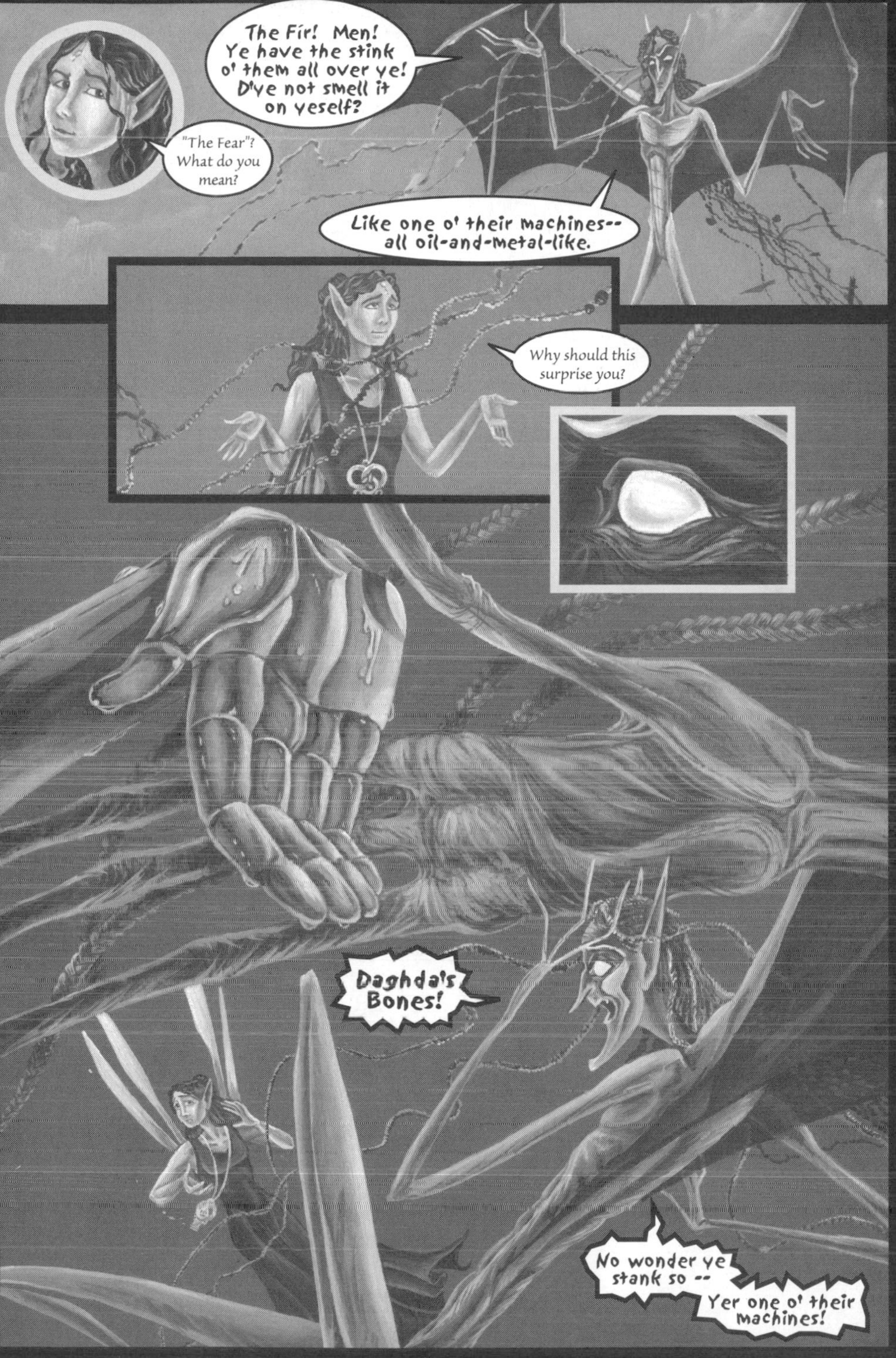

The Fir! Men! Ye have the stink o' them all over ye! D'ye not smell it on yeself?
"The Fear"? What do you mean?
Like one o' their machines-- all oil-and-metal-like.
Why should this surprise you?
Daghda's Bones!
No wonder ye stank so --
Yer one o' their machines!

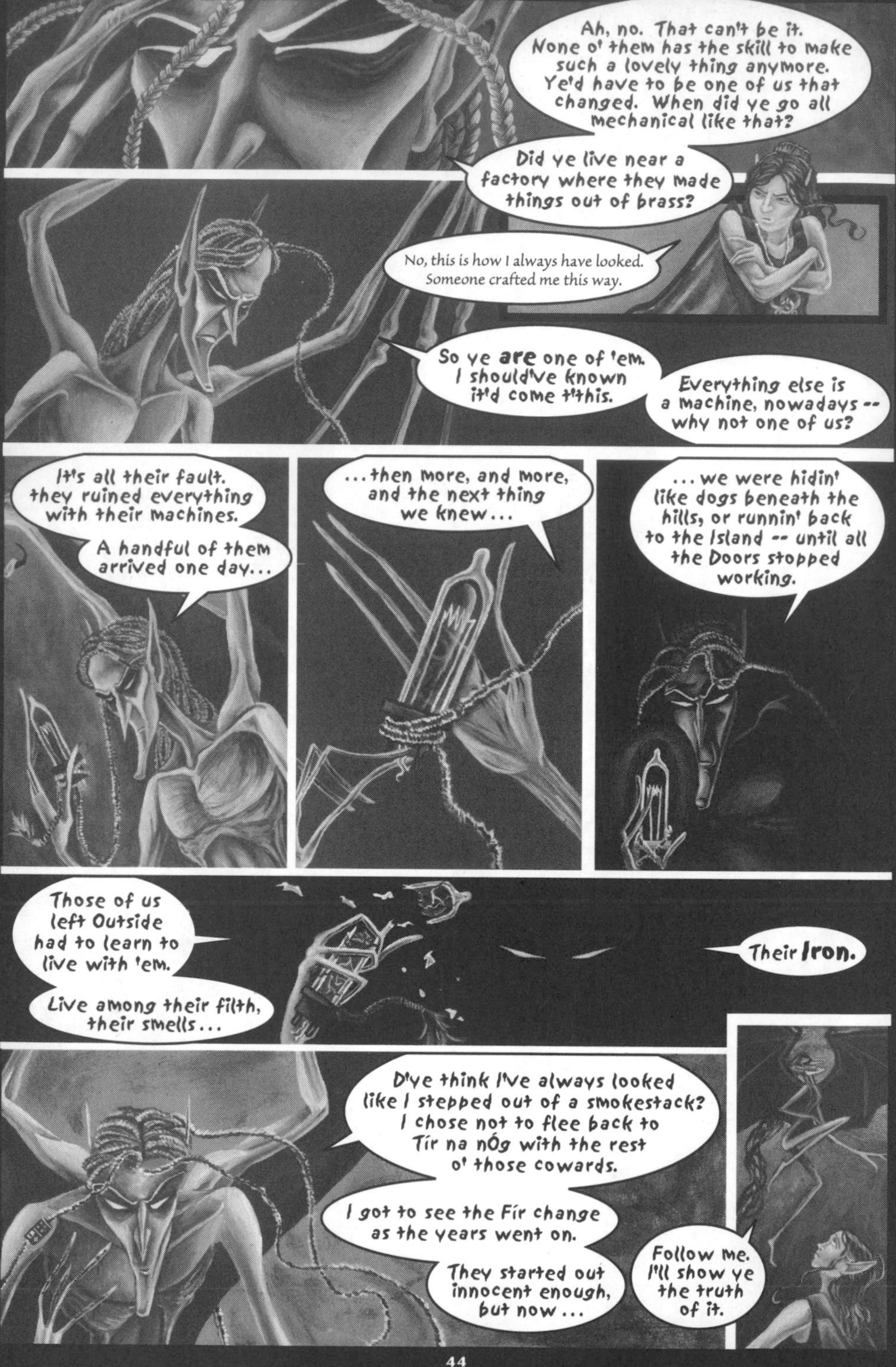
Ah, no. That can't be it. None o' them has the skill to make such a lovely thing anymore. Ye'd have to be one of us that changed. When did ye go all mechanical like that?
Did ye live near a factory where they made things out of brass?
No, this is how I always have looked. Someone crafted me this way.
So ye are one of 'em. I should've known it'd come t'this.
Everything else is a machine, nowadays -- why not one of us?
It's all their fault. they ruined everything with their machines.
A handful of them arrived one day...
...then more, and more, and the next thing we knew...
...we were hidin' like dogs beneath the hills, or runnin' back to the Island -- until all the Doors stopped working.
Those of us left Outside had to learn to live with 'em.
Live among their filth, their smells...
Their Iron.
D'ye think I've always looked like I stepped out of a smokestack? I chose not to flee back to Tír na nÓg with the rest o' those cowards.
I got to see the Fír change as the years went on.
They started out innocent enough, but now...
Follow me. I'll show ye the truth of it.

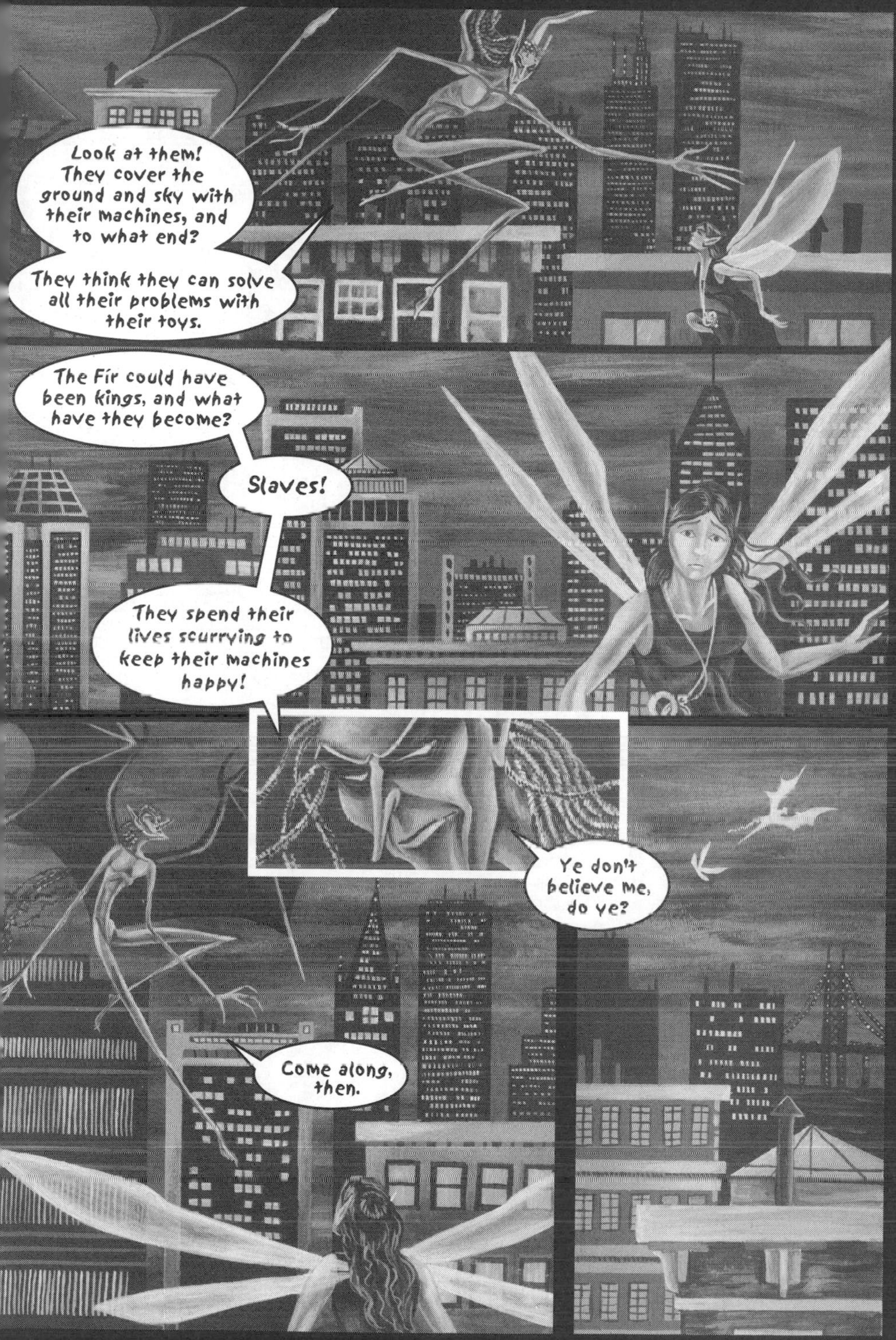
Look at them! They cover the ground and sky with their machines, and to what end?
They think they can solve all their problems with their toys.
The Fír could have been kings, and what have they become?
Slaves!
They spend their lives scurrying to keep their machines happy!
Ye don't believe me, do ye?
Come along, then.

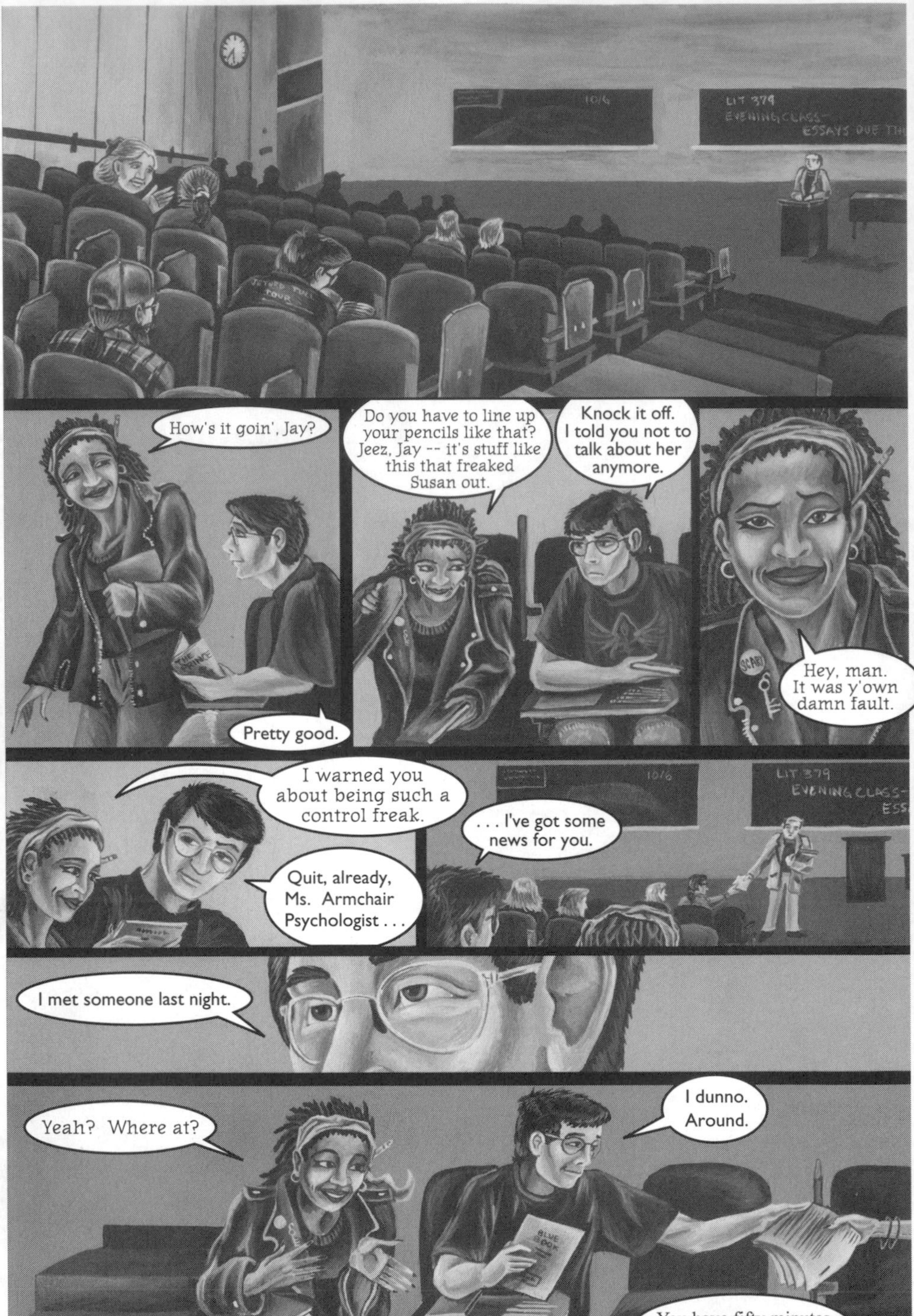
10/6
LIT 379
EVENING CLASS—
How's it goin', Jay?
THE PRINCE
Pretty good.
Do you have to line up your pencils like that? Jeez, Jay -- it's stuff like this that freaked Susan out.
Knock it off. I told you not to talk about her anymore.
SCARY
Hey, man. It was y'own damn fault.
I warned you about being such a control freak.
Quit, already, Ms. Armchair Psychologist . . .
. . . I've got some news for you.
I met someone last night.
Yeah? Where at?
I dunno. Around.
BLUE BOOK
You have fifty minutes to complete the exam.

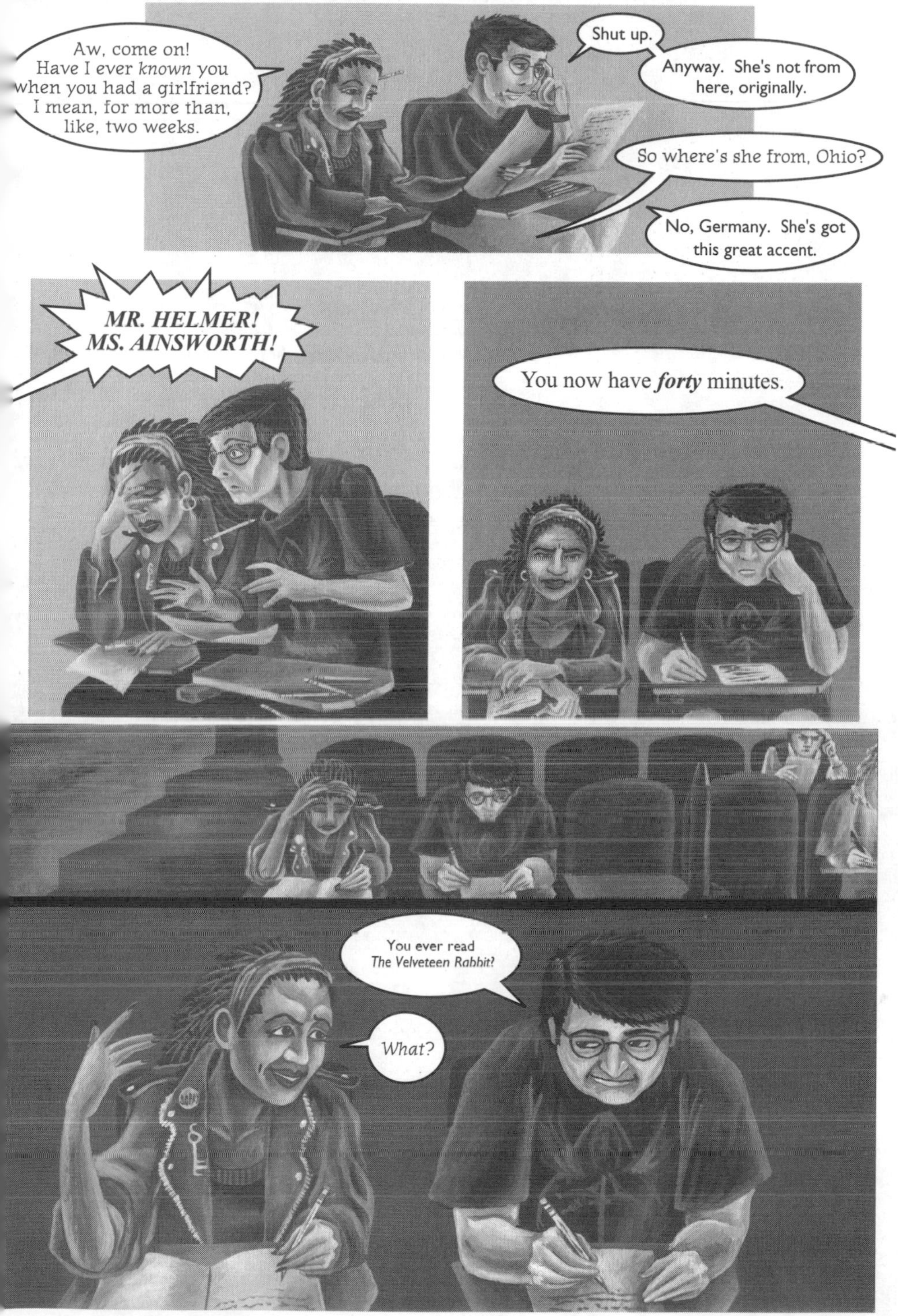
Aw, come on! Have I ever *known* you when you had a girlfriend? I mean, for more than, like, two weeks.
Shut up.
Anyway. She's not from here, originally.
So where's she from, Ohio?
No, Germany. She's got this great accent.
MR. HELMER! MS. AINSWORTH!
You now have ***forty*** minutes.
You ever read *The Velveteen Rabbit?*
What?

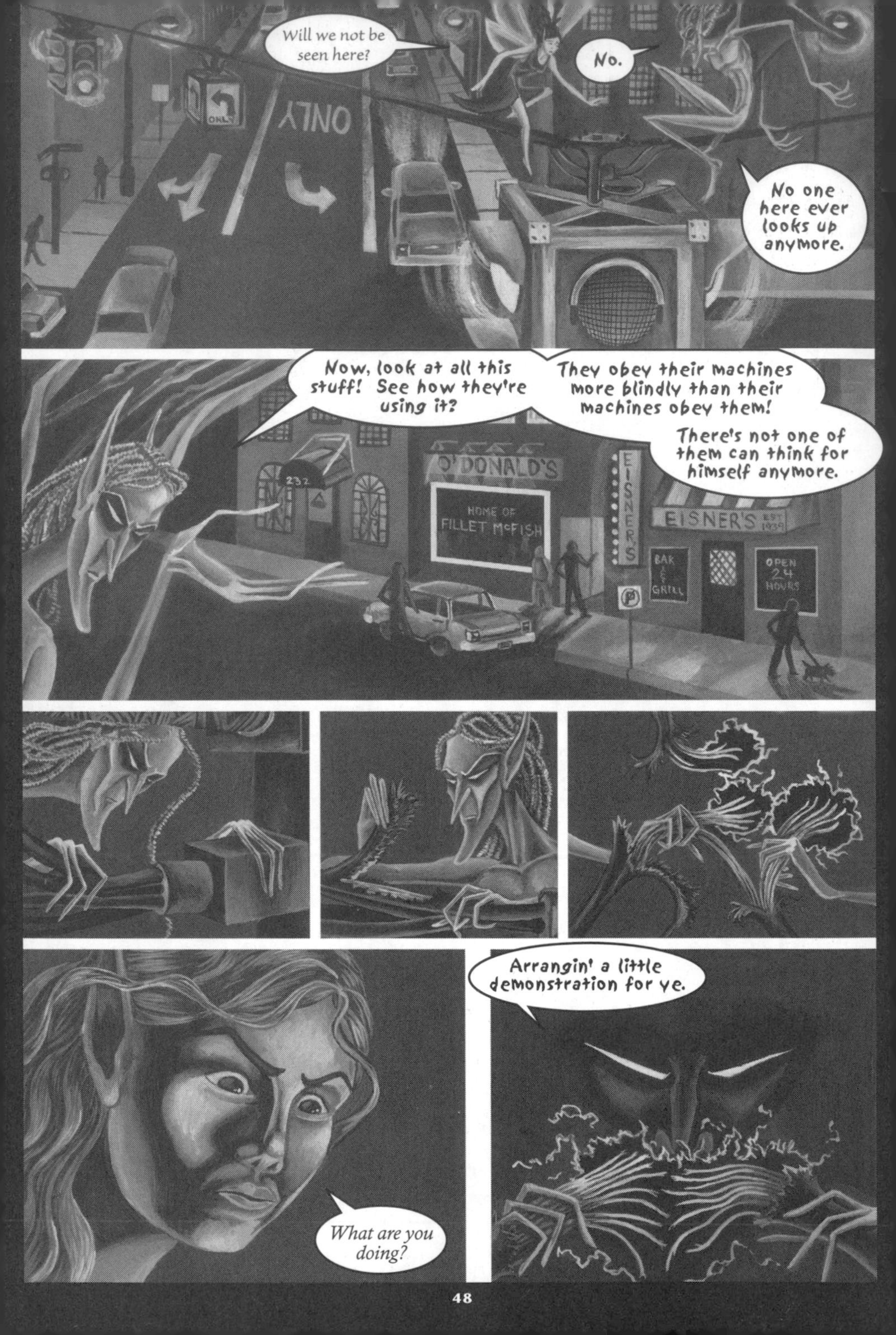
Will we not be seen here?
No.
ONLY
No one here ever looks up anymore.
Now, look at all this stuff! See how they're using it?
They obey their machines more blindly than their machines obey them!
There's not one of them can think for himself anymore.
232
O'DONALD'S
HOME OF FILLET McFISH
EISNER'S
EISNER'S
OPEN 24 HOURS
What are you doing?
Arrangin' a little demonstration for ye.

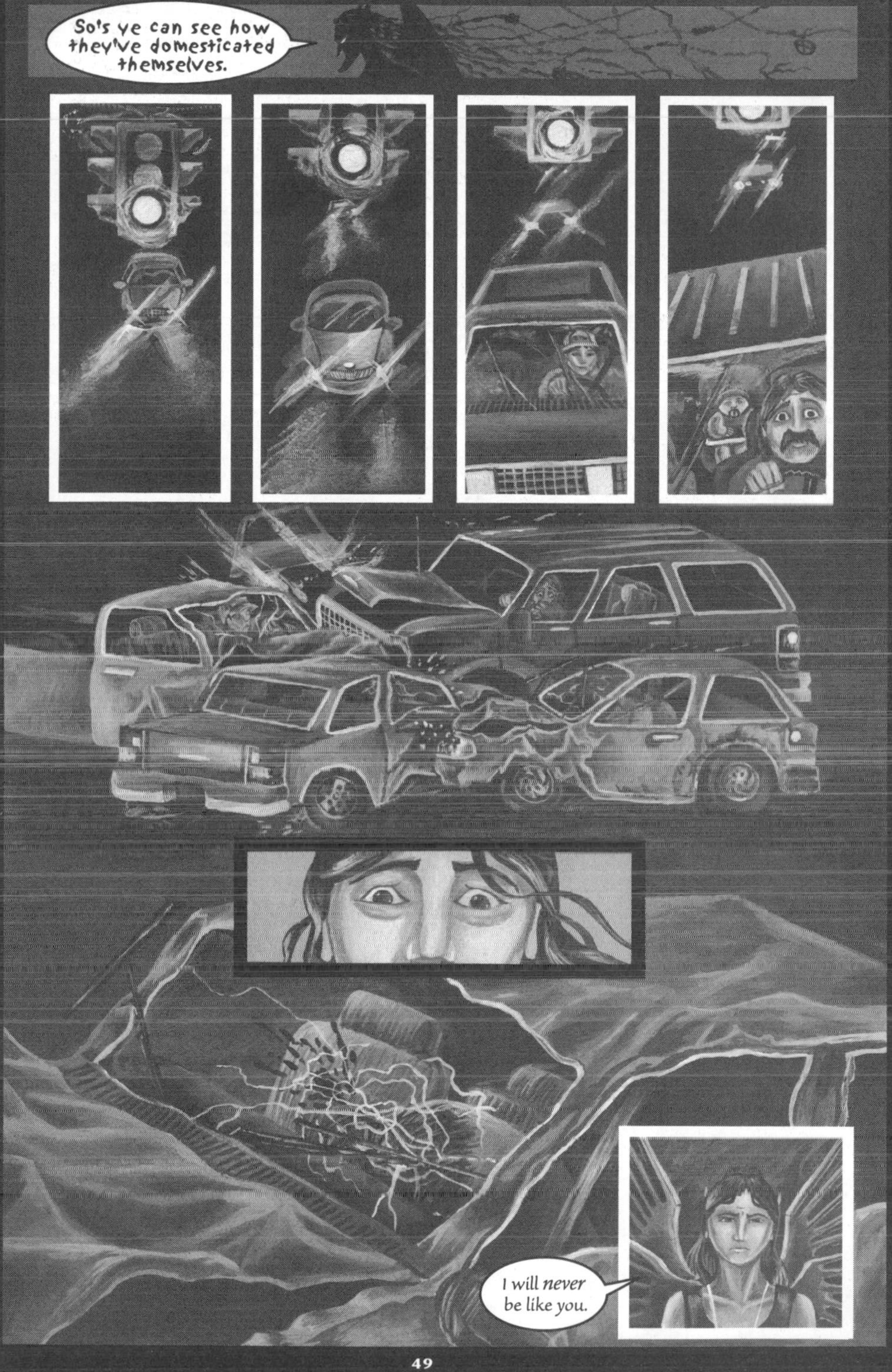

So's ye can see how they've domesticated themselves.
I will *never* be like you.

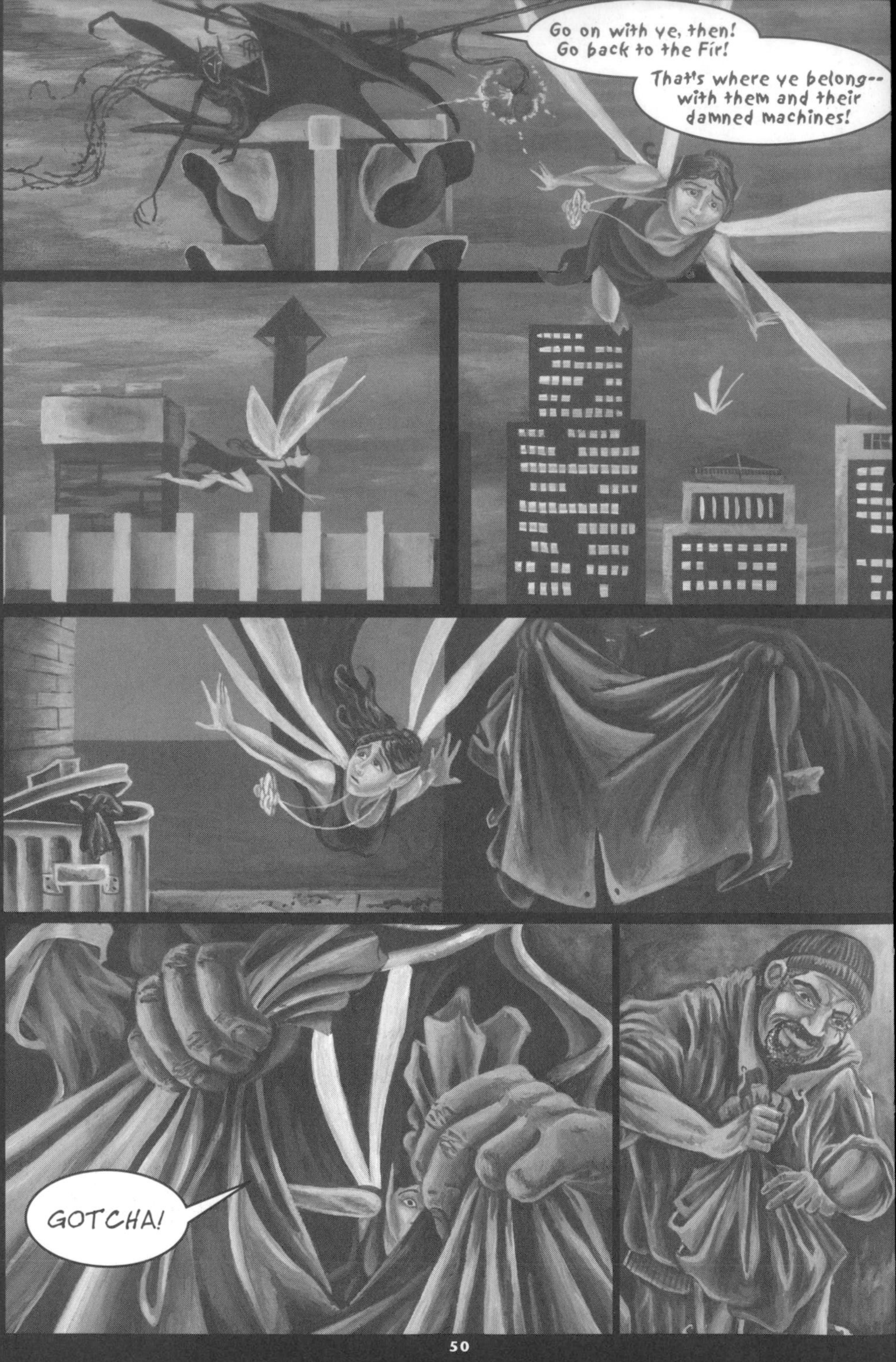
Go on with ye, then! Go back to the Fir!
That's where ye belong-- with them and their damned machines!
GOTCHA!

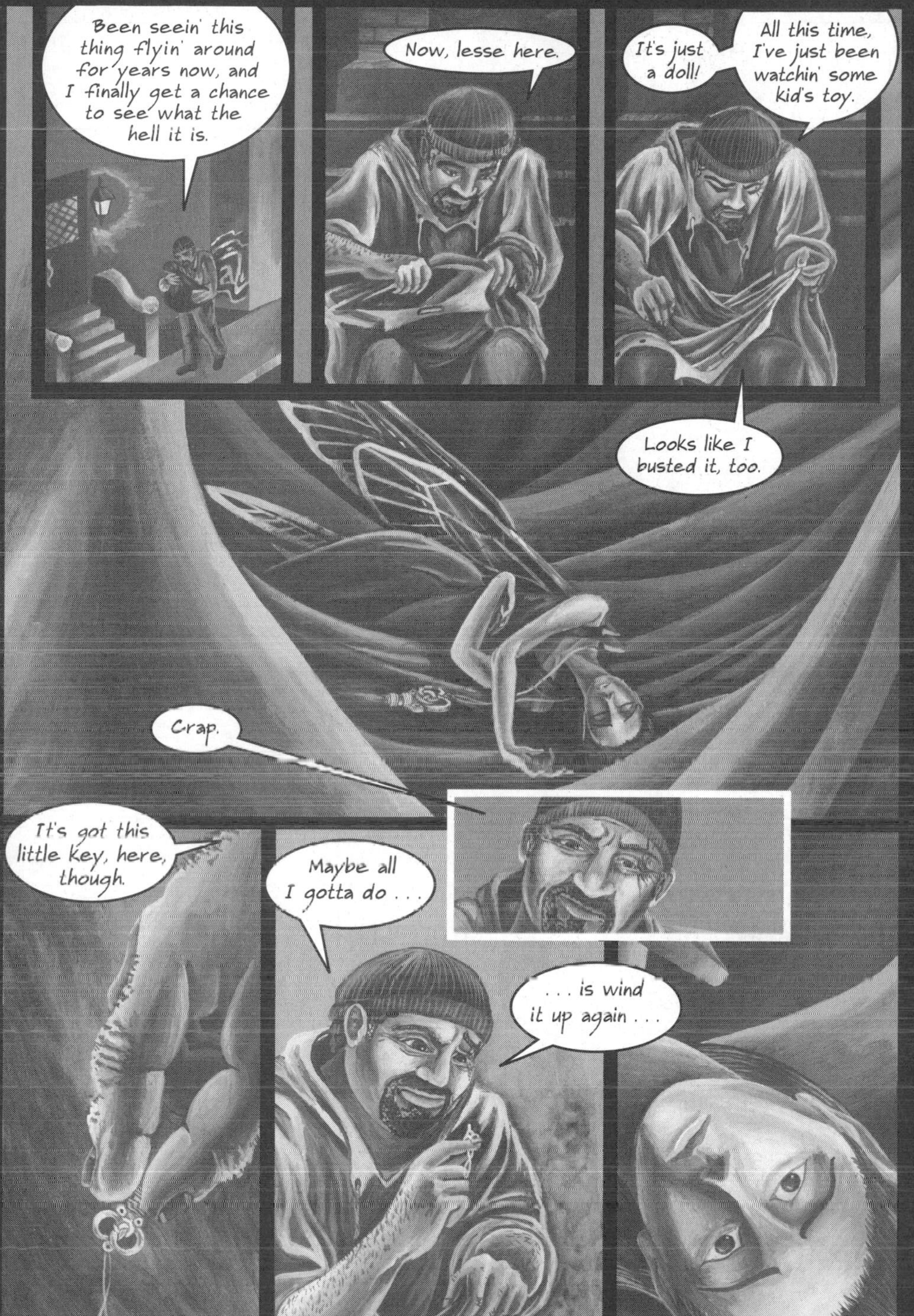
Been seein' this thing flyin' around for years now, and I finally get a chance to see what the hell it is.
Now, lesse here.
It's just a doll!
All this time, I've just been watchin' some kid's toy.
Looks like I busted it, too.
Crap.
It's got this little key, here, though.
Maybe all I gotta do . . .
. . . is wind it up again . . .

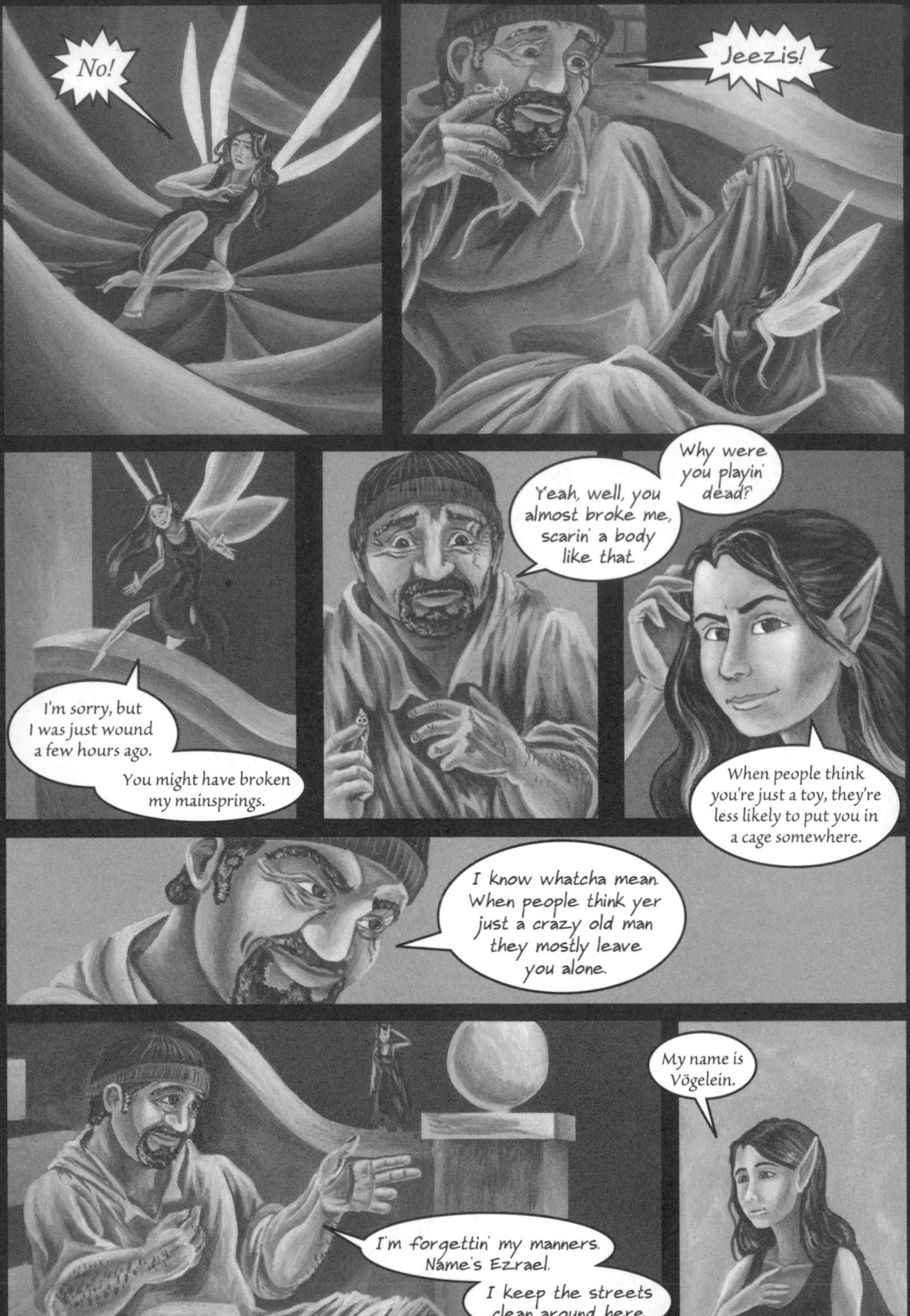
No!
Jeezis!
I'm sorry, but I was just wound a few hours ago.
You might have broken my mainsprings.
Yeah, well, you almost broke me, scarin' a body like that.
Why were you playin' dead?
When people think you're just a toy, they're less likely to put you in a cage somewhere.
I know whatcha mean. When people think yer just a crazy old man they mostly leave you alone.
I'm forgettin' my manners. Name's Ezrael.
I keep the streets clean around here.
My name is Vögelein.

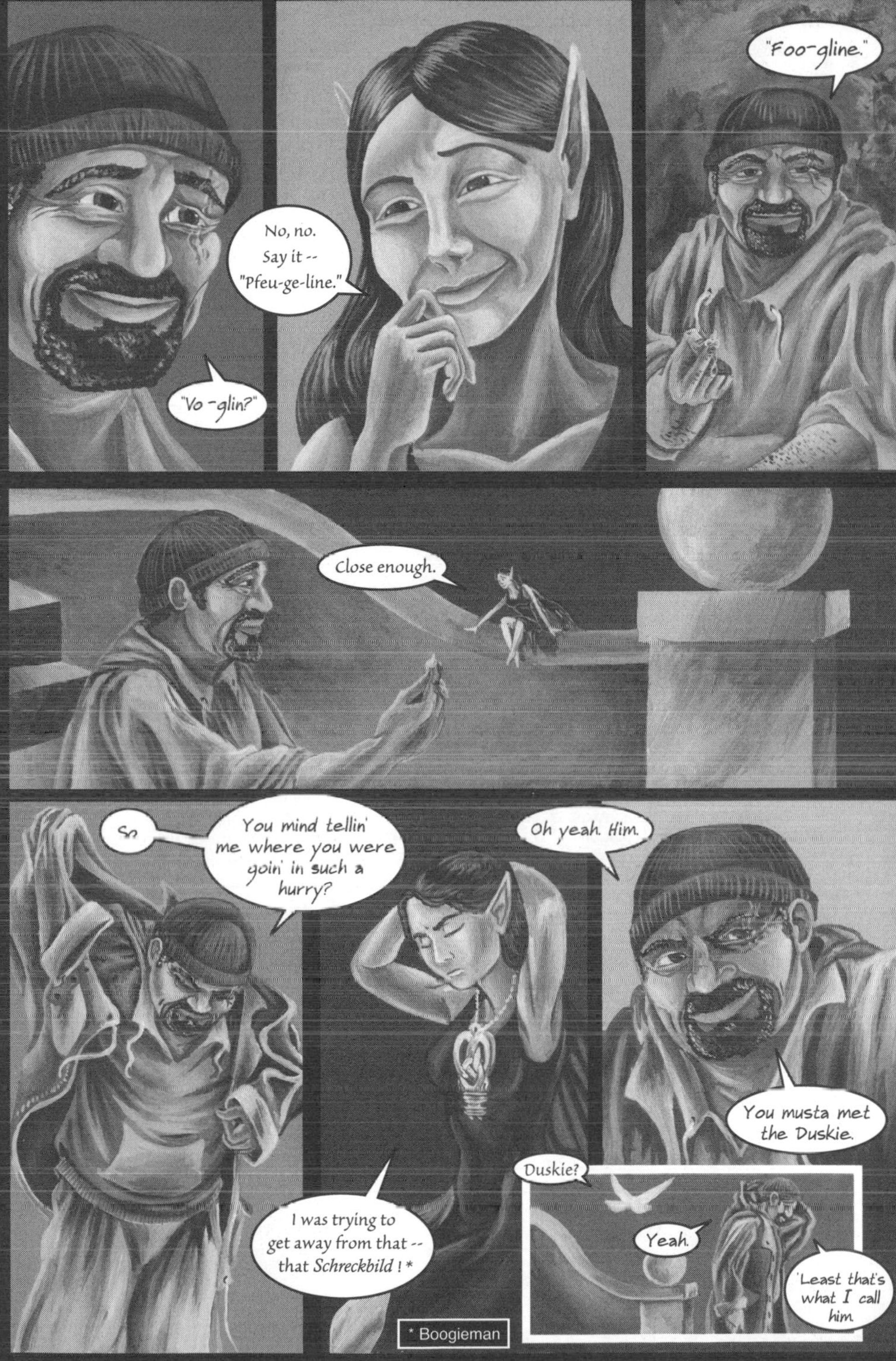
"Vo -glin?"
No, no. Say it -- "Pfeu-ge-line."
"Foo-gline."
Close enough.
So
You mind tellin' me where you were goin' in such a hurry?
I was trying to get away from that -- that *Schreckbild* ! *
Oh yeah. Him.
You musta met the Duskie.
Duskie?
Yeah.
'Least that's what I call him.
* Boogieman

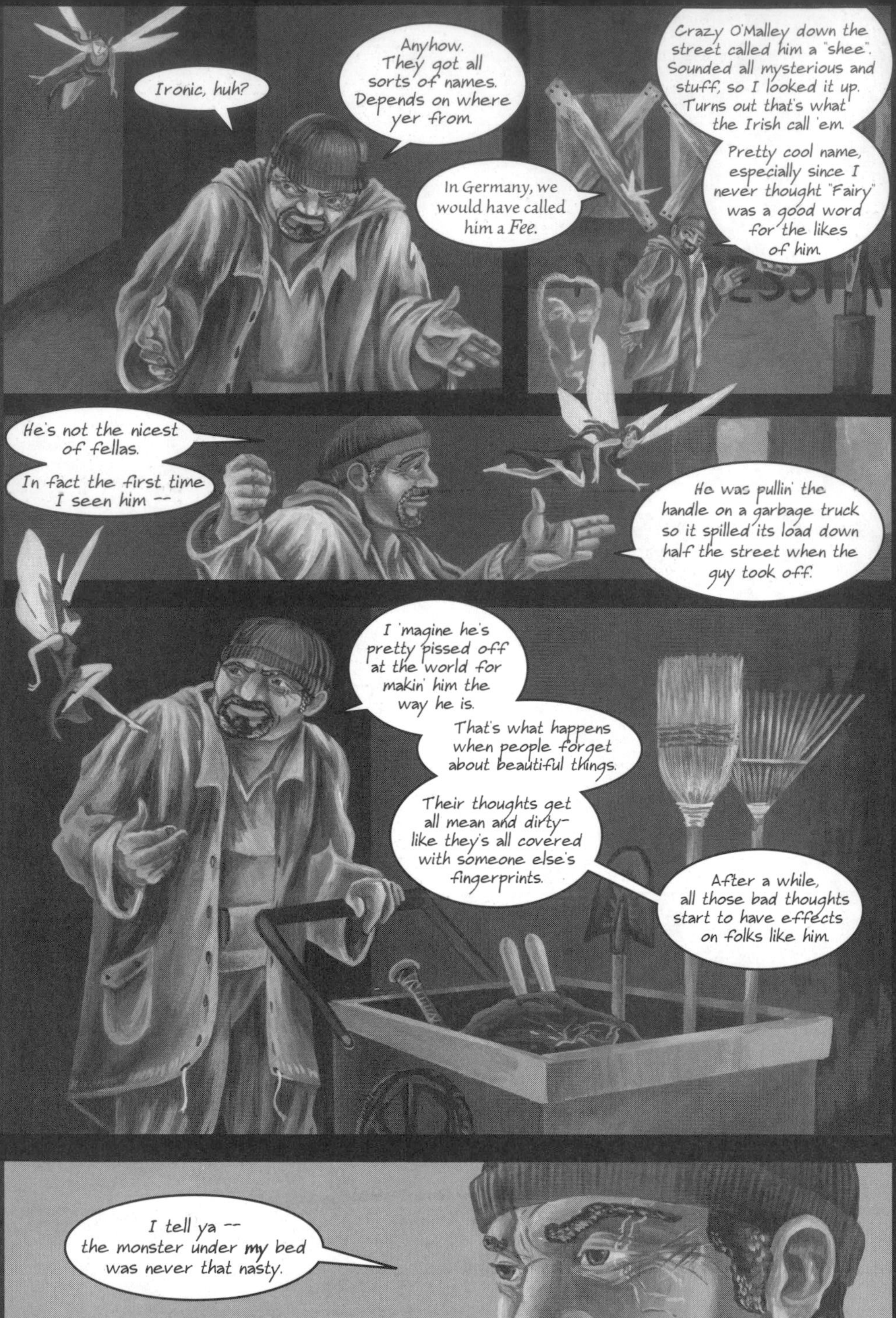
Ironic, huh?
Anyhow. They got all sorts of names. Depends on where yer from.
In Germany, we would have called him a *Fee*.
Crazy O'Malley down the street called him a "shee". Sounded all mysterious and stuff, so I looked it up. Turns out that's what the Irish call 'em.
Pretty cool name, especially since I never thought "Fairy" was a good word for the likes of him.
He's not the nicest of fellas.
In fact the first time I seen him --
He was pullin' the handle on a garbage truck so it spilled its load down half the street when the guy took off.
I 'magine he's pretty pissed off at the world for makin' him the way he is.
That's what happens when people forget about beautiful things.
Their thoughts get all mean and dirty- like they's all covered with someone else's fingerprints.
After a while, all those bad thoughts start to have effects on folks like him.
I tell ya -- the monster under **my** bed was never that nasty.

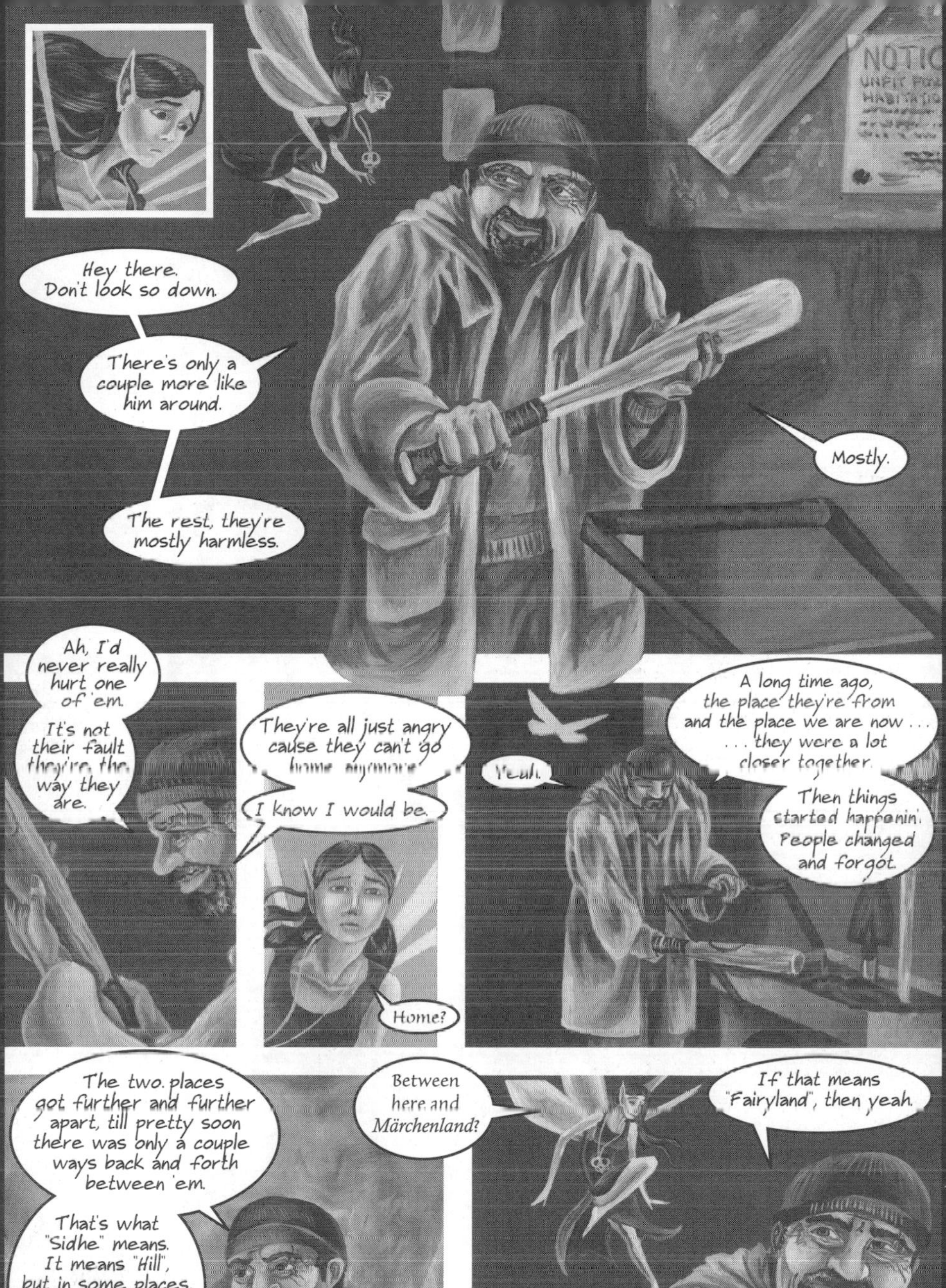

Hey there. Don't look so down.
There's only a couple more like him around.
The rest, they're mostly harmless.
Mostly.
Ah, I'd never really hurt one of 'em.
It's not their fault they're the way they are.
They're all just angry cause they can't go home anymore.
I know I would be.
Home?
Yeah.
A long time ago, the place they're from and the place we are now . . .
. . . they were a lot closer together.
Then things started happenin'. People changed and forgot.
The two places got further and further apart, till pretty soon there was only a couple ways back and forth between 'em.
That's what "Sidhe" means. It means "Hill", but in some places, those hills are doors, too: Doors between here and there.
Between here and *Märchenland?*
If that means "Fairyland", then yeah.
After a while, most of the Doors went closed.
Now there's no way back for him, or any of them.

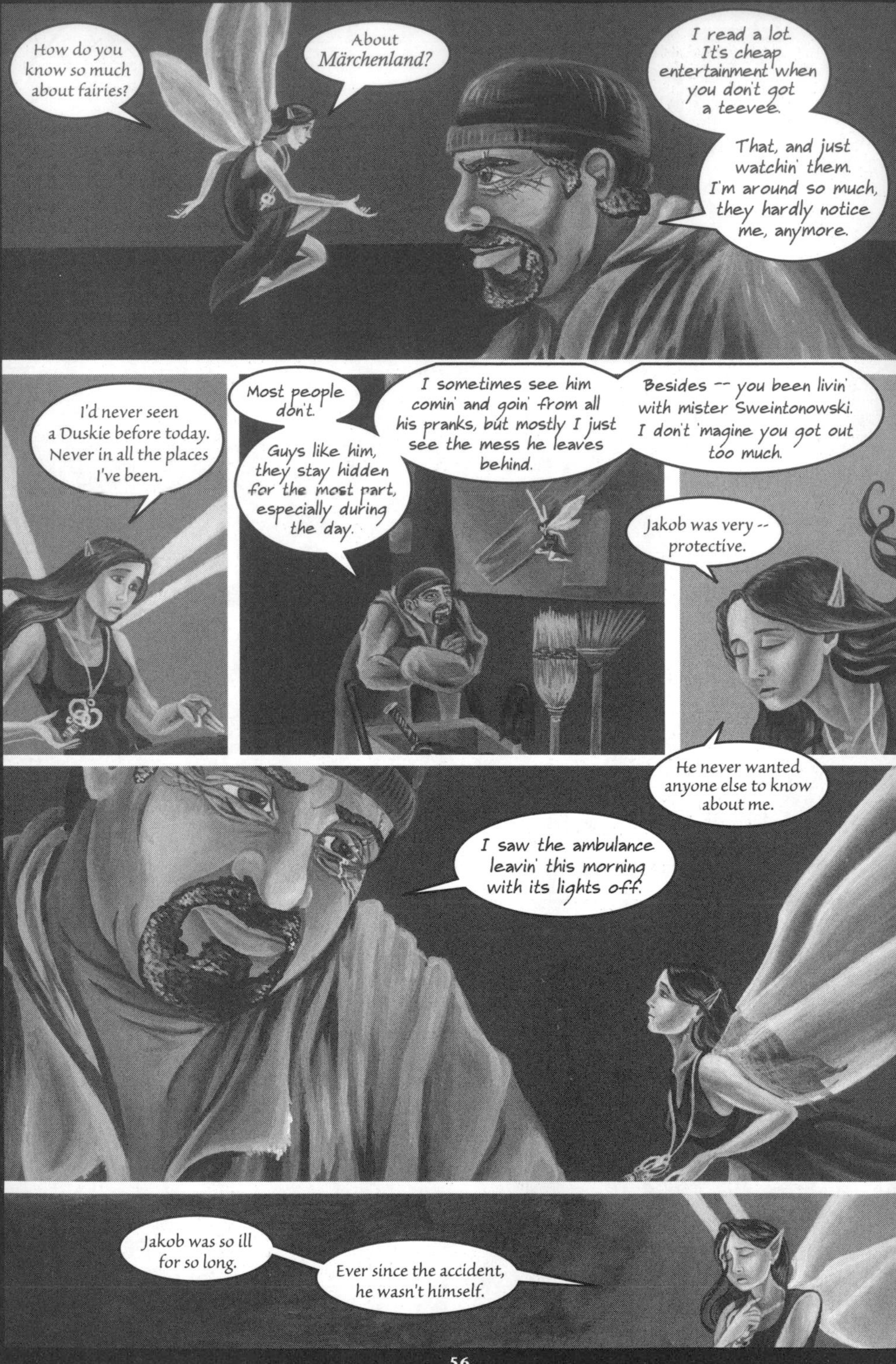
How do you know so much about fairies?
About Märchenland?
I read a lot. It's cheap entertainment when you don't got a teevee.
That, and just watchin' them. I'm around so much, they hardly notice me, anymore.
I'd never seen a Duskie before today. Never in all the places I've been.
Most people don't.
Guys like him, they stay hidden for the most part, especially during the day.
I sometimes see him comin' and goin' from all his pranks, but mostly I just see the mess he leaves behind.
Besides -- you been livin' with mister Sweintonowski. I don't 'magine you got out too much.
Jakob was very -- protective.
He never wanted anyone else to know about me.
I saw the ambulance leavin' this morning with its lights off.
Jakob was so ill for so long.
Ever since the accident, he wasn't himself.

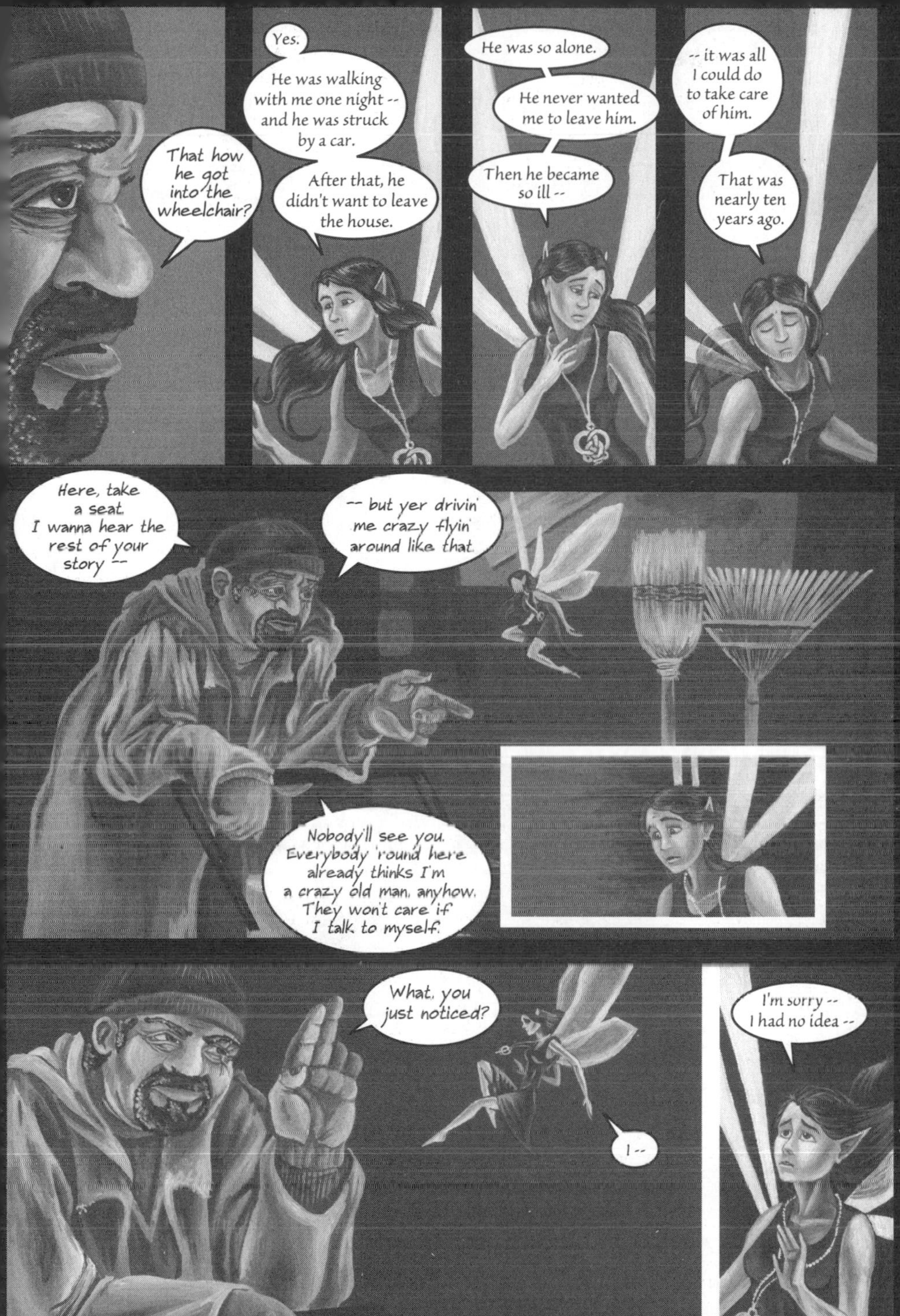

That how he got into the wheelchair?
Yes.
He was walking with me one night -- and he was struck by a car.
After that, he didn't want to leave the house.
He was so alone.
He never wanted me to leave him.
Then he became so ill --
-- it was all I could do to take care of him.
That was nearly ten years ago.
Here, take a seat. I wanna hear the rest of your story --
-- but yer drivin' me crazy flyin' around like that.
Nobody'll see you. Everybody 'round here already thinks I'm a crazy old man, anyhow. They won't care if I talk to myself.
What, you just noticed?
I --
I'm sorry -- I had no idea --

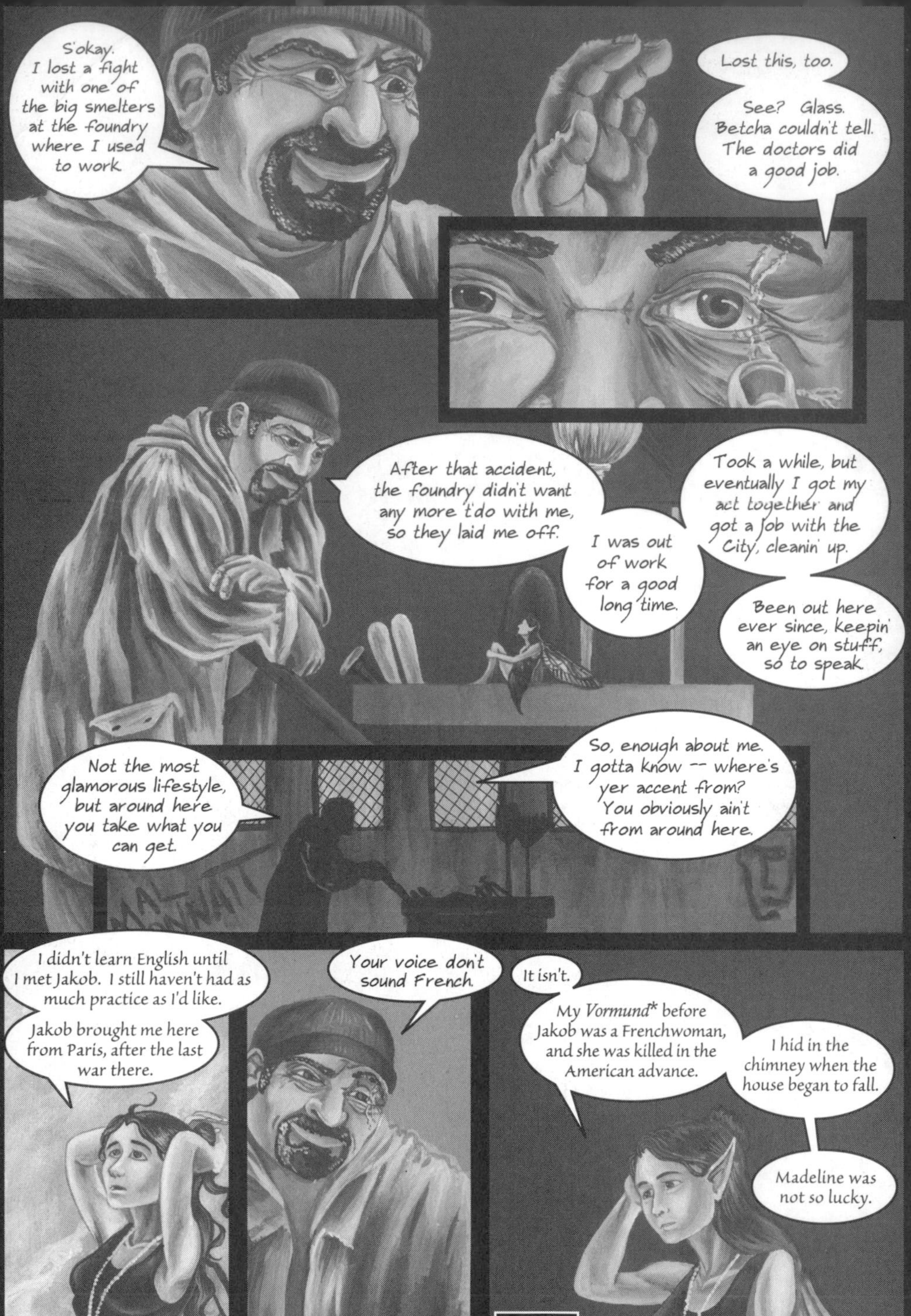
S'okay. I lost a fight with one of the big smelters at the foundry where I used to work.
Lost this, too.
See? Glass. Betcha couldn't tell. The doctors did a good job.
After that accident, the foundry didn't want any more t'do with me, so they laid me off.
I was out of work for a good long time.
Took a while, but eventually I got my act together and got a job with the City, cleanin' up.
Been out here ever since, keepin' an eye on stuff, so to speak.
Not the most glamorous lifestyle, but around here you take what you can get.
So, enough about me. I gotta know -- where's yer accent from? You obviously ain't from around here.
I didn't learn English until I met Jakob. I still haven't had as much practice as I'd like.
Jakob brought me here from Paris, after the last war there.
Your voice don't sound French.
It isn't.
My *Vormund** before Jakob was a Frenchwoman, and she was killed in the American advance.
I hid in the chimney when the house began to fall.
Madeline was not so lucky.
*Guardian

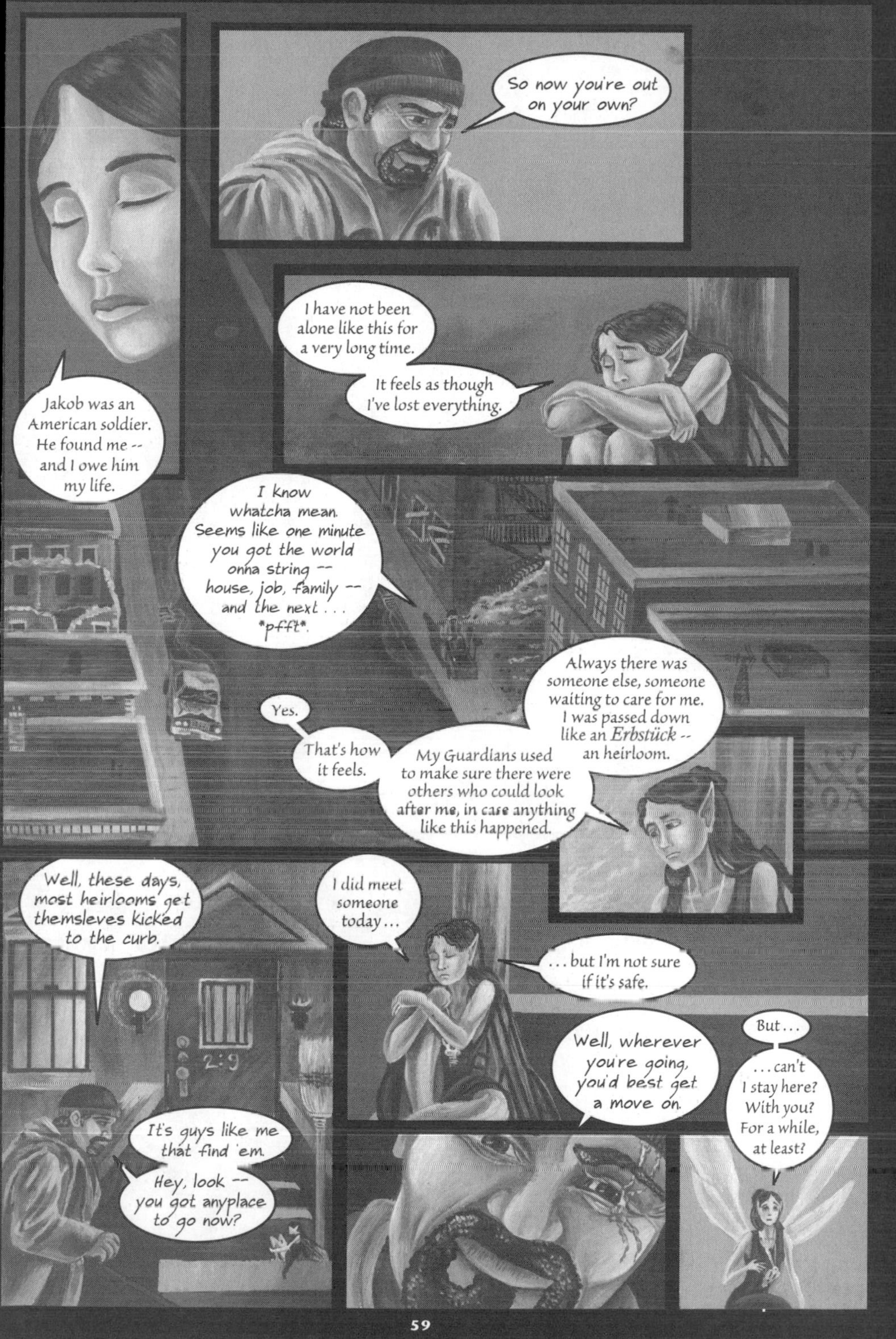
Jakob was an American soldier. He found me -- and I owe him my life.
So now you're out on your own?
I have not been alone like this for a very long time.
It feels as though I've lost everything.
I know whatcha mean. Seems like one minute you got the world onna string -- house, job, family -- and the next . . . *pfft*.
Always there was someone else, someone waiting to care for me. I was passed down like an *Erbstück* -- an heirloom.
Yes.
That's how it feels.
My Guardians used to make sure there were others who could look after me, in case anything like this happened.
Well, these days, most heirlooms get themsleves kicked to the curb.
It's guys like me that find 'em.
Hey, look -- you got anyplace to go now?
I did meet someone today...
... but I'm not sure if it's safe.
Well, wherever you're going, you'd best get a move on.
But...
... can't I stay here? With you? For a while, at least?

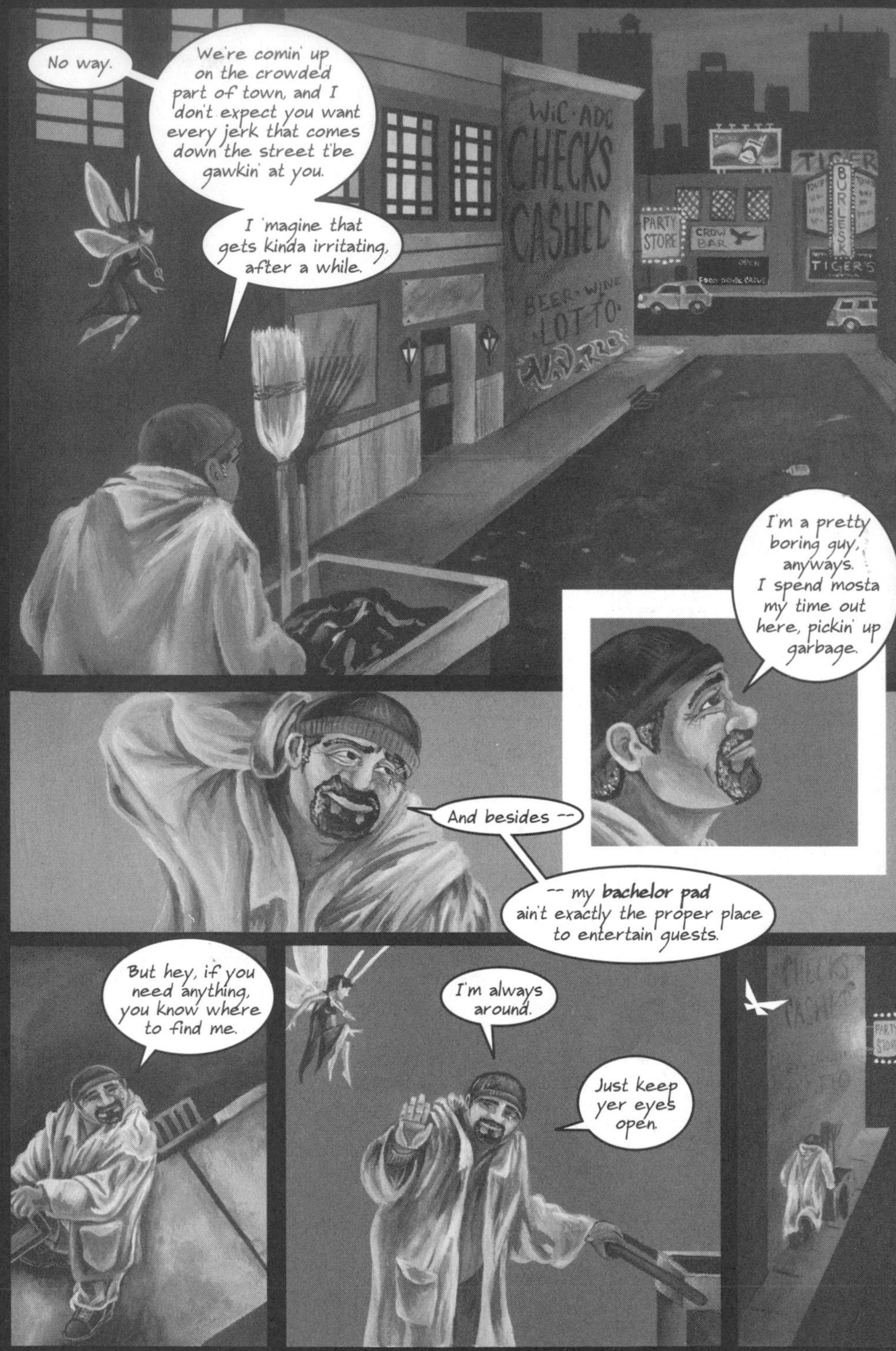
No way.
We're comin' up on the crowded part of town, and I don't expect you want every jerk that comes down the street t'be gawkin' at you.
I 'magine that gets kinda irritating, after a while.
WIC·ADC
CHECKS CASHED
BEER·WINE
·LOTTO·
PARTY STORE
CROW BAR
TIGER
BURLESK
TIGER'S
I'm a pretty boring guy, anyways. I spend mosta my time out here, pickin' up garbage.
And besides --
-- my **bachelor pad** ain't exactly the proper place to entertain guests.
But hey, if you need anything, you know where to find me.
I'm always around.
Just keep yer eyes open.

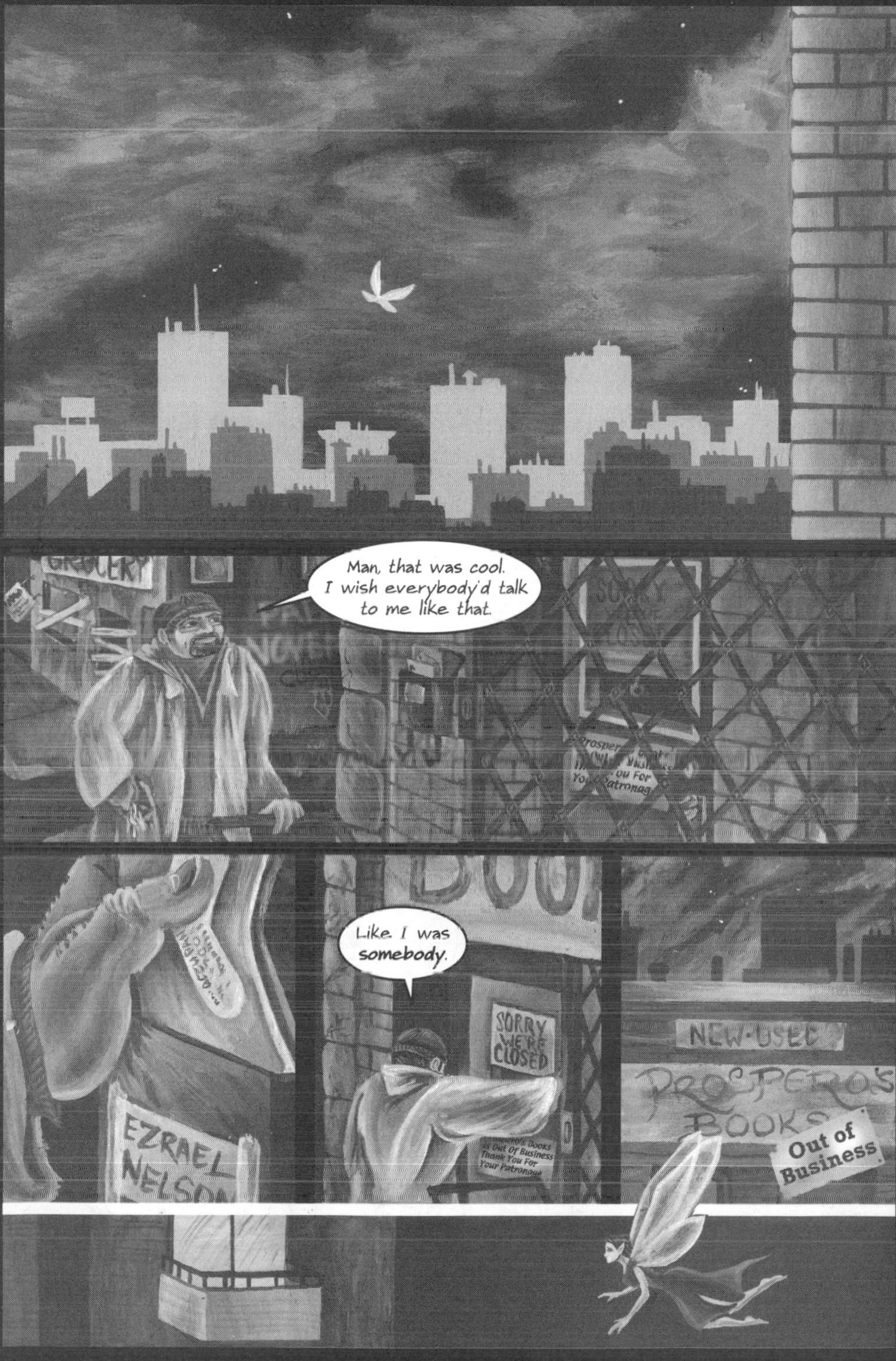
GROCERY
Man, that was cool. I wish everybody'd talk to me like that.
Thank You For
Your Patronag
EZRAEL
NELSO
Like I was **somebody**.
SORRY WE'RE CLOSED
Is Out Of Business
Thank You For
Your Patronage
NEW-USED
PROSPERO'S
BOOKS
Out of Business

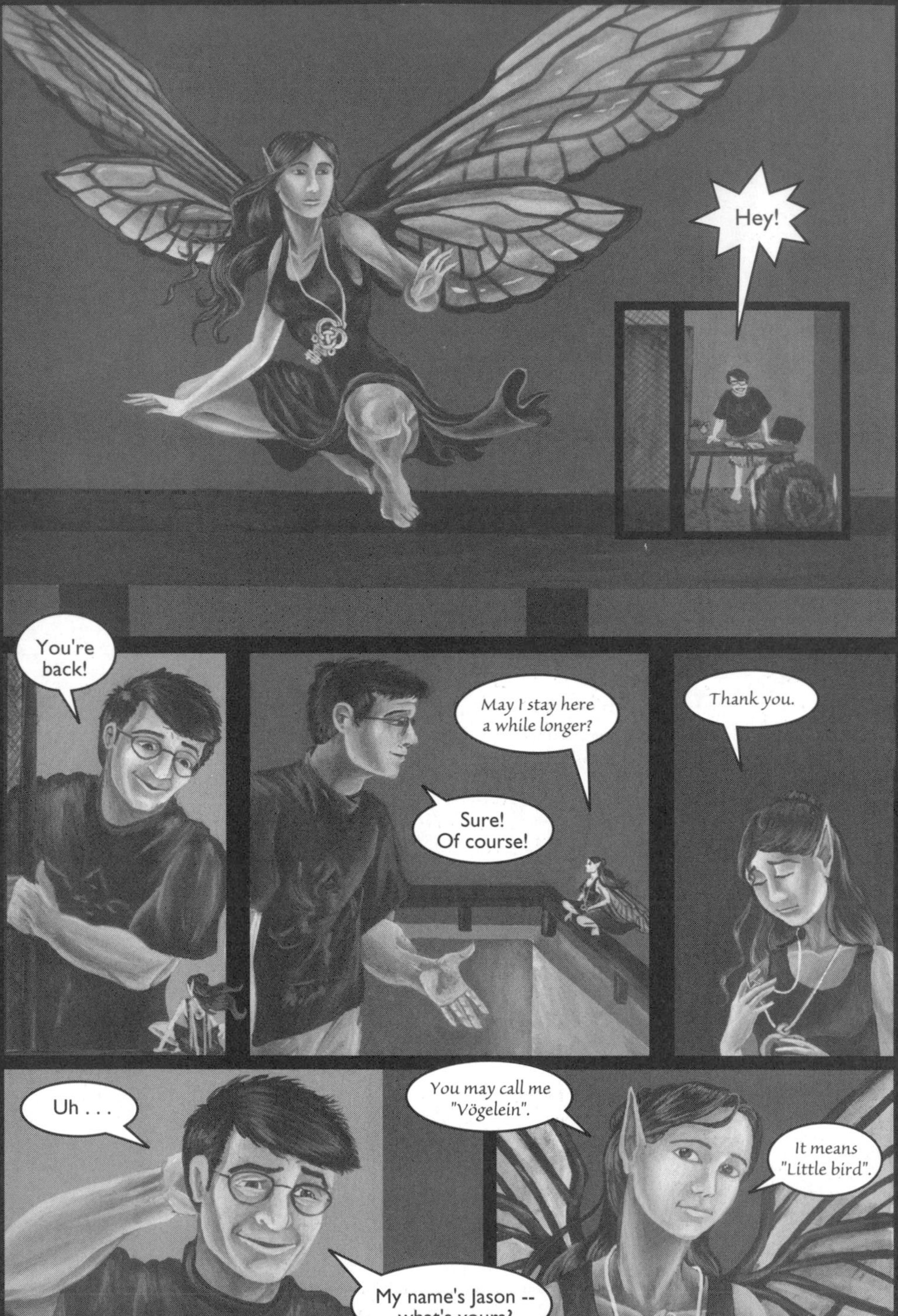
Hey!
You're back!
May I stay here a while longer?
Sure! Of course!
Thank you.
Uh . . .
My name's Jason -- what's yours?
You may call me "Vögelein".
It means "Little bird".

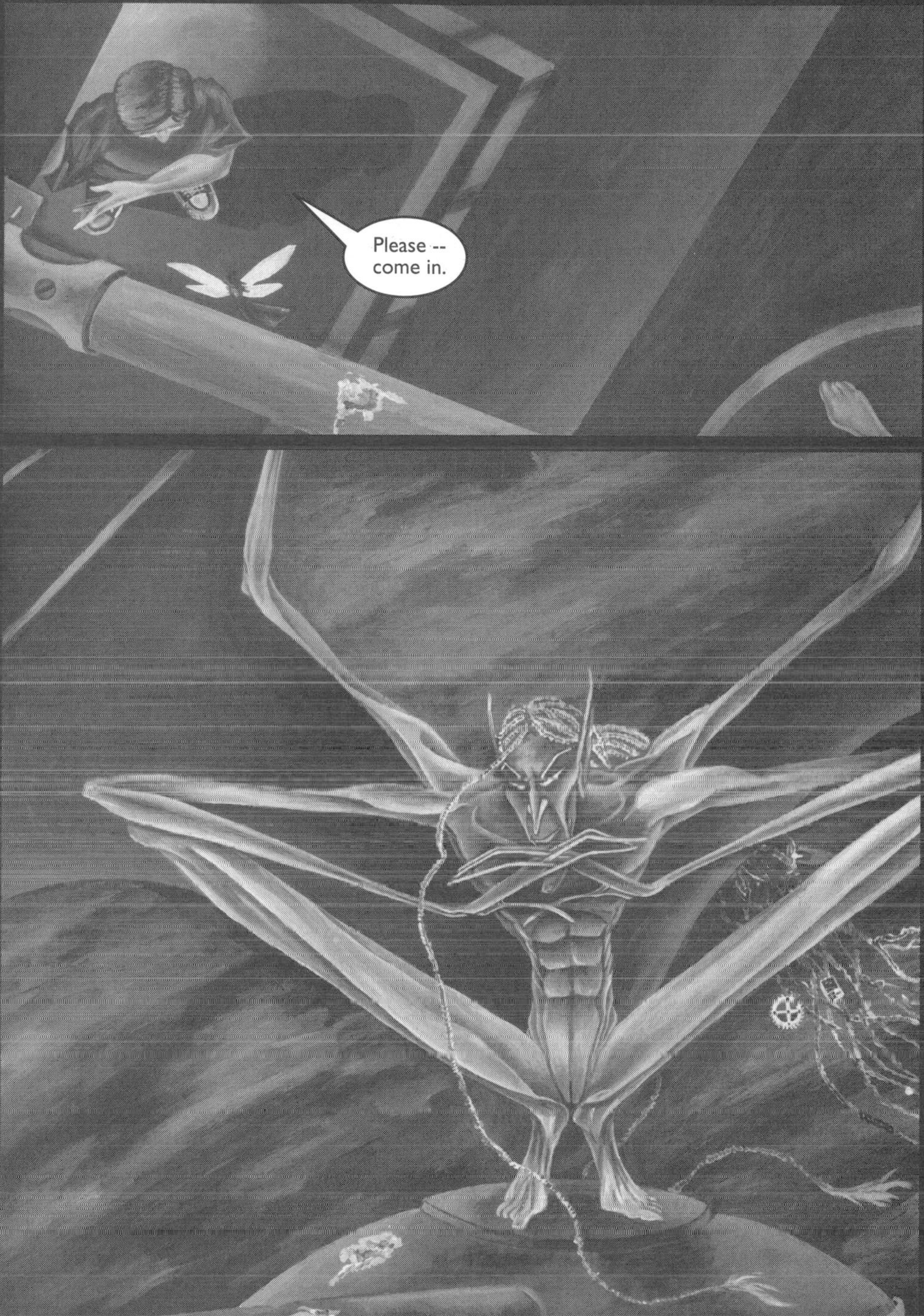
Please -- come in.

If a man is called to be a streetsweeper,
he should sweep streets even as Michaelangelo painted,
or Beethoven composed music,
or Shakespeare wrote poetry.

He should sweep streets so well that
all the hosts of heaven and earth will pause to say,
here lived a streetweeper who did his job well.

-- Martin Luther King, Jr.

- Chapter Three -

You cannot make Remembrance grow
When it has lost its Root --
The tightening the Soil around
And setting it upright
Deceives perhaps the Universe
But not retrieves the Plant --
Real Memory, like Cedar Feet
Is shod with Adamant --
Nor can you cut Remembrance down
When it shall once have grown --
Its Iron Buds will sprout anew
However overthrown -

-- Emily Dickinson

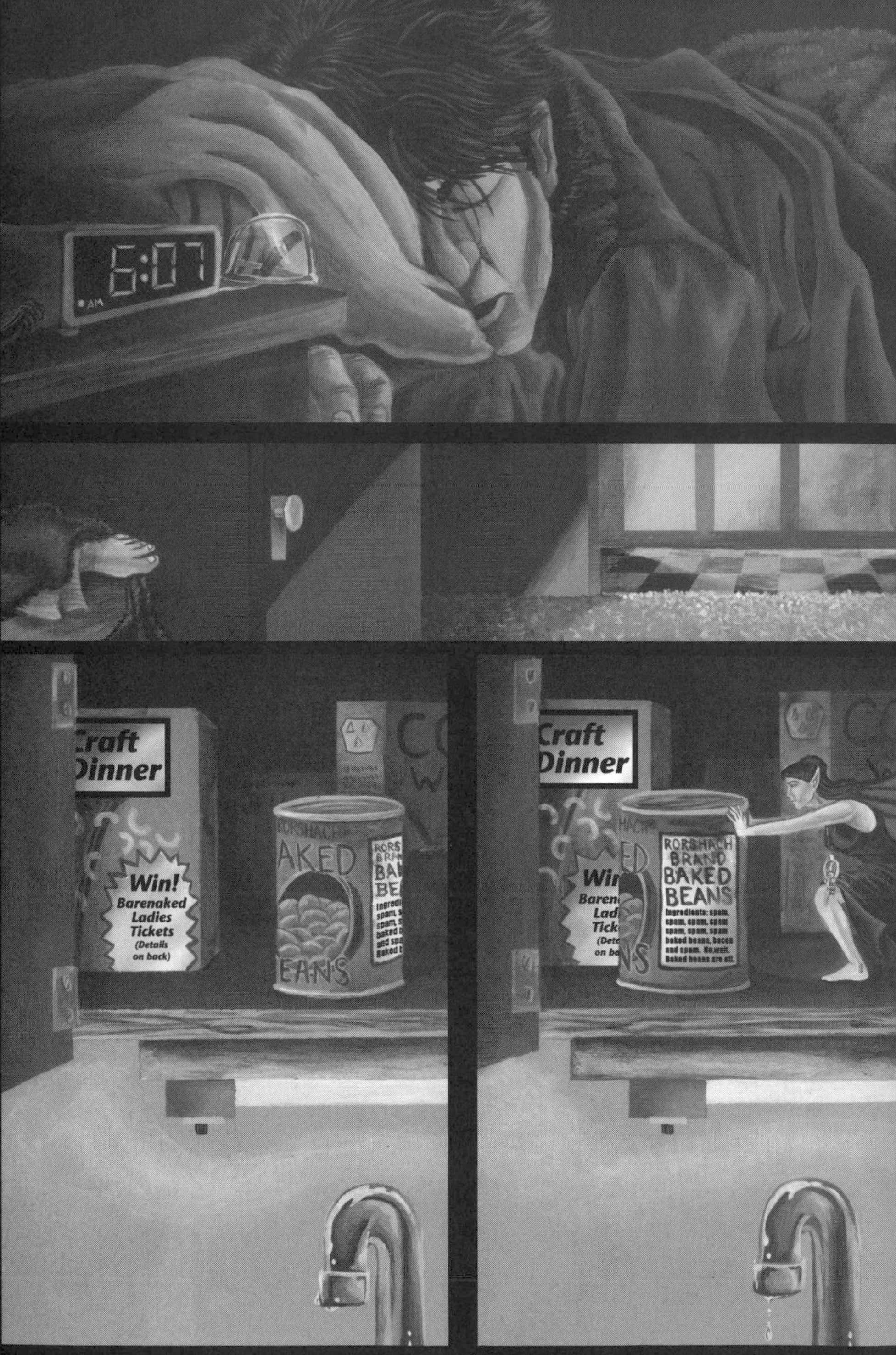
6:07
AM
Craft Dinner
Win!
Barenaked Ladies Tickets
(Details on back)
Craft Dinner
RORSHACH BRAND
BAKED BEANS
Ingredients: spam, spam, spam, spam spam, spam, spam baked beans, bacon and spam. No,wait. Baked beans are off.

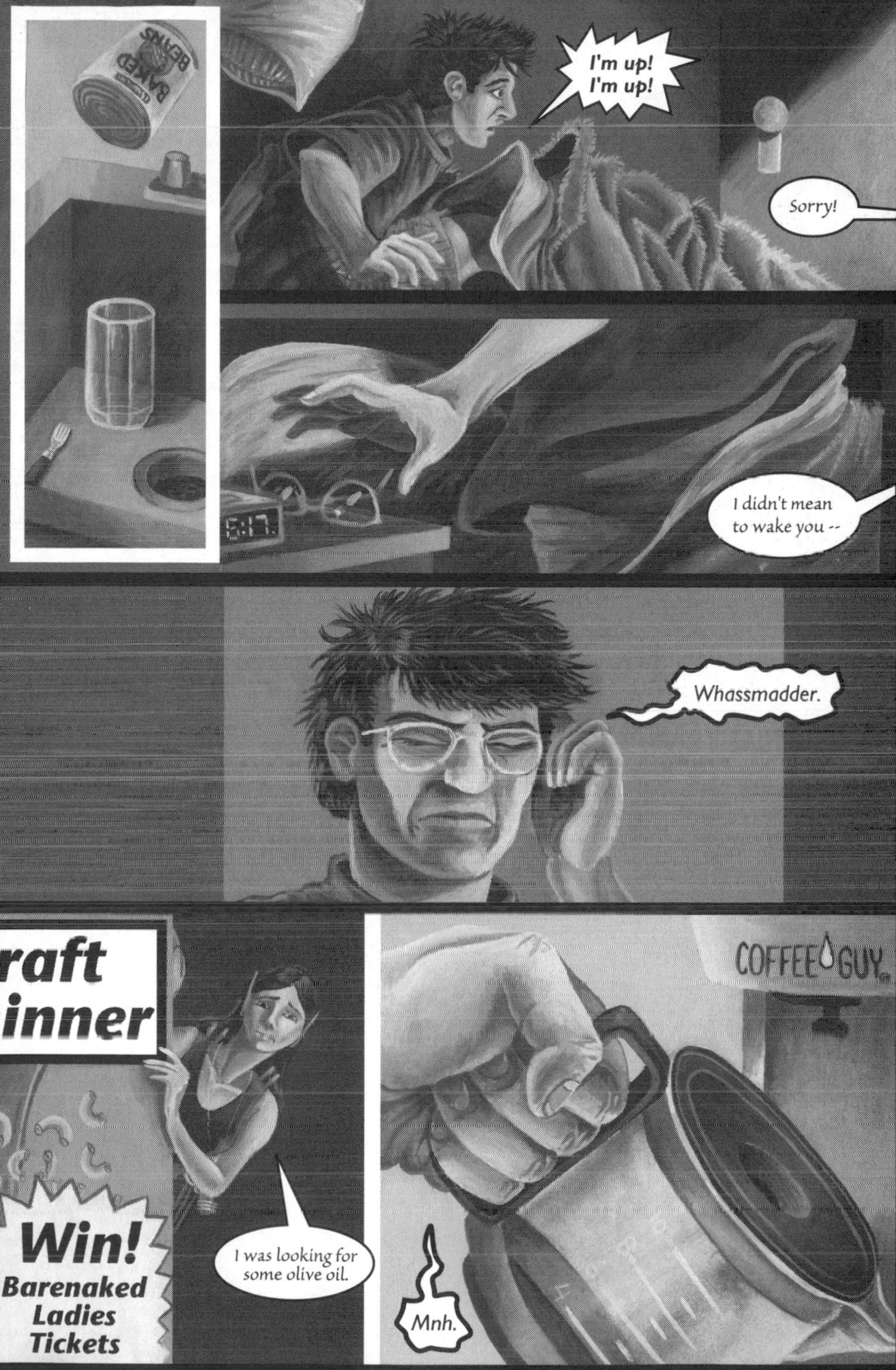
I'm up!
I'm up!
Sorry!
I didn't mean to wake you --
Whassmadder.
raft
inner
Win!
Barenaked Ladies Tickets
I was looking for some olive oil.
COFFEE GUY
Mnh.

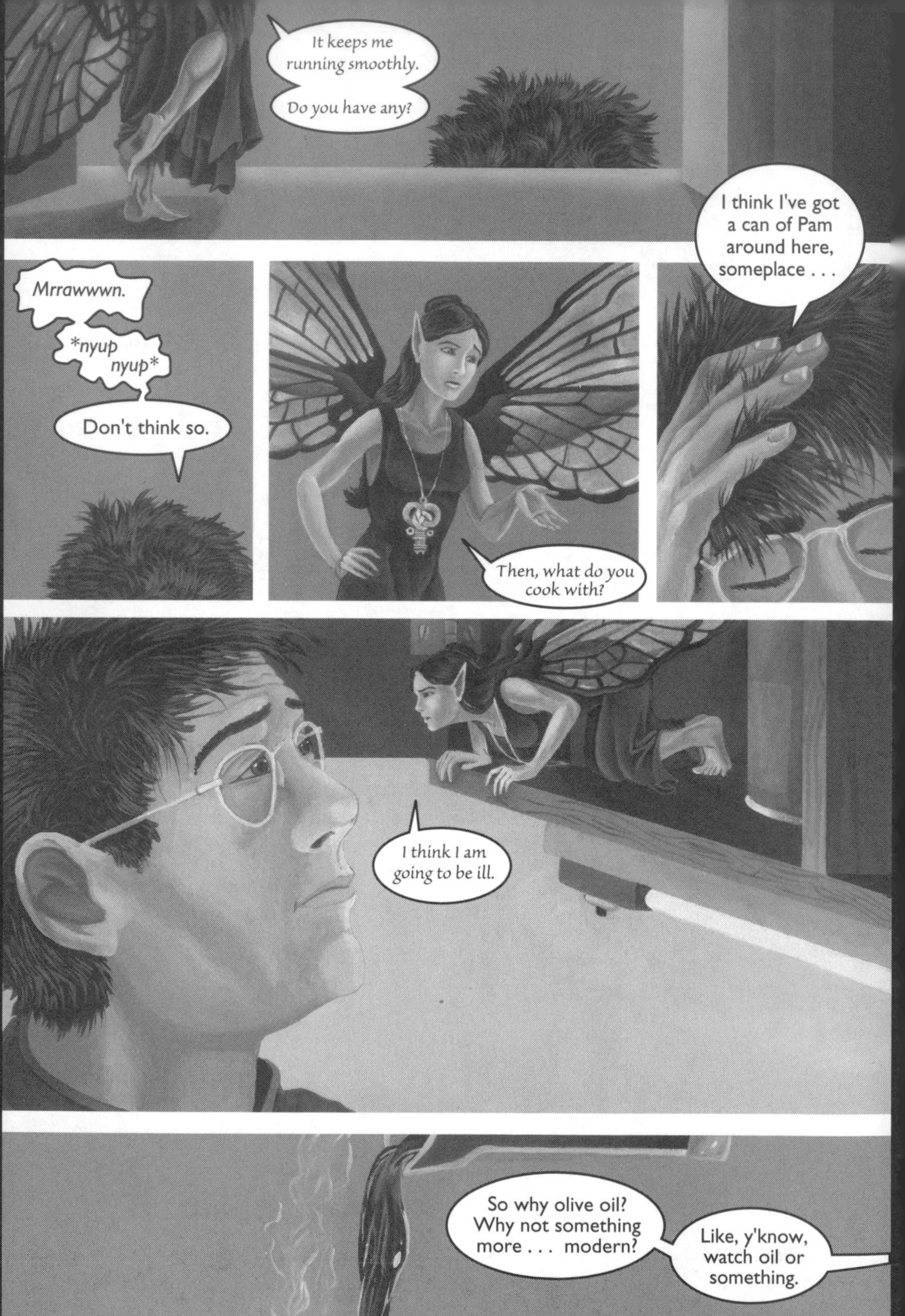
It keeps me running smoothly.
Do you have any?
I think I've got a can of Pam around here, someplace . . .
Mrrawwwn.
nyup nyup
Don't think so.
Then, what do you cook with?
I think I am going to be ill.
So why olive oil? Why not something more . . . modern?
Like, y'know, watch oil or something.

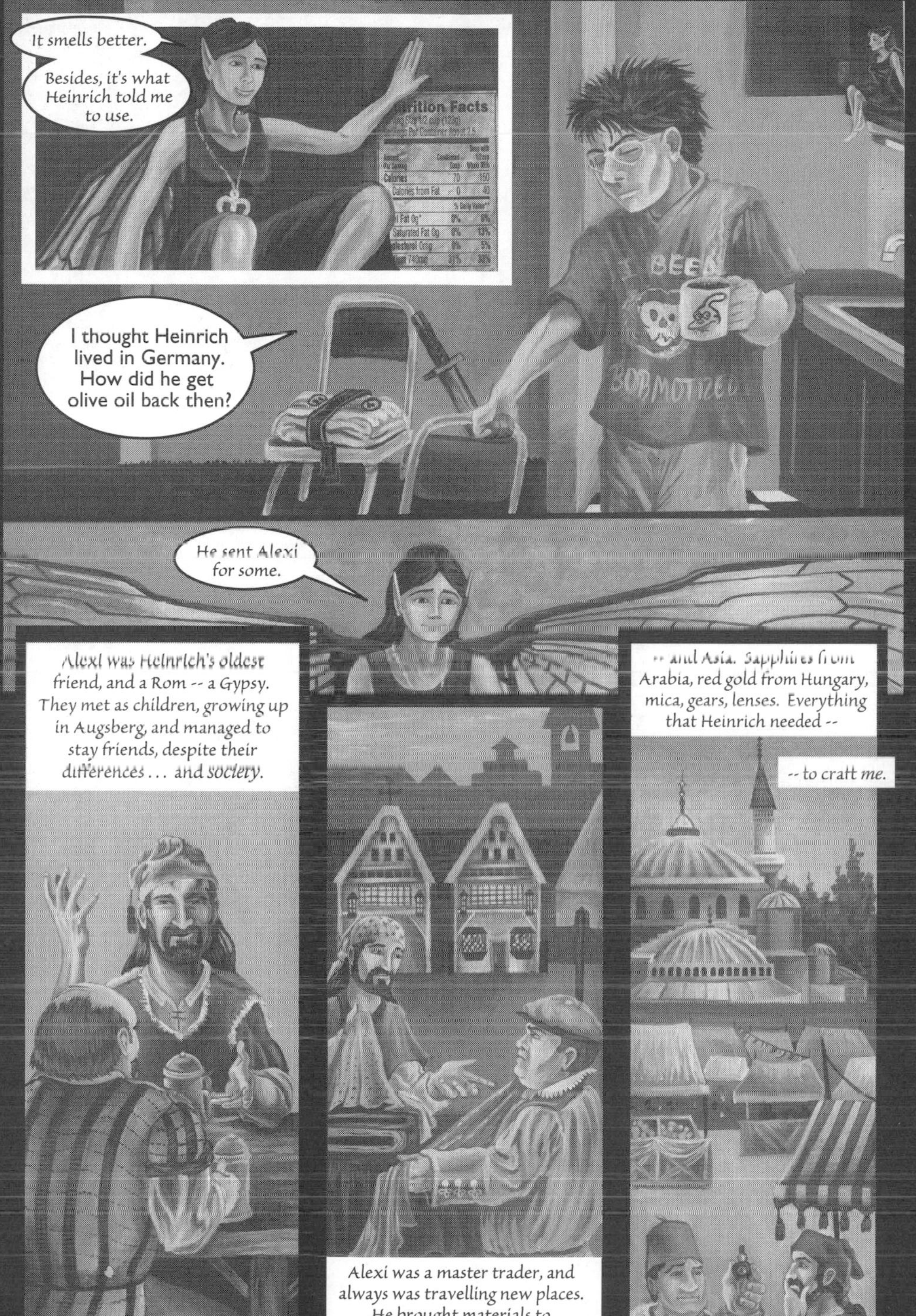
It smells better.
Besides, it's what Heinrich told me to use.
I thought Heinrich lived in Germany. How did he get olive oil back then?
He sent Alexi for some.
Alexi was Heinrich's oldest friend, and a Rom -- a Gypsy. They met as children, growing up in Augsberg, and managed to stay friends, despite their differences . . . and *society*.
Alexi was a master trader, and always was travelling new places. He brought materials to Heinrich from all across Europe --
-- and Asia. Sapphires from Arabia, red gold from Hungary, mica, gears, lenses. Everything that Heinrich needed --
-- to craft *me*.

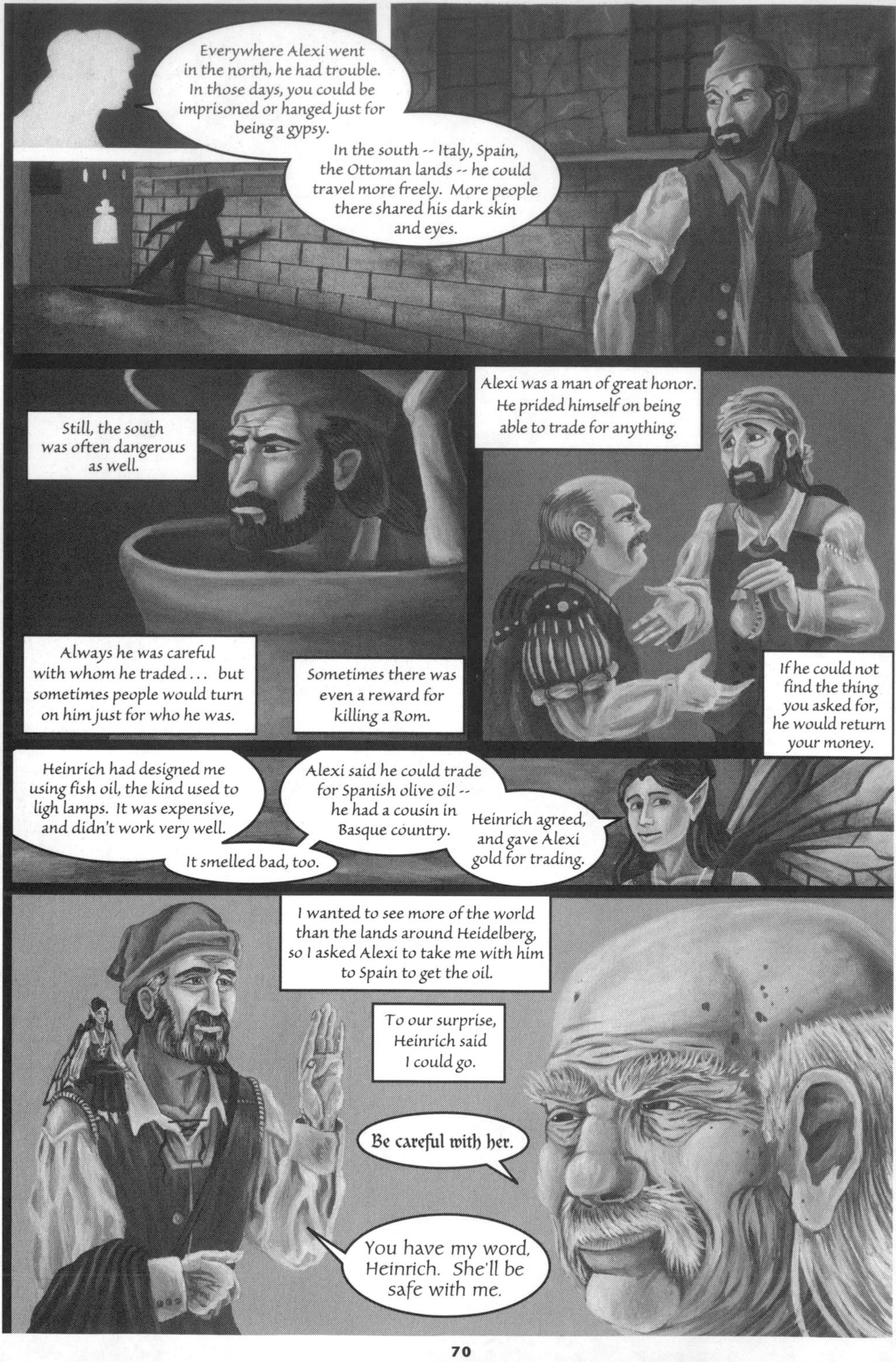
Everywhere Alexi went in the north, he had trouble. In those days, you could be imprisoned or hanged just for being a gypsy.
In the south -- Italy, Spain, the Ottoman lands -- he could travel more freely. More people there shared his dark skin and eyes.
Still, the south was often dangerous as well.
Always he was careful with whom he traded . . . but sometimes people would turn on him just for who he was.
Sometimes there was even a reward for killing a Rom.
Alexi was a man of great honor. He prided himself on being able to trade for anything.
If he could not find the thing you asked for, he would return your money.
Heinrich had designed me using fish oil, the kind used to ligh lamps. It was expensive, and didn't work very well.
It smelled bad, too.
Alexi said he could trade for Spanish olive oil -- he had a cousin in Basque country.
Heinrich agreed, and gave Alexi gold for trading.
I wanted to see more of the world than the lands around Heidelberg, so I asked Alexi to take me with him to Spain to get the oil.
To our surprise, Heinrich said I could go.
Be careful with her.
You have my word, Heinrich. She'll be safe with me.

And remember to wind her every day.

No exceptions.

"From dawn the first day until dusk the next." I know.

What Alexi didn't mention was that the oil casks would also be holding Spanish swords. A blacksmith in Heidelberg paid Alexi to get them -- so he could study Spanish craftsmanship. Alexi had traded for them honestly, but no one in the north would trust a Rom with weapons.

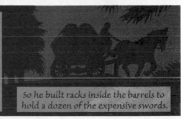

So he built racks inside the barrels to hold a dozen of the expensive swords.

The oil preserved the blades, and whenever a guard stopped him -

Hmm.

Olive oil, Signor.

Eventually, however, his luck ran out.

He had to abandon the wagon to escape.

Alexi told me that the guards persued him all day.

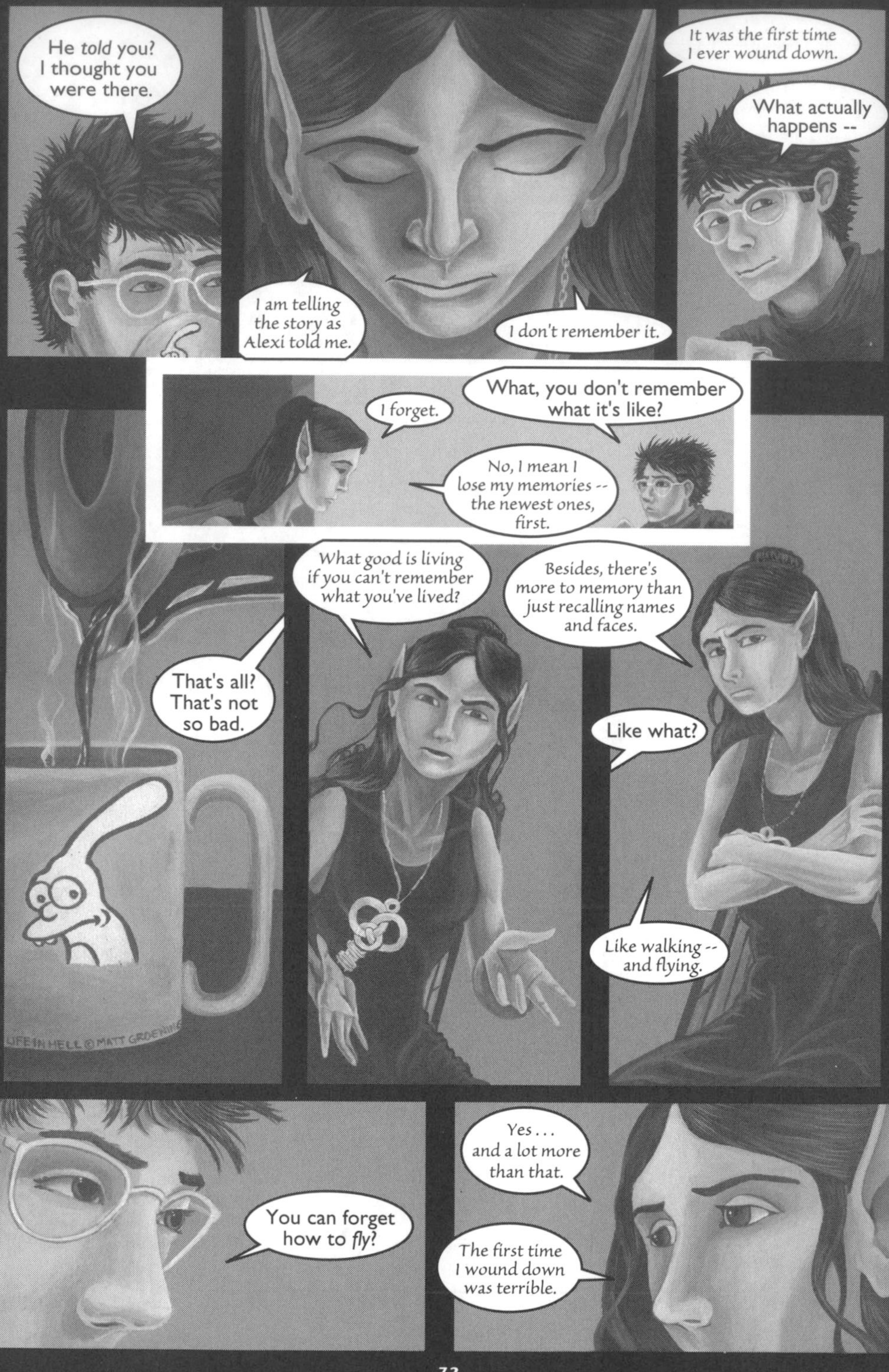
He *told* you? I thought you were there.
I am telling the story as Alexi told me.
I don't remember it.
It was the first time I ever wound down.
What actually happens --
What, you don't remember what it's like?
I forget.
No, I mean I lose my memories -- the newest ones, first.
That's all? That's not so bad.
LIFE IN HELL © MATT GROENING
What good is living if you can't remember what you've lived?
Besides, there's more to memory than just recalling names and faces.
Like what?
Like walking -- and flying.
You can forget how to *fly*?
Yes . . . and a lot more than that.
The first time I wound down was terrible.

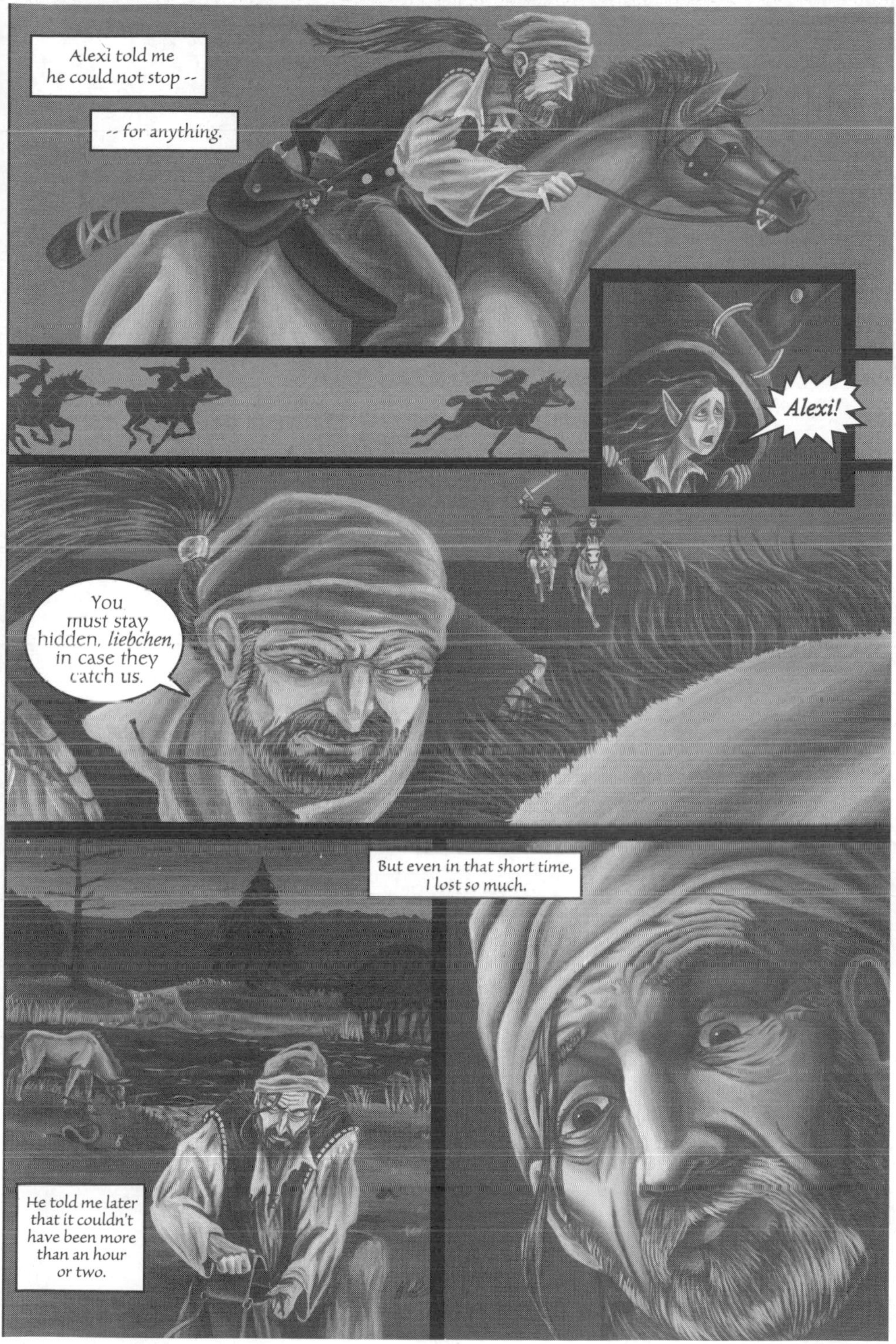
Alexi told me he could not stop --
-- for anything.
Alexi!
You must stay hidden, *liebchen*, in case they catch us.
But even in that short time, I lost so much.
He told me later that it couldn't have been more than an hour or two.

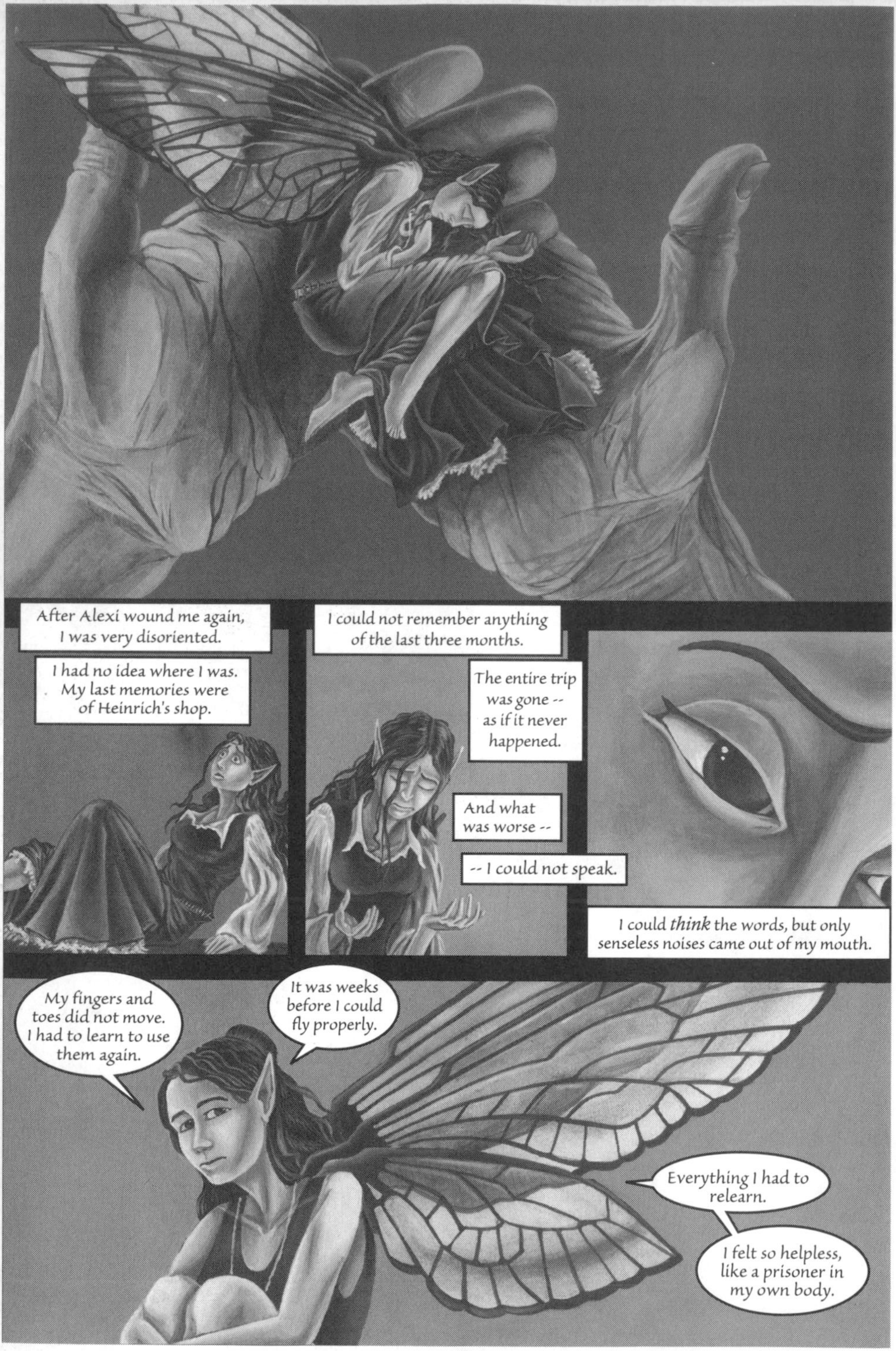
After Alexi wound me again, I was very disoriented.
I had no idea where I was. My last memories were of Heinrich's shop.
I could not remember anything of the last three months.
The entire trip was gone -- as if it never happened.
And what was worse --
-- I could not speak.
I could *think* the words, but only senseless noises came out of my mouth.
My fingers and toes did not move. I had to learn to use them again.
It was weeks before I could fly properly.
Everything I had to relearn.
I felt so helpless, like a prisoner in my own body.

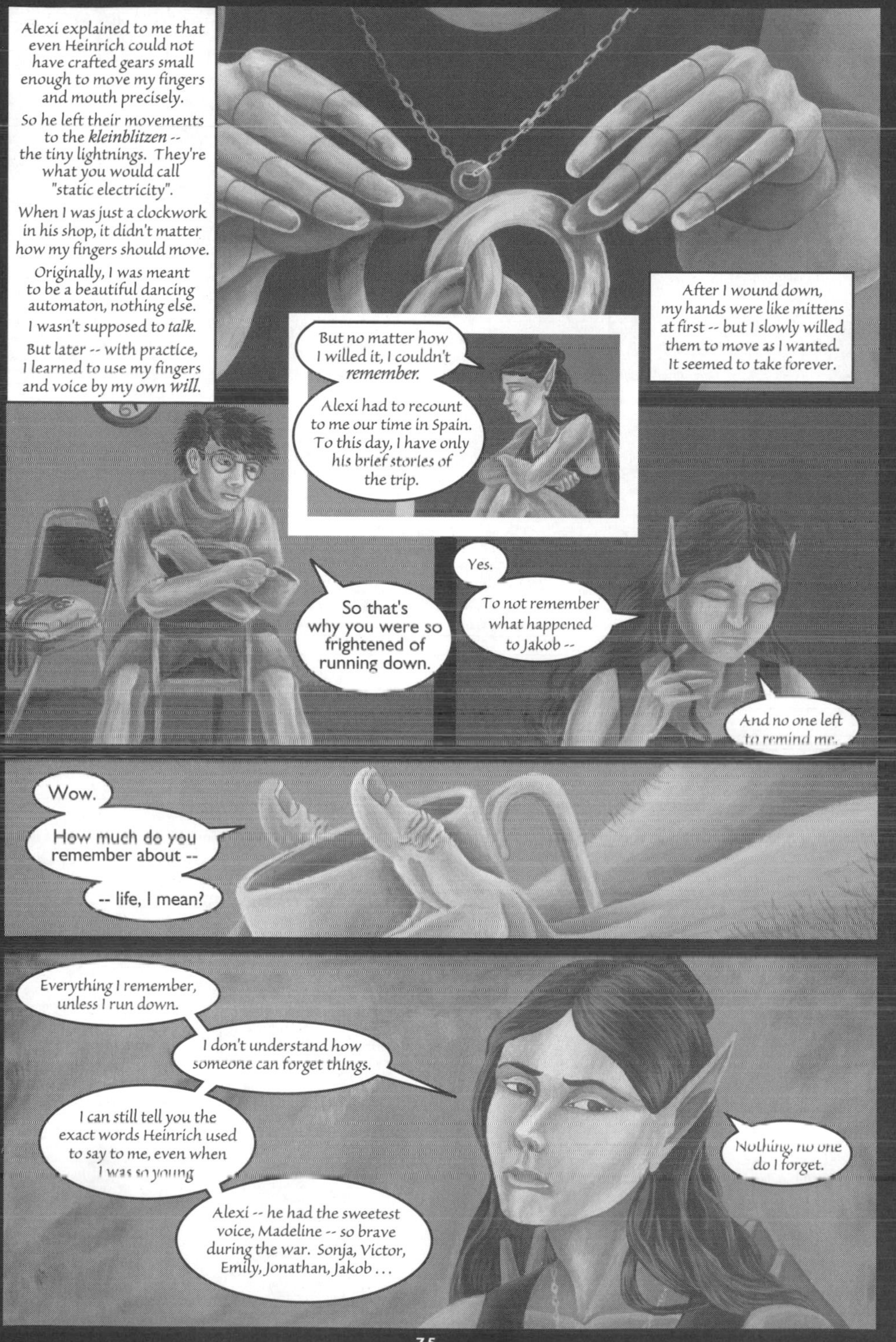
Alexi explained to me that even Heinrich could not have crafted gears small enough to move my fingers and mouth precisely.
So he left their movements to the *kleinblitzen* -- the tiny lightnings. They're what you would call "static electricity".
When I was just a clockwork in his shop, it didn't matter how my fingers should move.
Originally, I was meant to be a beautiful dancing automaton, nothing else.
I wasn't supposed to *talk*.
But later -- with practice, I learned to use my fingers and voice by my own *will*.
After I wound down, my hands were like mittens at first -- but I slowly willed them to move as I wanted. It seemed to take forever.
But no matter how I willed it, I couldn't *remember.*
Alexi had to recount to me our time in Spain. To this day, I have only his brief stories of the trip.
So that's why you were so frightened of running down.
Yes.
To not remember what happened to Jakob --
And no one left to remind me.
Wow.
How much do you remember about --
-- life, I mean?
Everything I remember, unless I run down.
I don't understand how someone can forget things.
I can still tell you the exact words Heinrich used to say to me, even when I was so young
Alexi -- he had the sweetest voice, Madeline -- so brave during the war. Sonja, Victor, Emily, Jonathan, Jakob . . .
Nothing, no one do I forget.

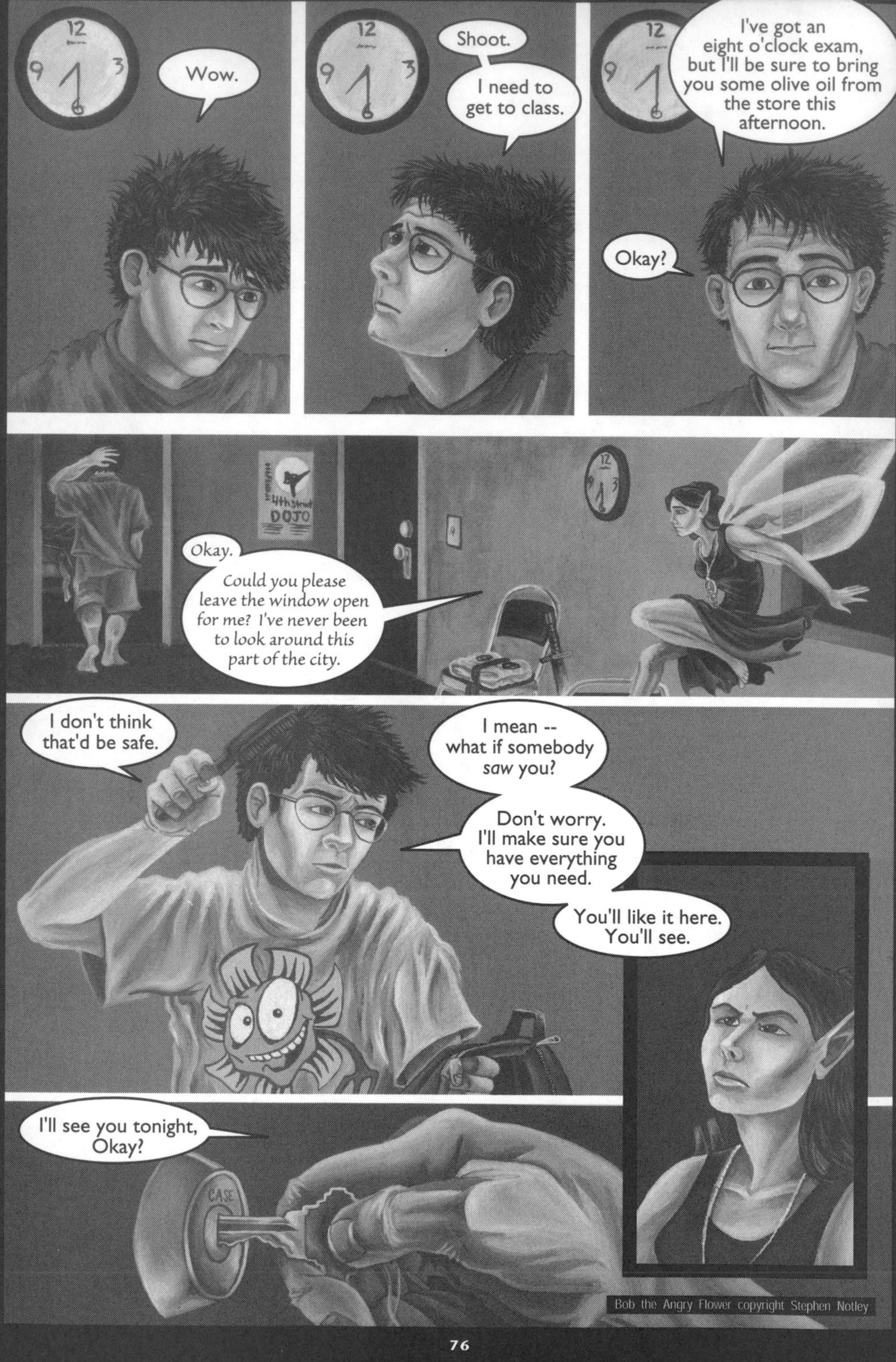
12
9
3
6
Wow.
Shoot.
I need to get to class.
I've got an eight o'clock exam, but I'll be sure to bring you some olive oil from the store this afternoon.
Okay?
4th Street DOJO
Okay.
Could you please leave the window open for me? I've never been to look around this part of the city.
I don't think that'd be safe.
I mean -- what if somebody *saw* you?
Don't worry. I'll make sure you have everything you need.
You'll like it here. You'll see.
I'll see you tonight, Okay?
CASE
Bob the Angry Flower copyright Stephen Notley

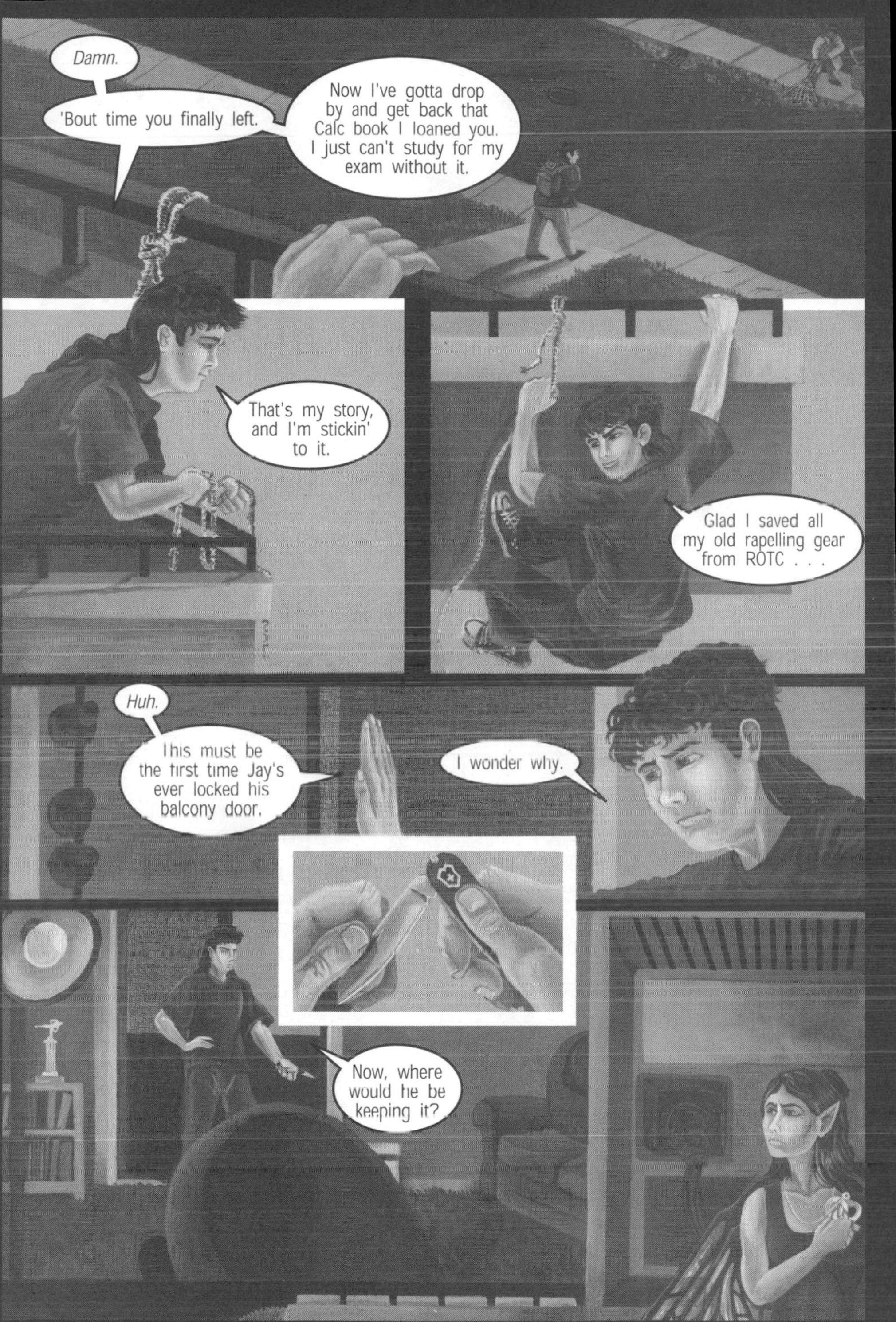
Damn.
'Bout time you finally left.
Now I've gotta drop by and get back that Calc book I loaned you. I just can't study for my exam without it.
That's my story, and I'm stickin' to it.
Glad I saved all my old rapelling gear from ROTC . . .
Huh.
This must be the first time Jay's ever locked his balcony door.
I wonder why.
Now, where would he be keeping it?

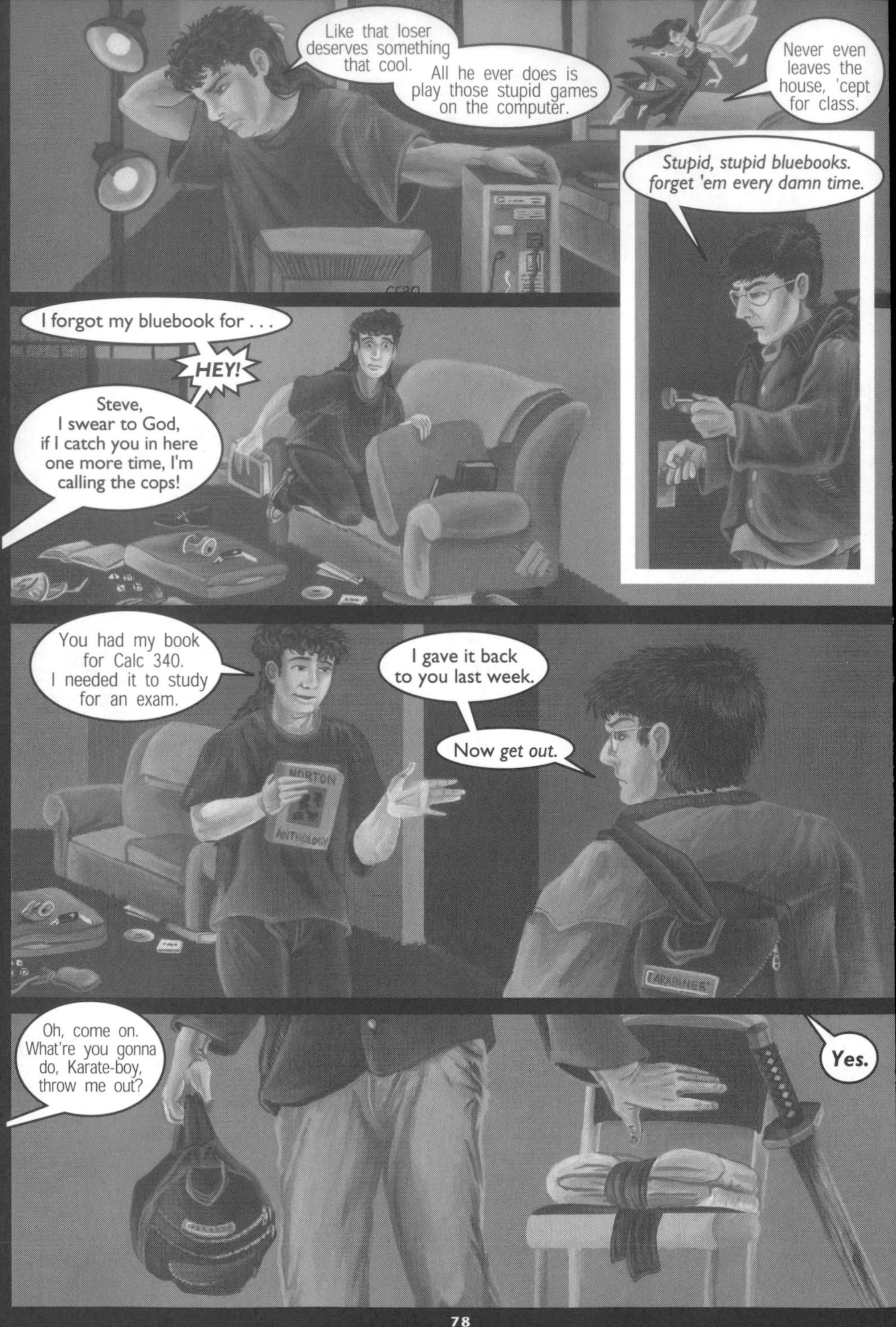
Like that loser deserves something that cool.
All he ever does is play those stupid games on the computer.
Never even leaves the house, 'cept for class.
I forgot my bluebook for . . .
HEY!
Steve, I swear to God, if I catch you in here one more time, I'm calling the cops!
Stupid, stupid bluebooks. forget 'em every damn time.
You had my book for Calc 340. I needed it to study for an exam.
I gave it back to you last week.
Now *get out.*
NORTON ANTHOLOGY
CARABINER
Oh, come on. What're you gonna do, Karate-boy, throw me out?
Yes.

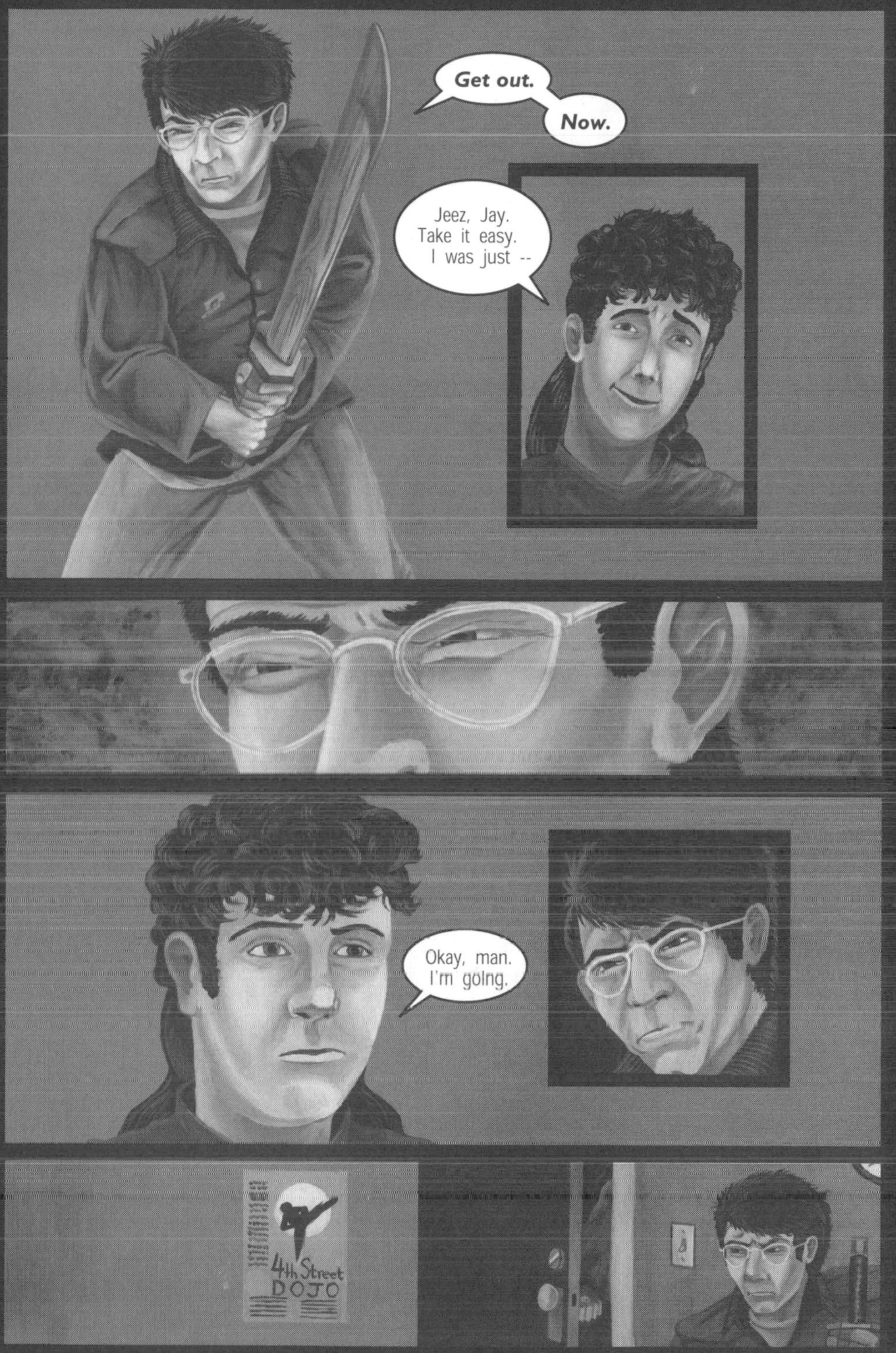
Get out.
Now.
Jeez, Jay. Take it easy. I was just --
Okay, man. I'm going.
4th Street DOJO

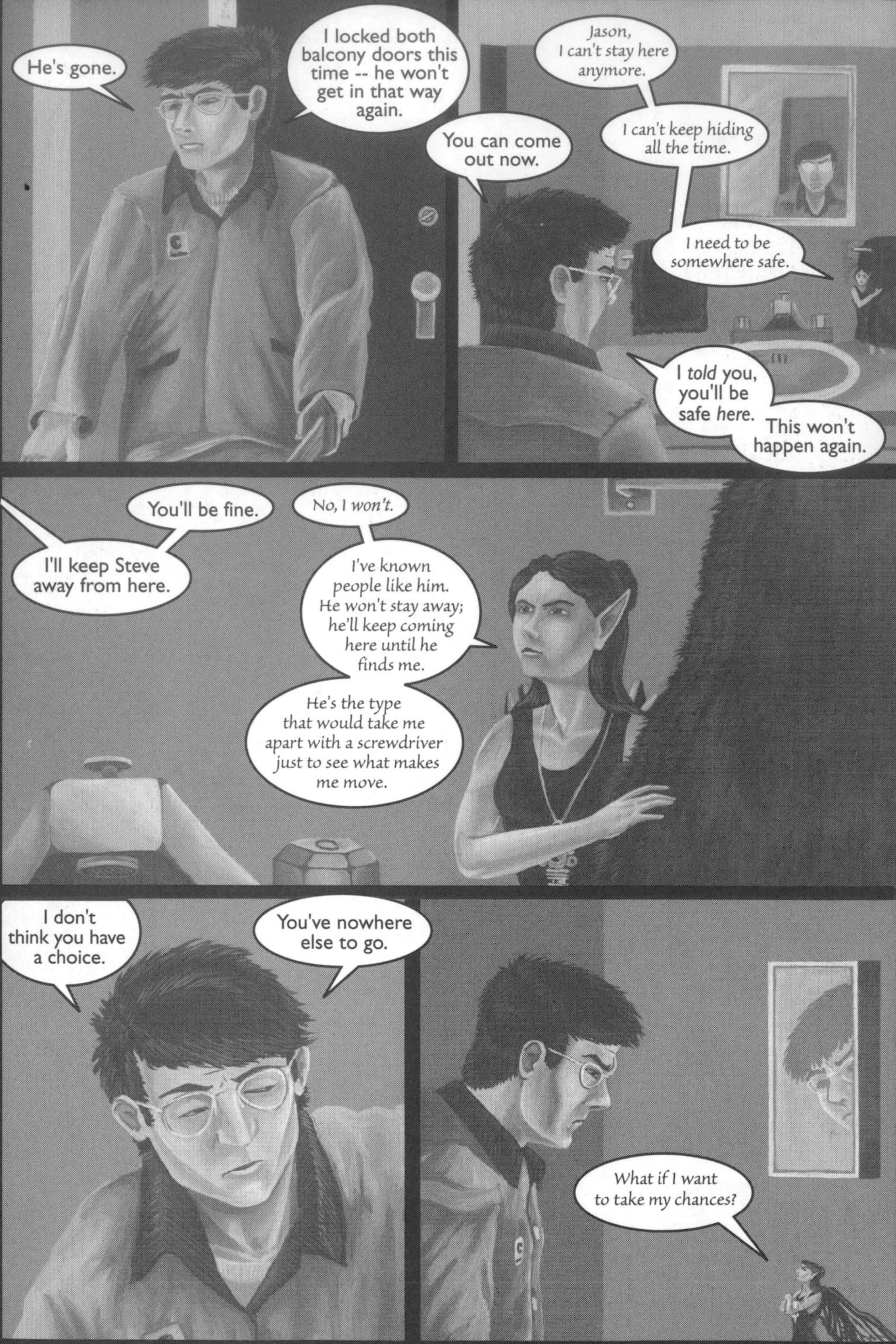
He's gone.
I locked both balcony doors this time -- he won't get in that way again.
You can come out now.
Jason, I can't stay here anymore.
I can't keep hiding all the time.
I need to be somewhere safe.
I *told* you, you'll be safe *here*.
This won't happen again.
You'll be fine.
I'll keep Steve away from here.
No, I *won't*.
I've known people like him. He won't stay away; he'll keep coming here until he finds me.
He's the type that would take me apart with a screwdriver just to see what makes me move.
I don't think you have a choice.
You've nowhere else to go.
What if I want to take my chances?

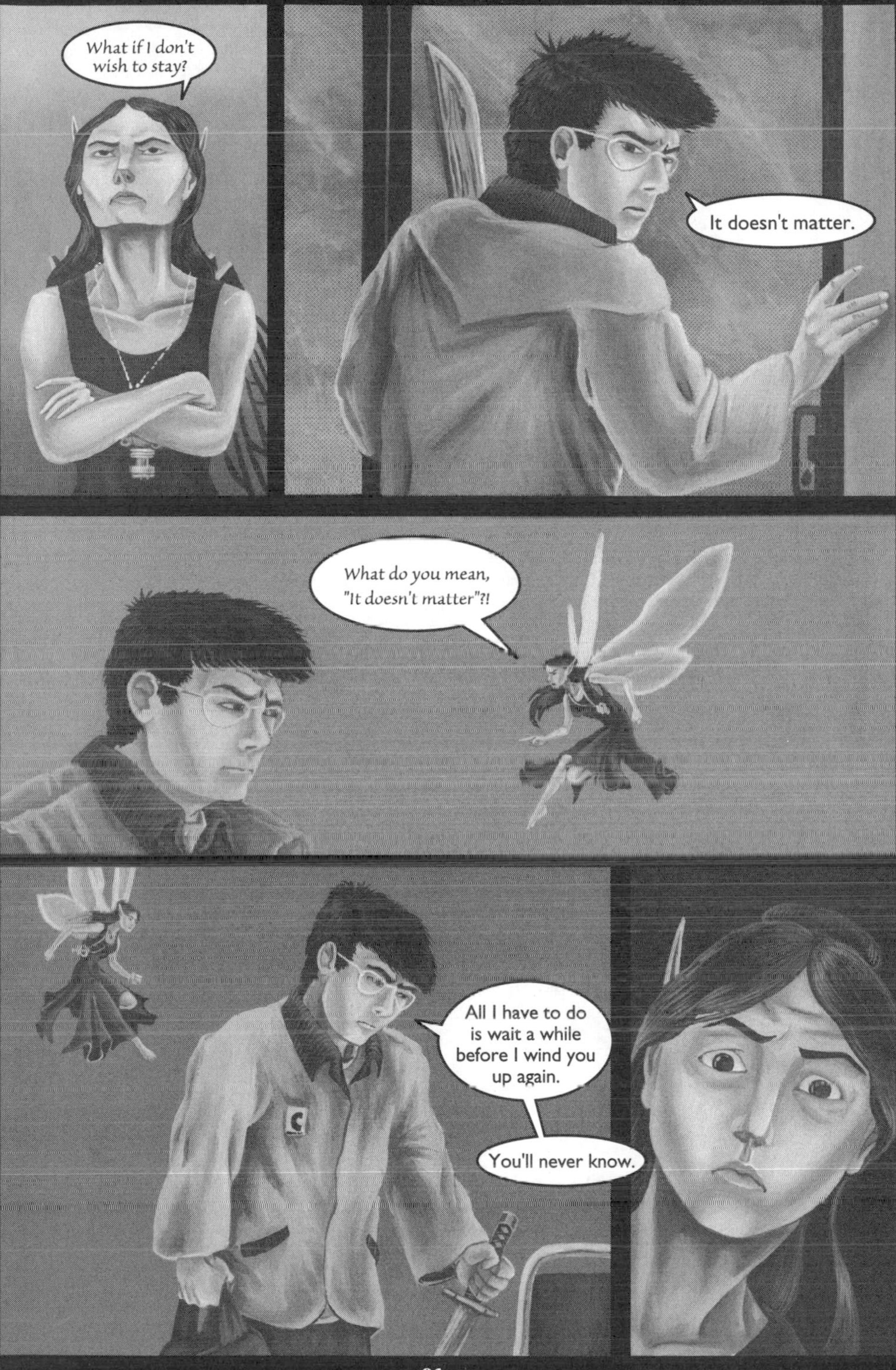
What if I don't wish to stay?
It doesn't matter.
What do you mean, "It doesn't matter"?!
All I have to do is wait a while before I wind you up again.
You'll never know.

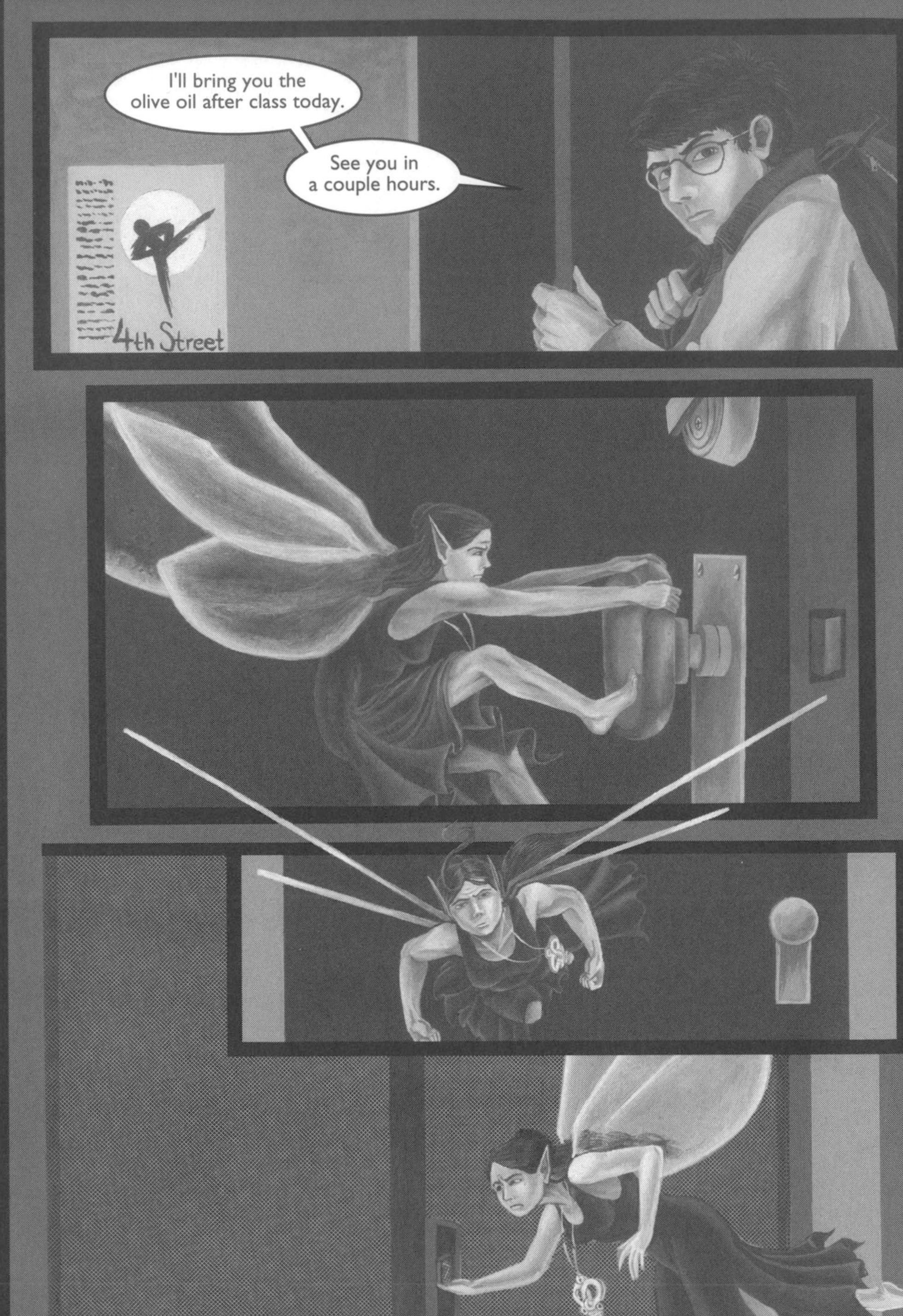
I'll bring you the olive oil after class today.
See you in a couple hours.
4th Street

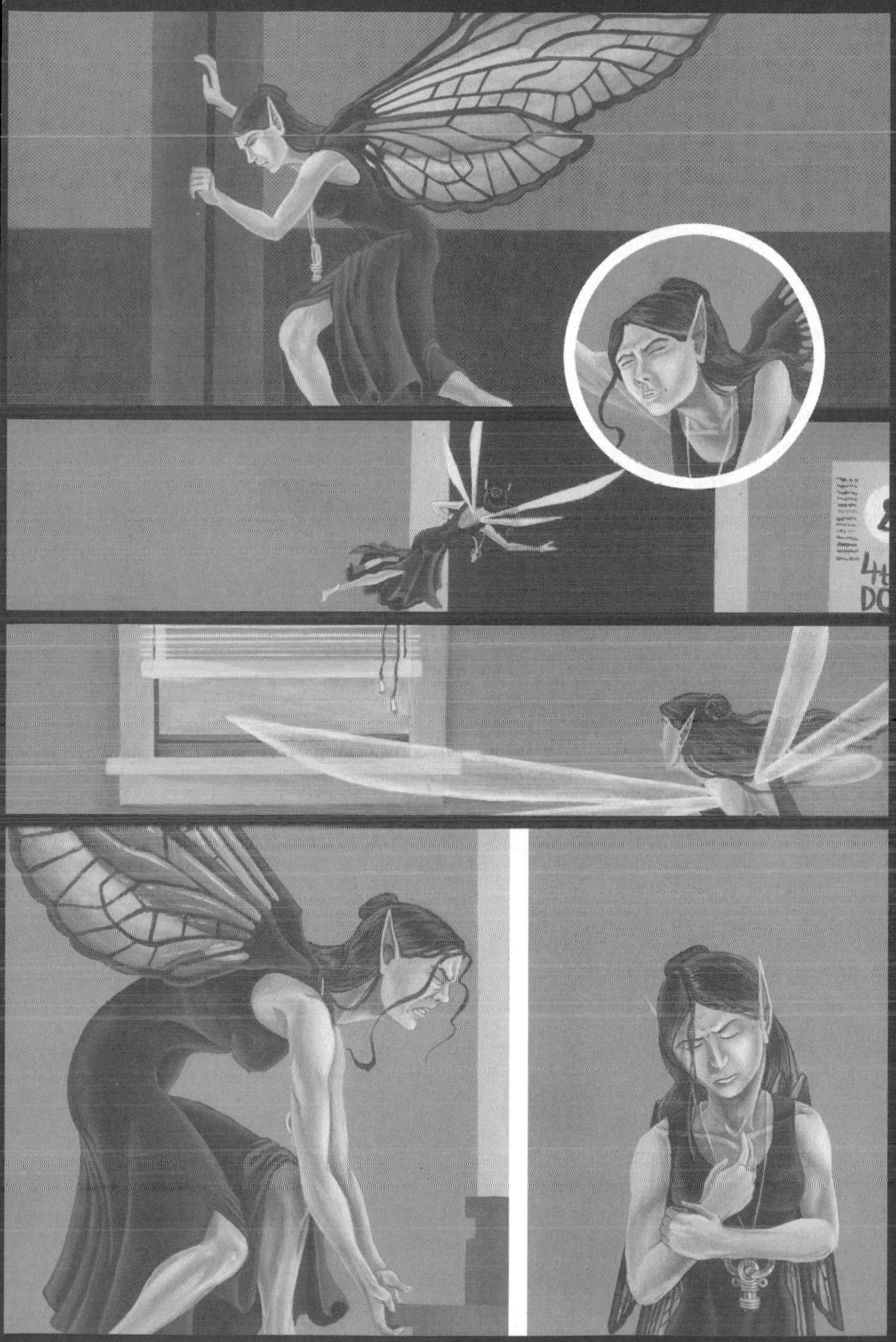

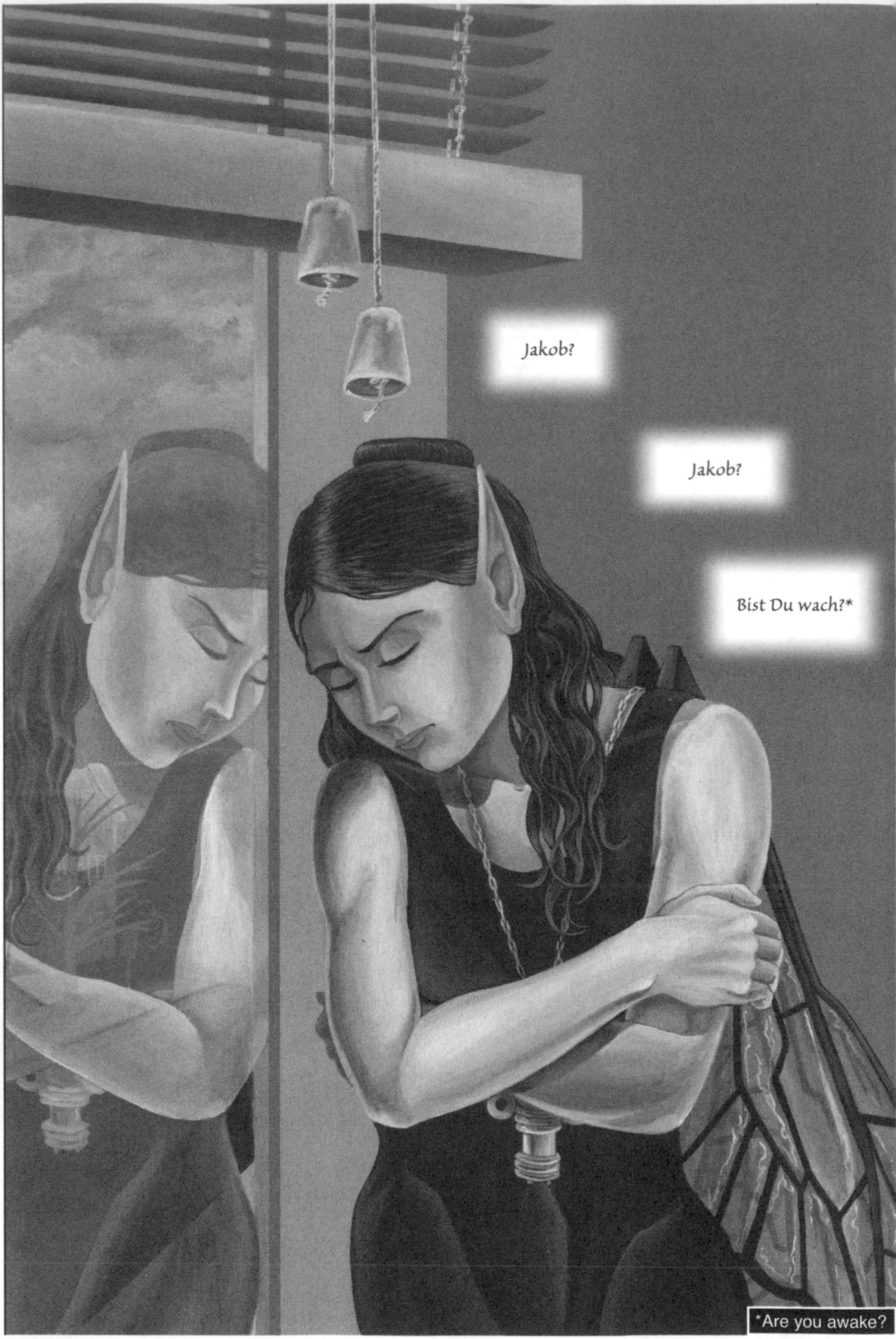
Jakob?
Jakob?
Bist Du wach?*
*Are you awake?

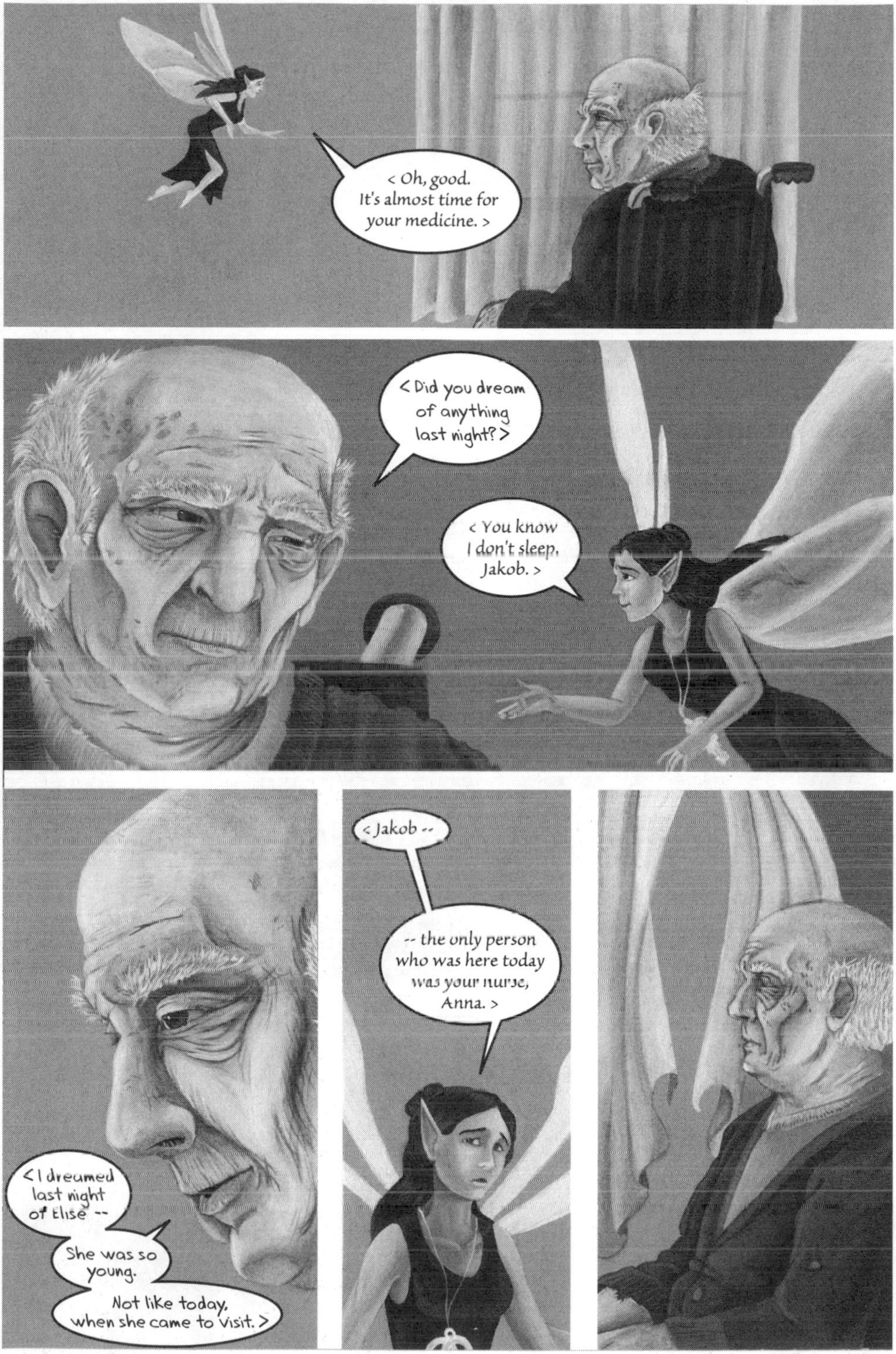

< Oh, good. It's almost time for your medicine. >
< Did you dream of anything last night? >
< You know I don't sleep, Jakob. >
< I dreamed last night of Elise --
She was so young.
Not like today, when she came to visit. >
< Jakob --
-- the only person who was here today was your nurse, Anna. >

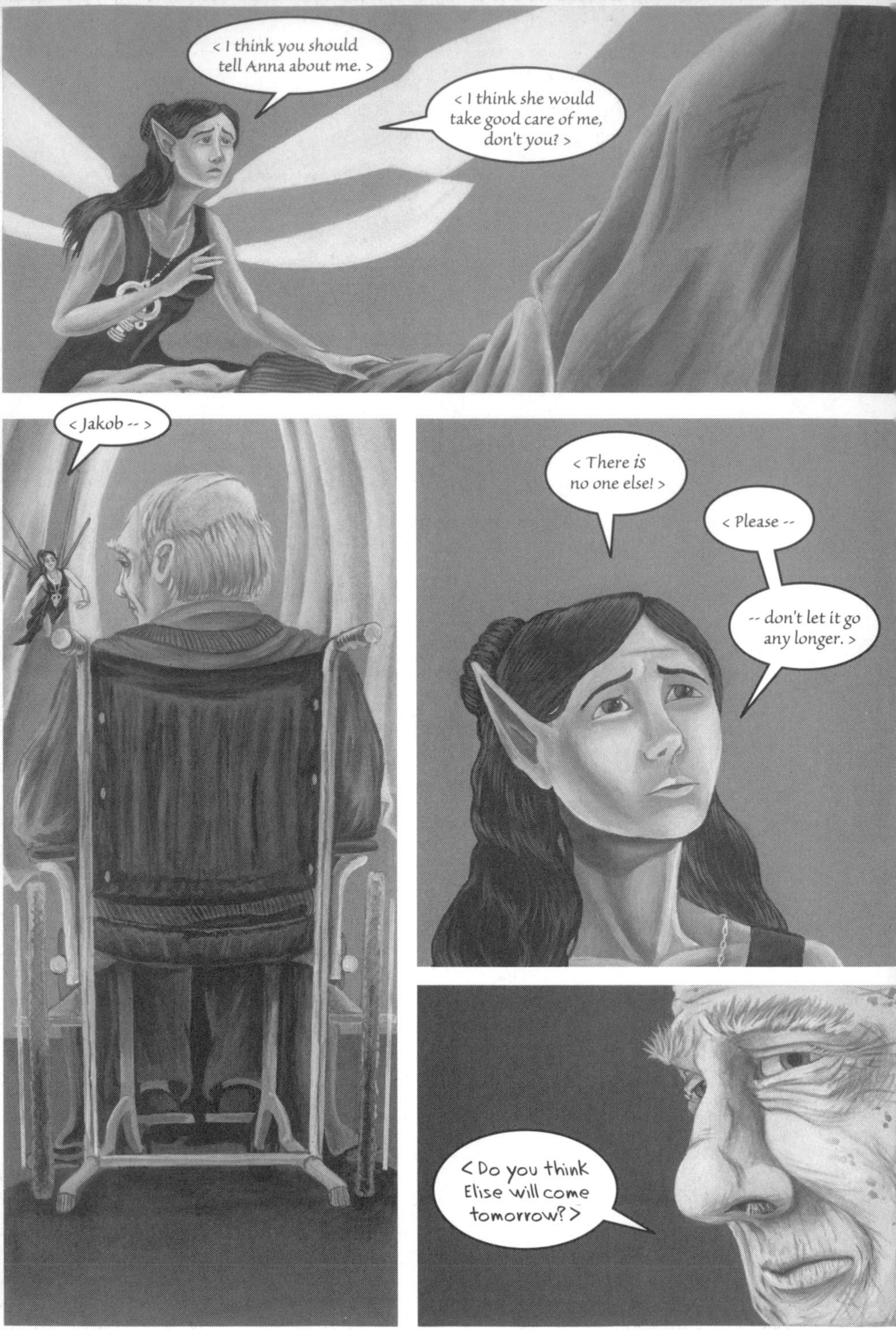
< I think you should tell Anna about me. >
< I think she would take good care of me, don't you? >
< Jakob -- >
< There *is* no one else! >
< Please --
-- don't let it go any longer. >
< Do you think Elise will come tomorrow? >

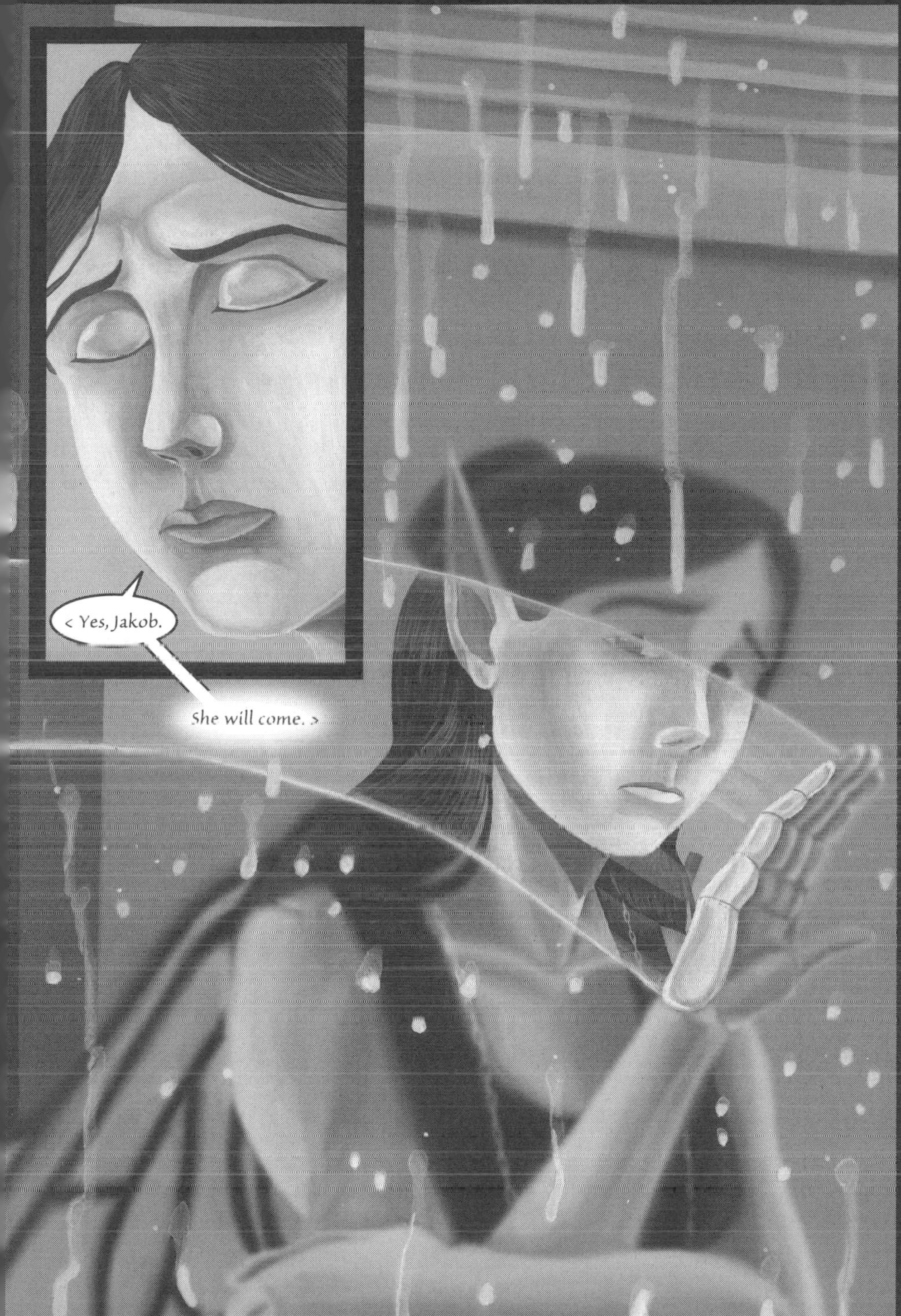
< Yes, Jakob.
She will come. >

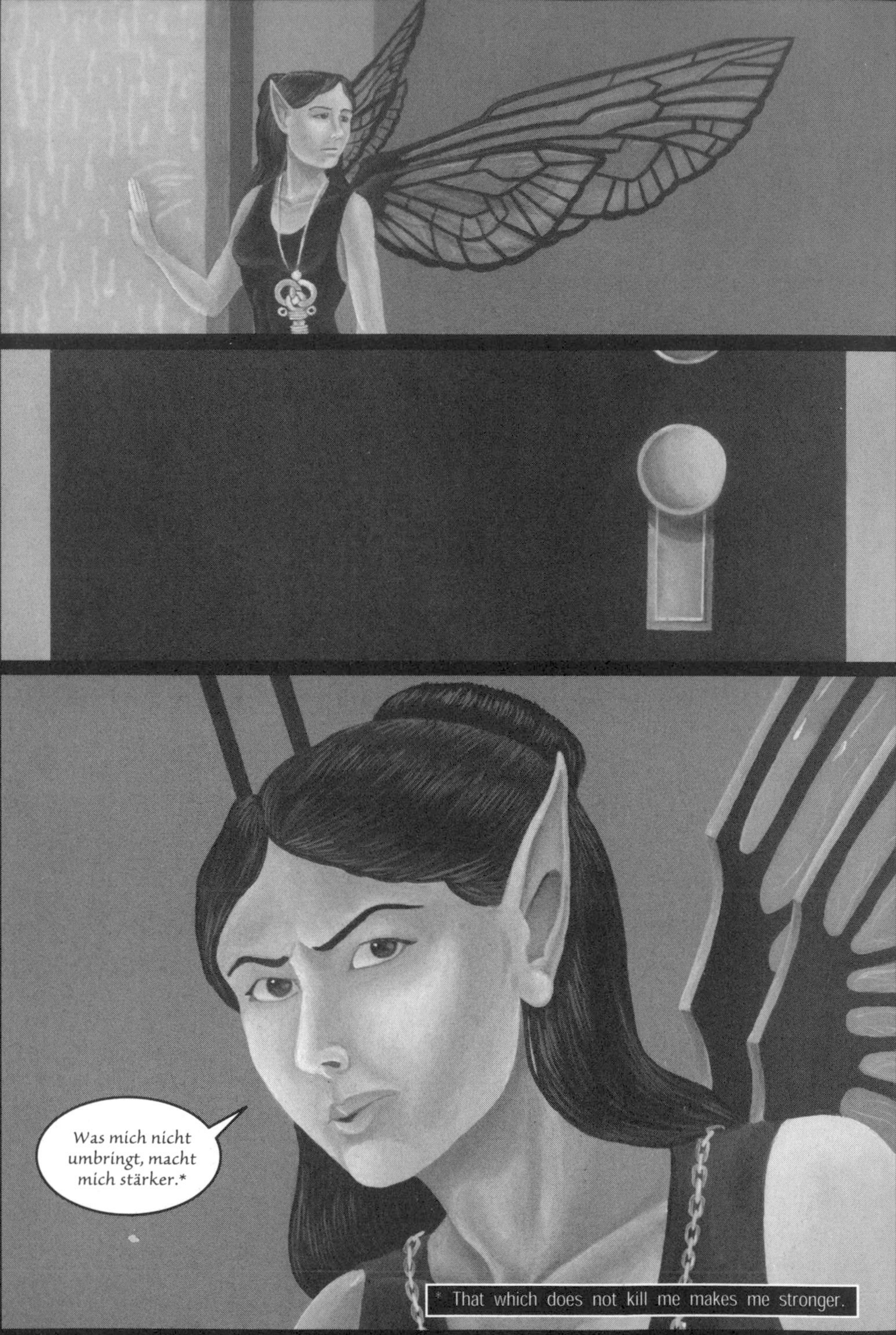
Was mich nicht umbringt, macht mich stärker.*
* That which does not kill me makes me stronger.

- Chapter Four-

Though tenderest roses were round you,
The soul of the pitiless place
With pitiless magic has bound you --
Ah! woe for the loss of your face,
And loss of your laugh and its lightness --
Ah! woe for your wings and your head --
Ah! woe for your eyes and their brightness --
Ah! woe for your slippers of red.

-- W.B. Yeats

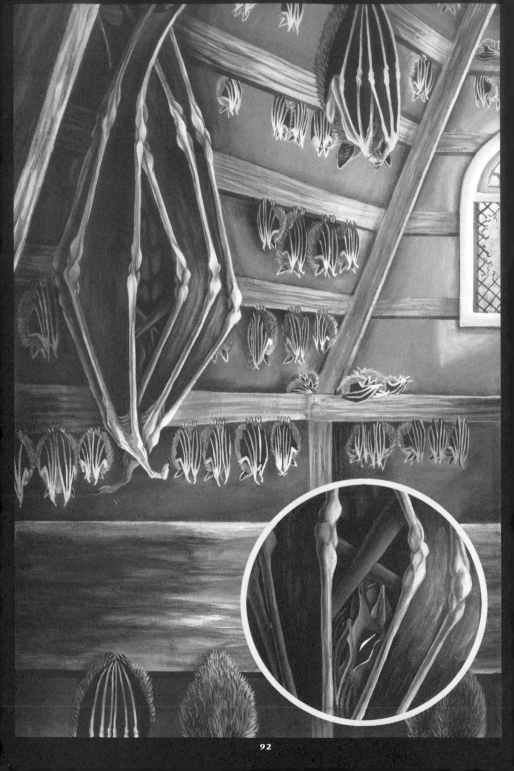

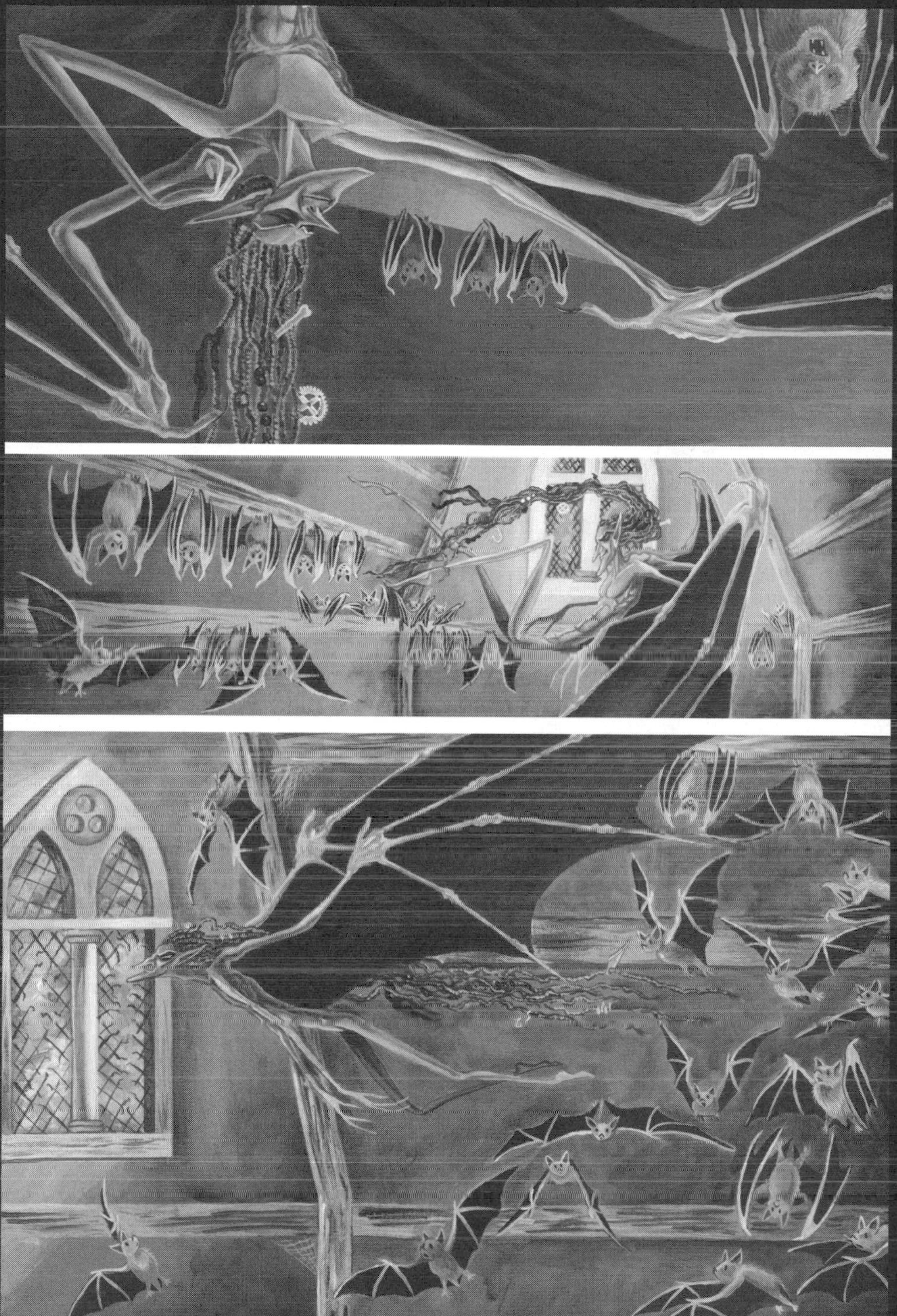

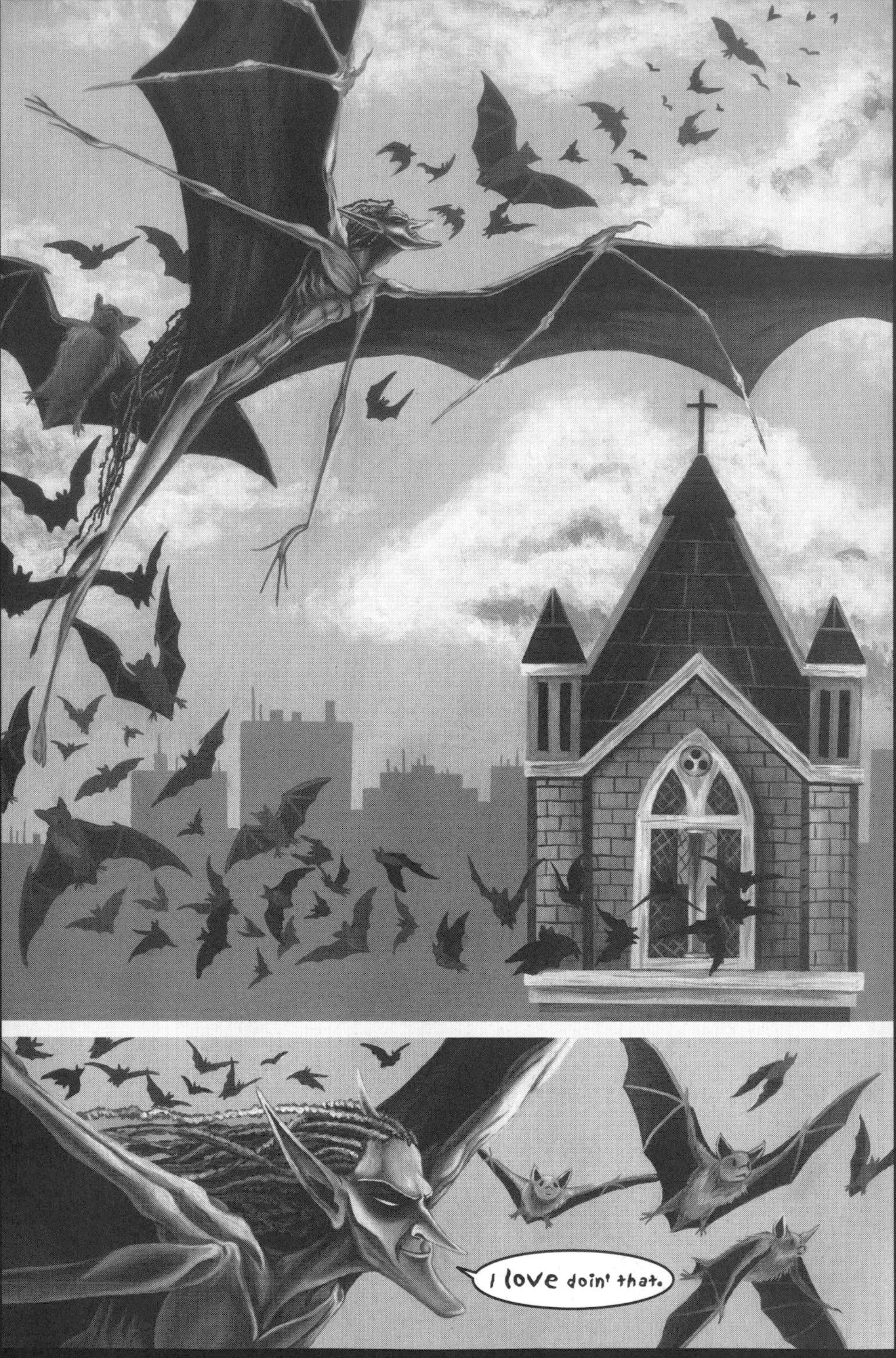
I love doin' that.

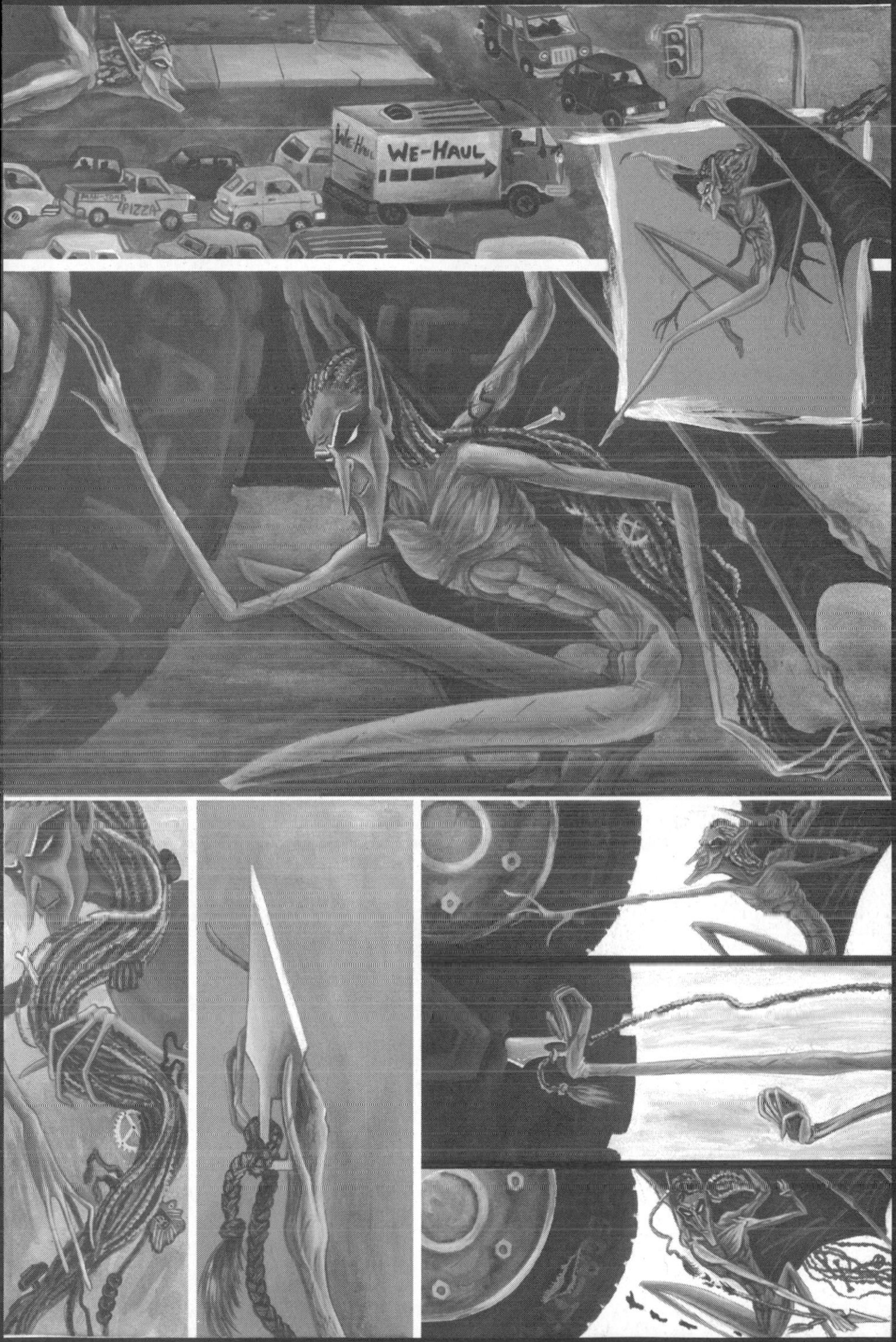
We-Haul
WE-HAUL
PIZZA

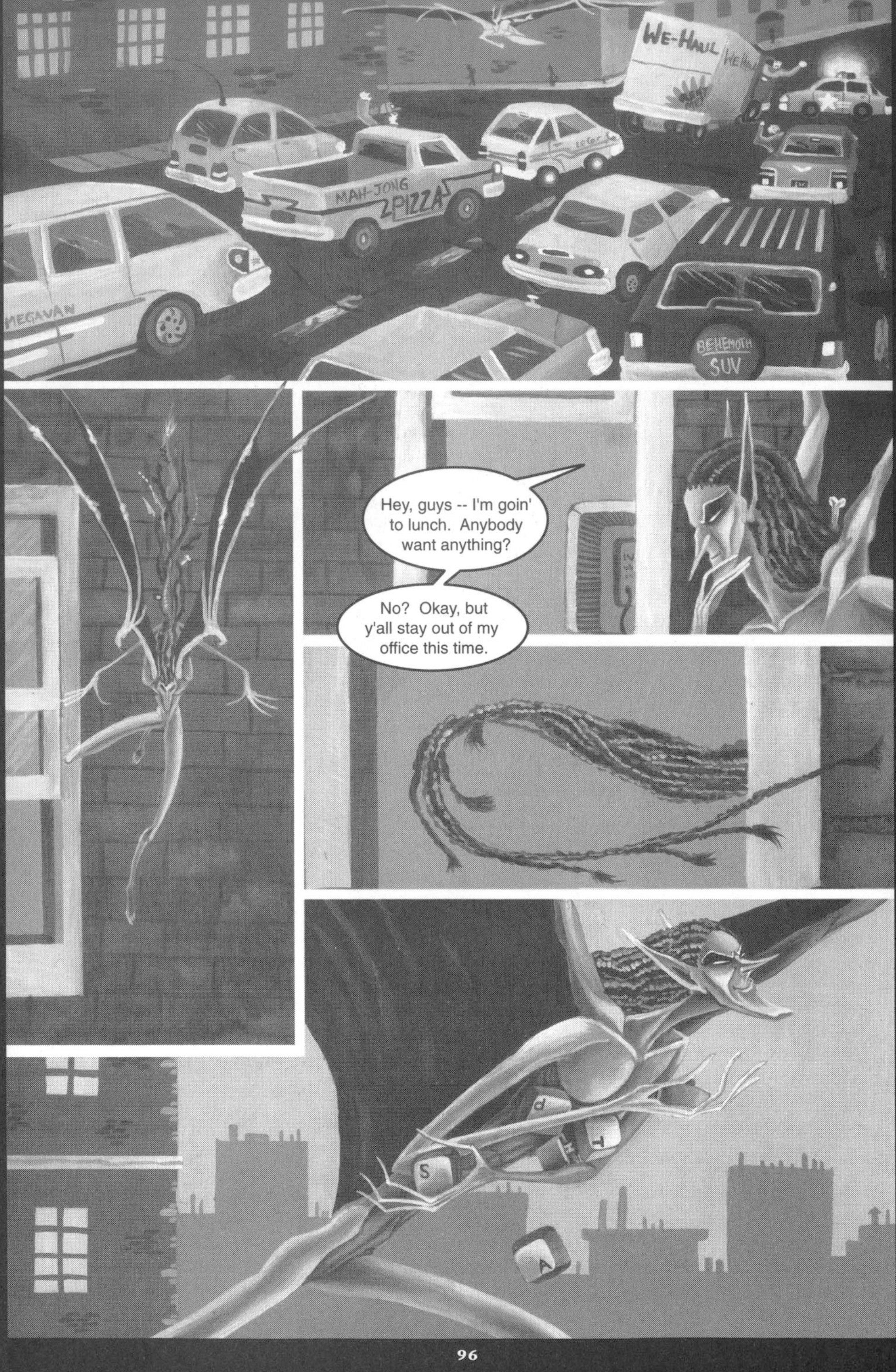
WE-HAUL
MAH-JONG PIZZA
MEGAVAN
BEHEMOTH SUV
Hey, guys -- I'm goin' to lunch. Anybody want anything?
No? Okay, but y'all stay out of my office this time.

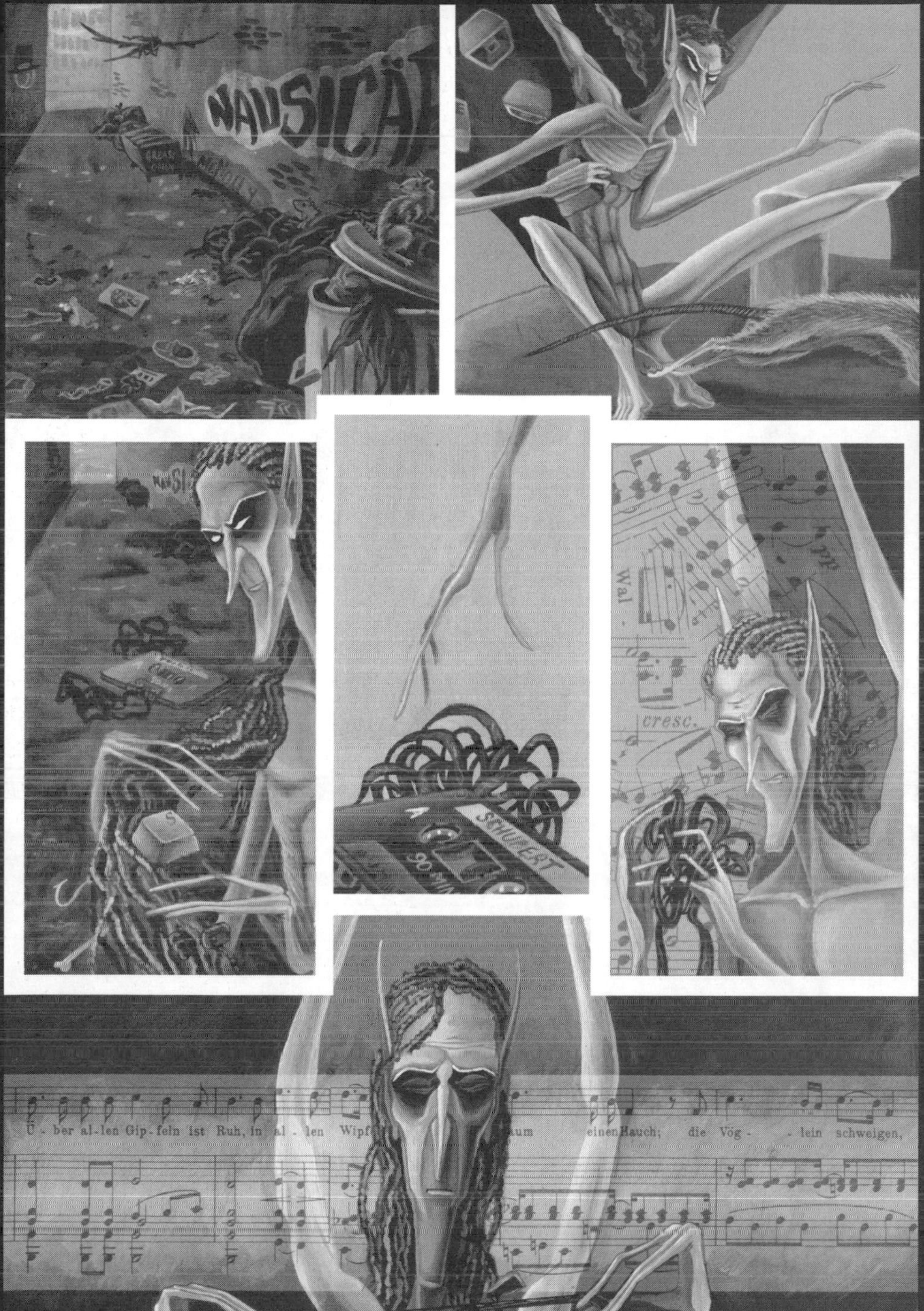
NAUSICAÄ
SCHUBERT
Wal -
cresc.
Ü - ber al - len Gip - feln ist Ruh, in al - len Wipf
aum
einen Hauch; die Vög - lein schweigen,

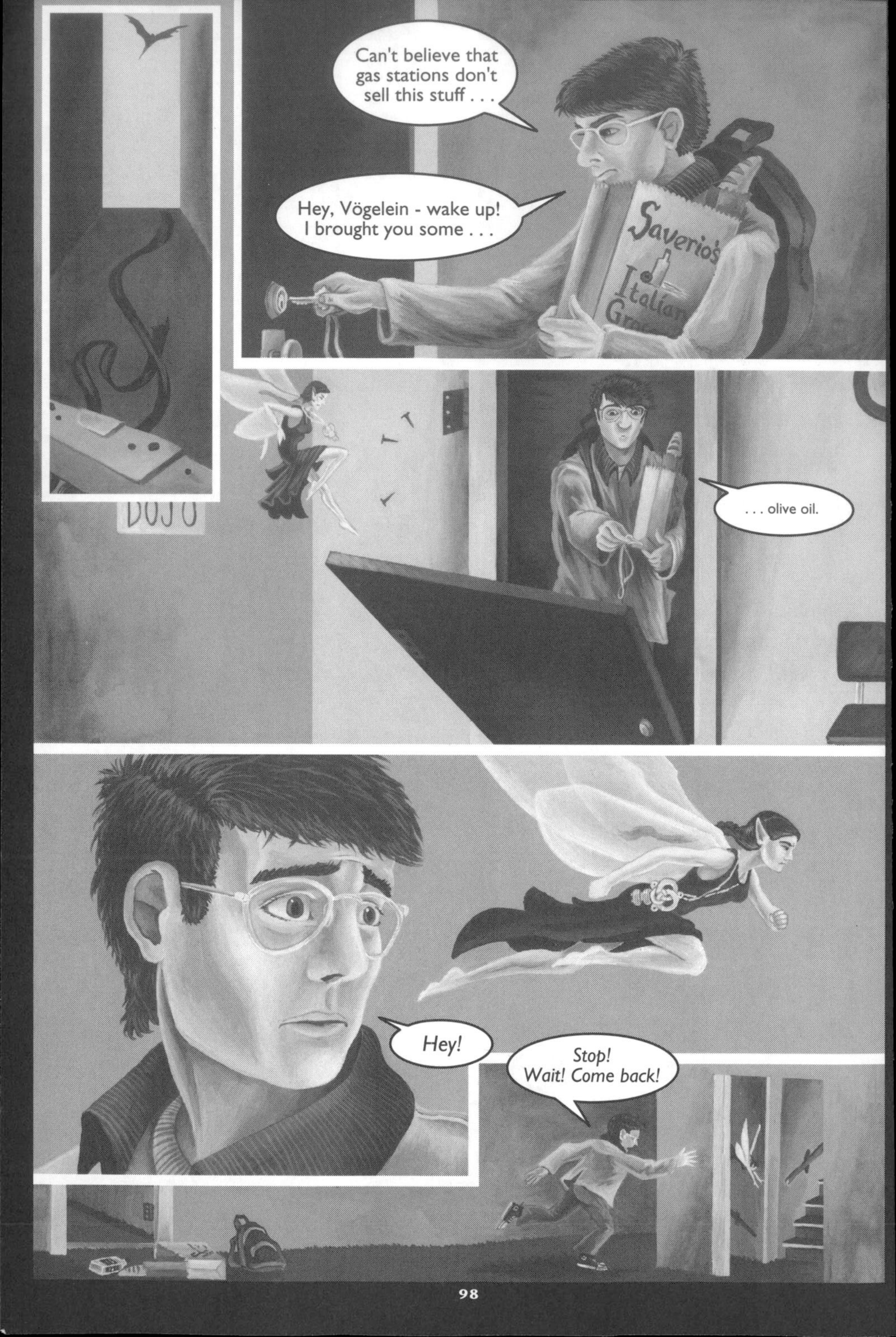
Can't believe that gas stations don't sell this stuff . . .
Hey, Vögelein - wake up! I brought you some . . .
Saverio's Italian Groc
DOJO
. . . olive oil.
Hey!
Stop! Wait! Come back!

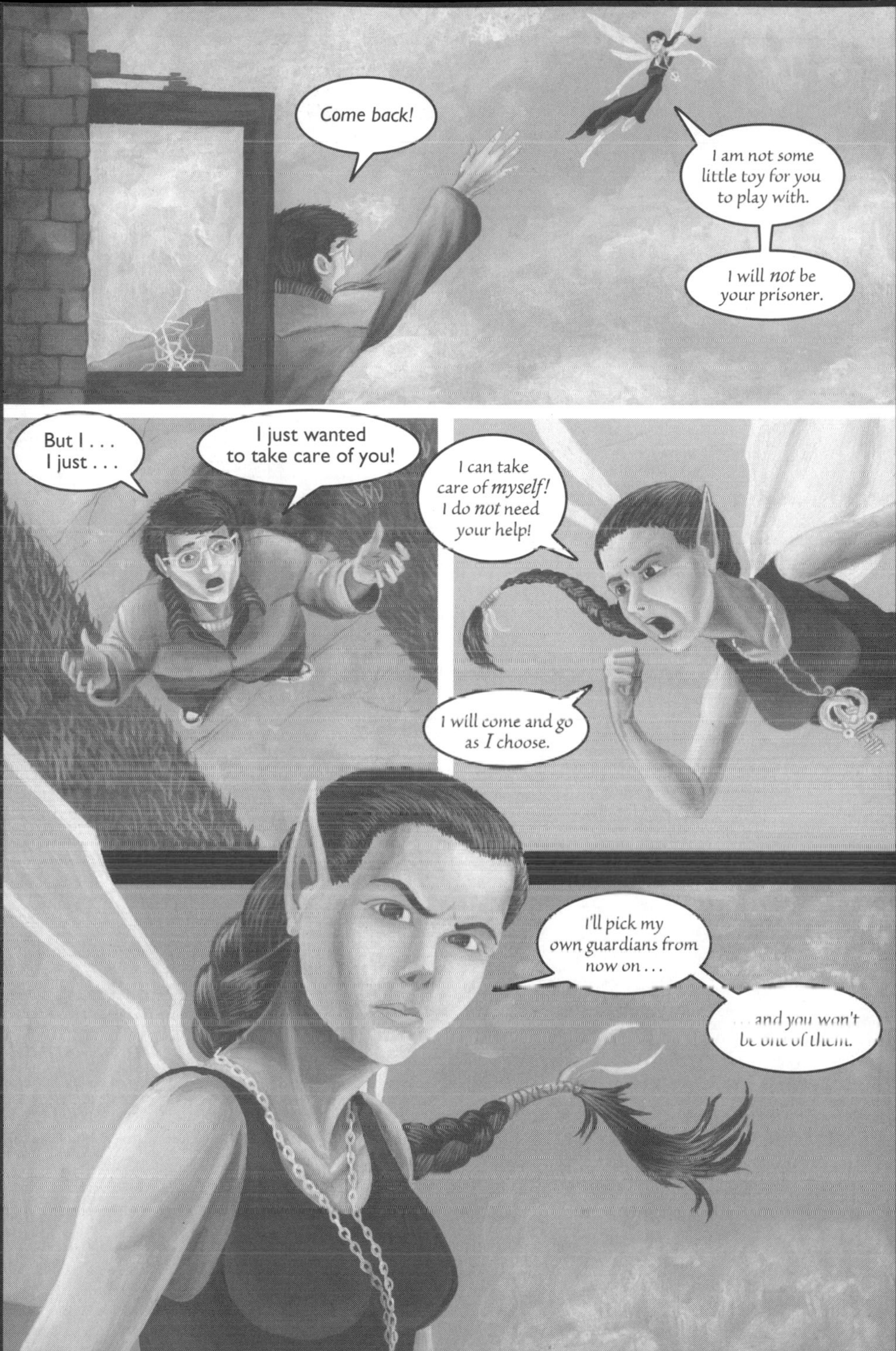
Come back!
I am not some little toy for you to play with.
I will *not* be your prisoner.
But I . . . I just . . .
I just wanted to take care of you!
I can take care of *myself*! I do *not* need your help!
I will come and go as *I* choose.
I'll pick my own guardians from now on . . .
. . . and you won't be one of them.

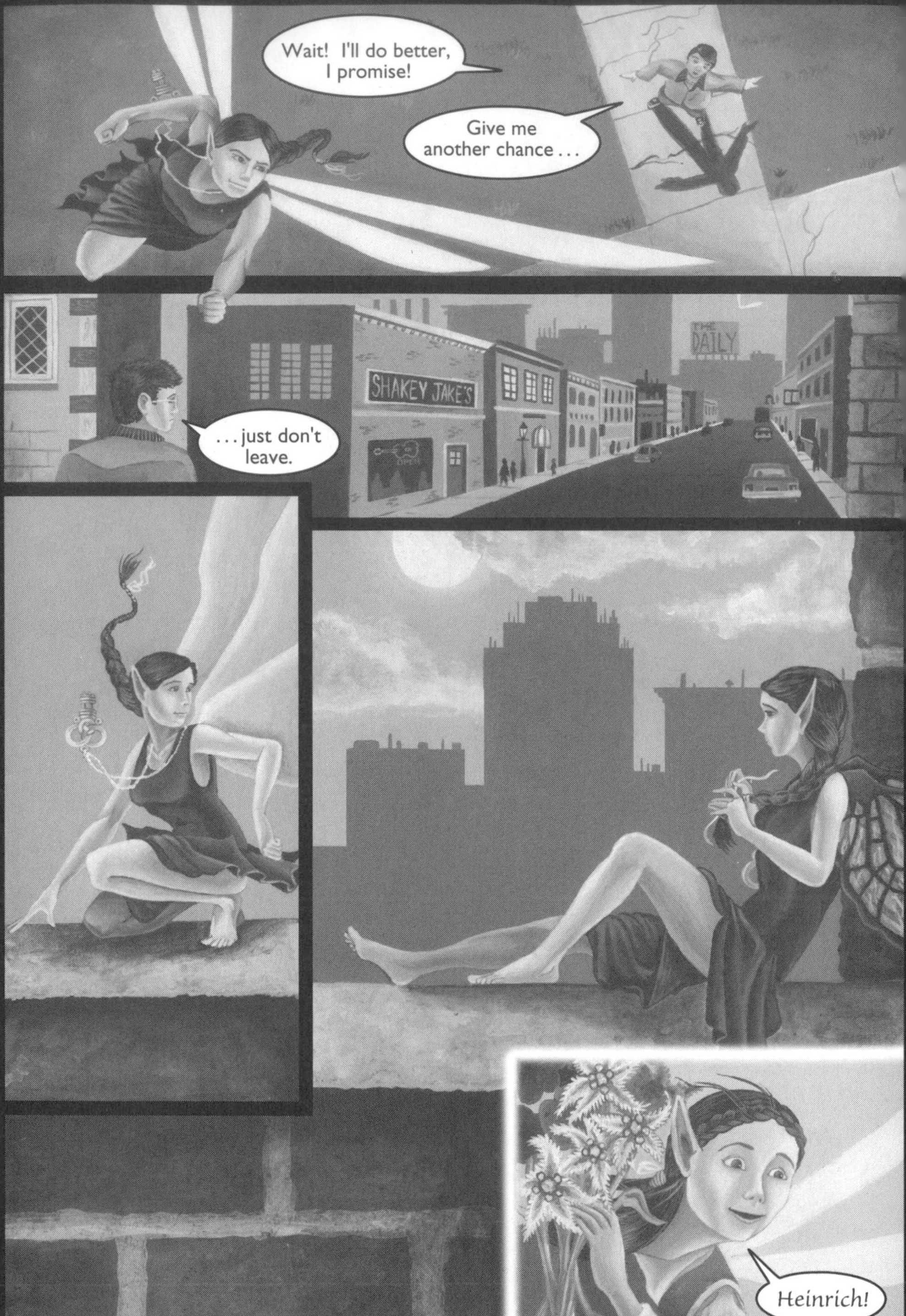
Wait! I'll do better, I promise!
Give me another chance . . .
. . . just don't leave.
SHAKEY JAKE'S
THE DAILY
Heinrich!

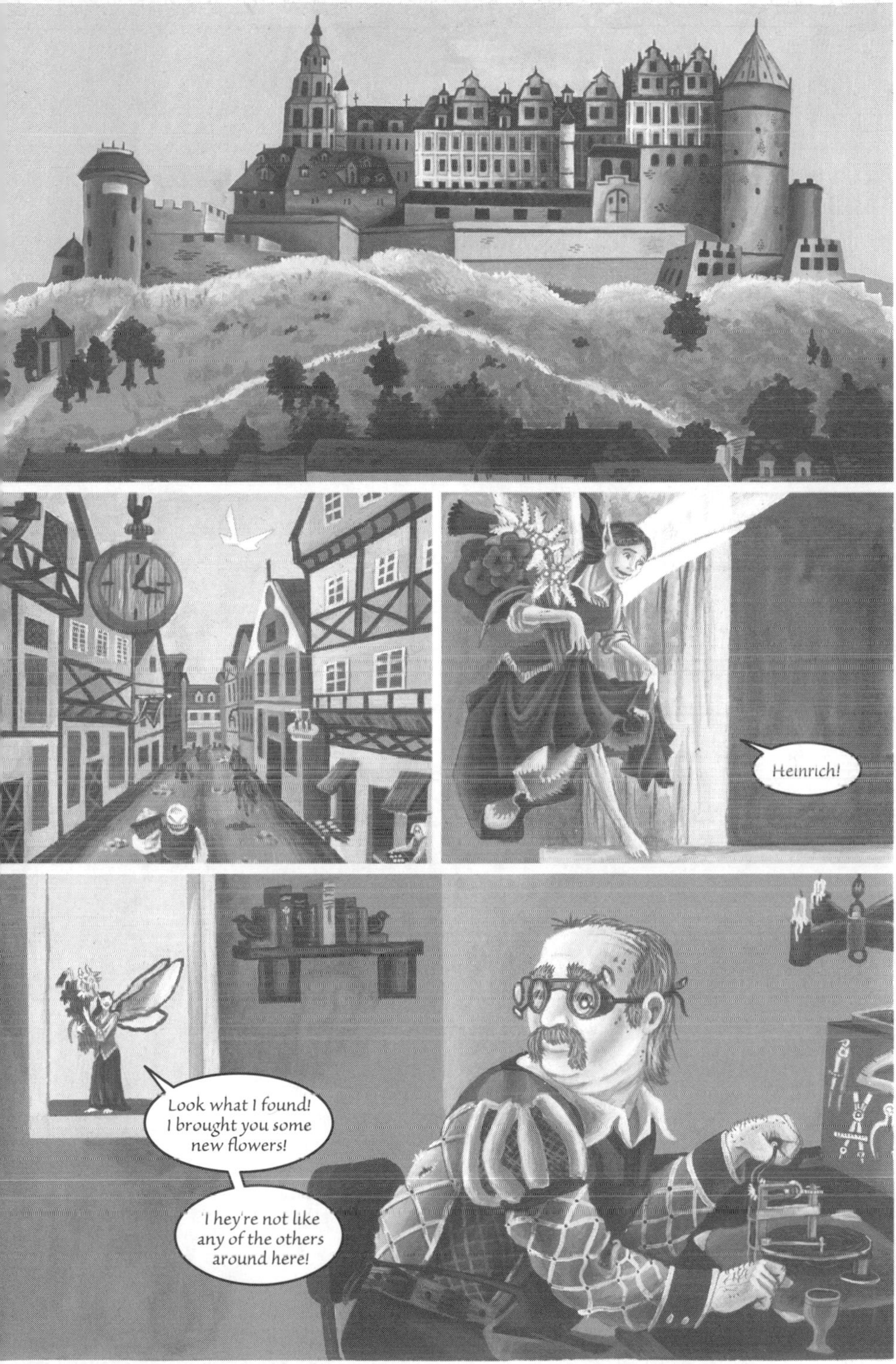
Heinrich!
Look what I found! I brought you some new flowers!
They're not like any of the others around here!

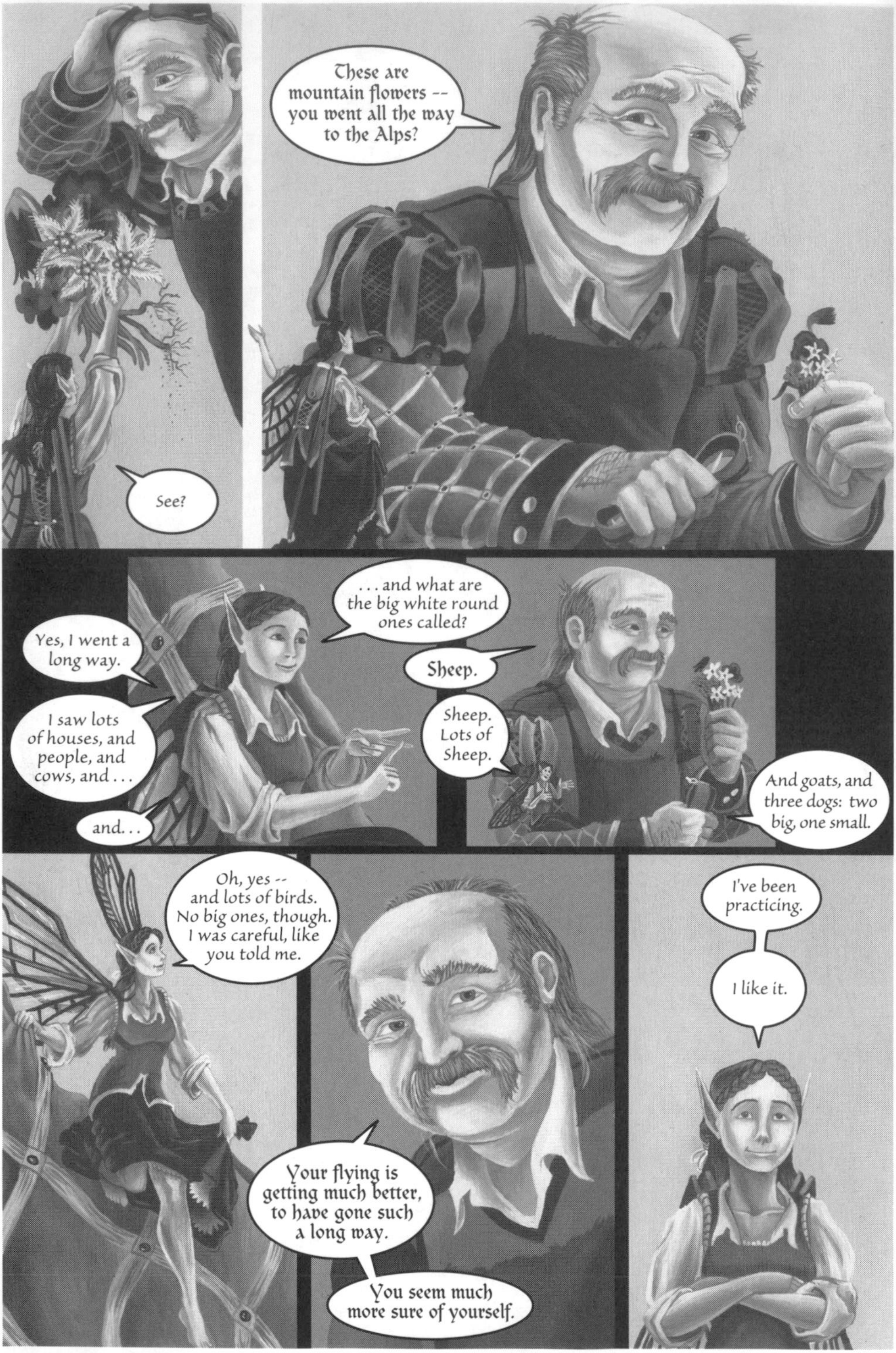
See?
These are mountain flowers -- you went all the way to the Alps?
Yes, I went a long way.
I saw lots of houses, and people, and cows, and . . .
and. . .
. . . and what are the big white round ones called?
Sheep.
Sheep. Lots of Sheep.
And goats, and three dogs: two big, one small.
Oh, yes -- and lots of birds. No big ones, though. I was careful, like you told me.
Your flying is getting much better, to have gone such a long way.
You seem much more sure of yourself.
I've been practicing.
I like it.

I like these, too. What are they called?

These are a kind of primrose --

-- and these are called 'edelweiss'. Its petals are wooly-- -- like a sheep.

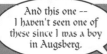

And this one -- I haven't seen one of these since I was a boy in Augsberg.

A gentian.

Look how the blue is so deep --

-- like the sapphires in your eyes.

That's why I liked it so much.

I will put them right here, so I can see them while I work.

What are you working on?

I am fixing a watch -- come see how it is done.

Someone wound it too hard and stripped the gears. This is a new gear I cut, to replace a broken one.

Now I must check my work to make sure all the teeth are cut correctly.

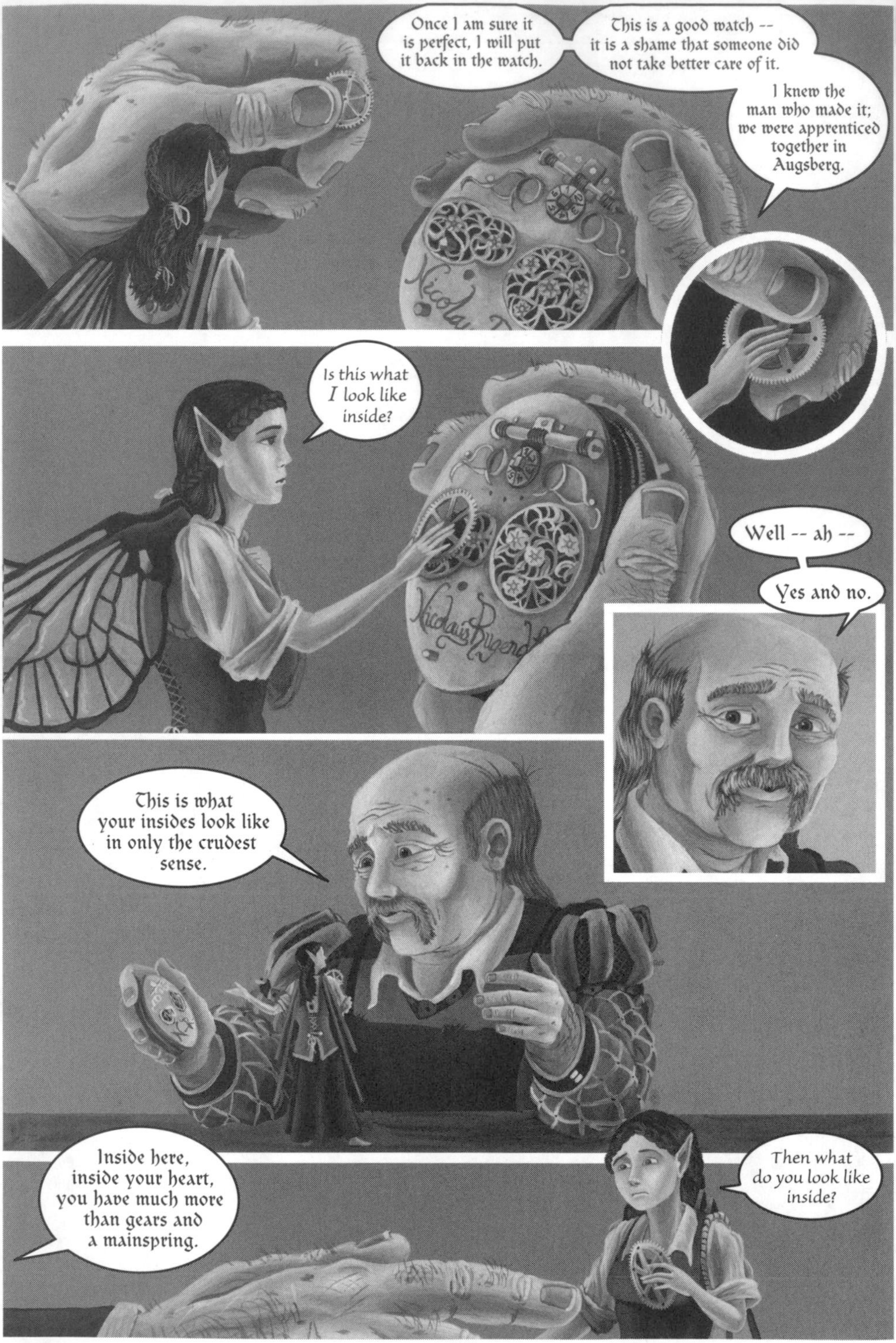
Once I am sure it is perfect, I will put it back in the watch.
This is a good watch -- it is a shame that someone did not take better care of it.
I knew the man who made it; we were apprenticed together in Augsberg.
Is this what I look like inside?
Well -- ah --
Yes and no.
This is what your insides look like in only the crudest sense.
Inside here, inside your heart, you have much more than gears and a mainspring.
Then what do you look like inside?

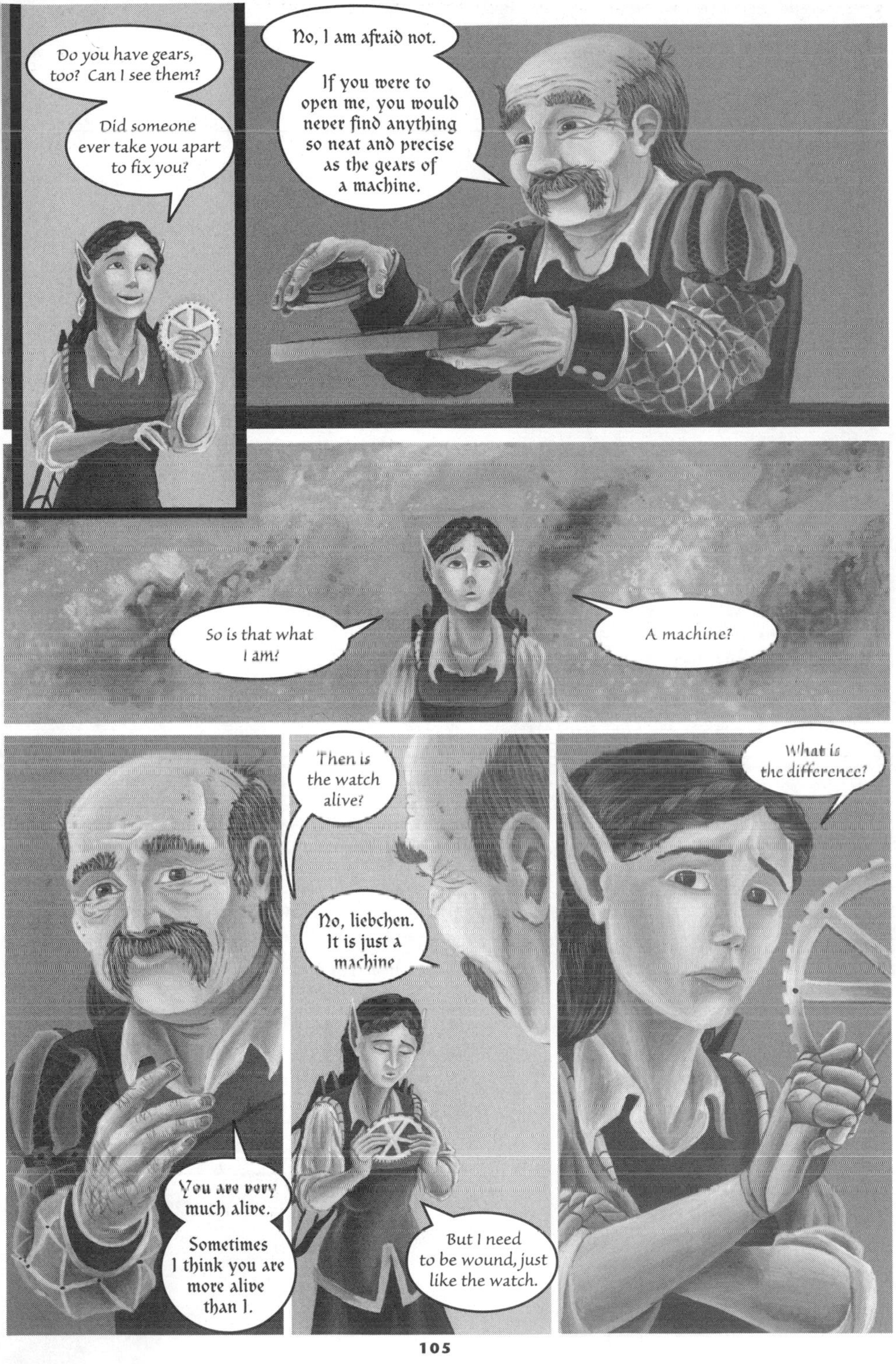

Do you have gears, too? Can I see them?
Did someone ever take you apart to fix you?
No, I am afraid not.
If you were to open me, you would never find anything so neat and precise as the gears of a machine.
So is that what I am?
A machine?
You are very much alive.
Sometimes I think you are more alive than I.
Then is the watch alive?
No, liebchen. It is just a machine
But I need to be wound, just like the watch.
What is the difference?

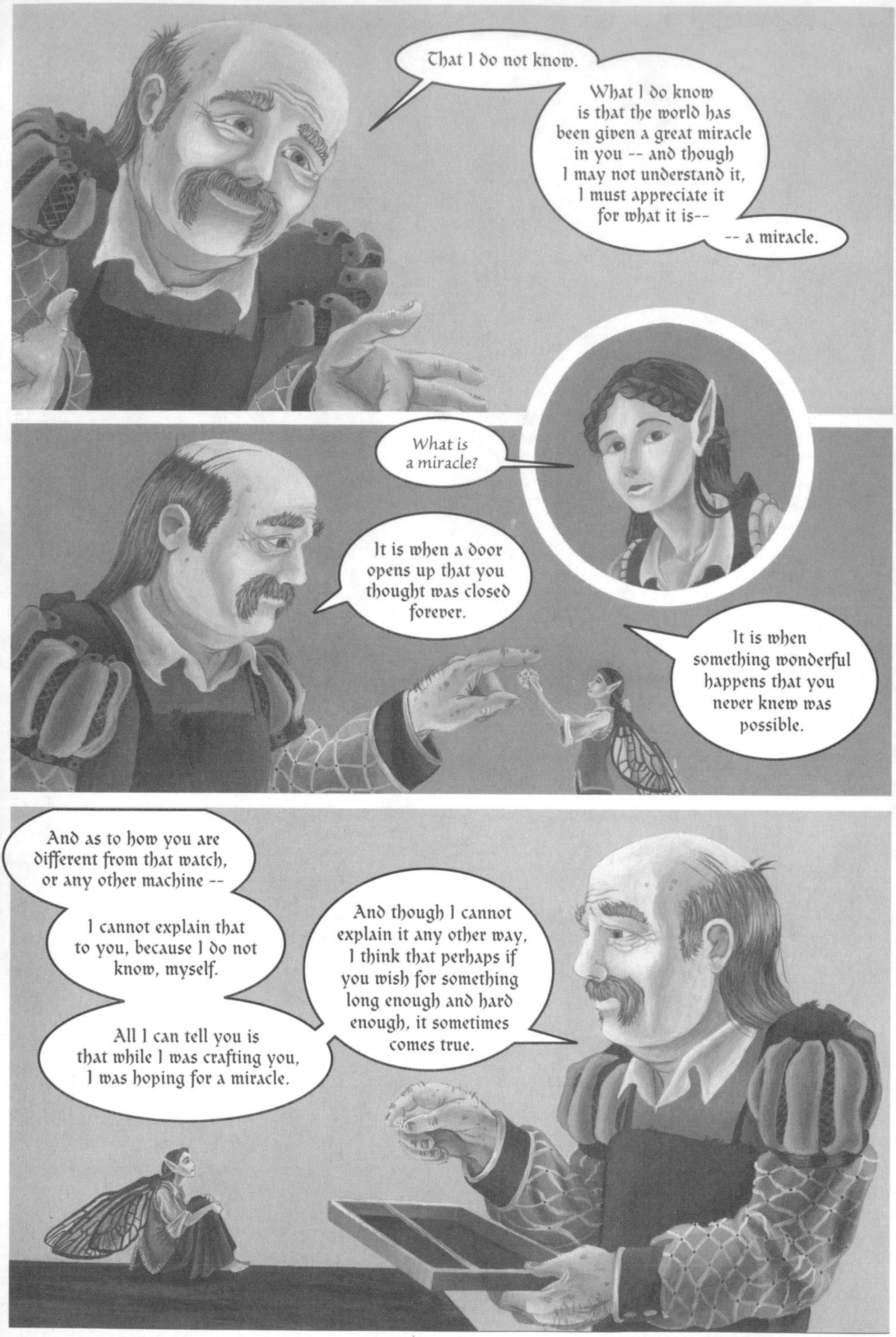
That I do not know.
What I do know is that the world has been given a great miracle in you -- and though I may not understand it, I must appreciate it for what it is--
-- a miracle.
What is a miracle?
It is when a door opens up that you thought was closed forever.
It is when something wonderful happens that you never knew was possible.
And as to how you are different from that watch, or any other machine --
I cannot explain that to you, because I do not know, myself.
All I can tell you is that while I was crafting you, I was hoping for a miracle.
And though I cannot explain it any other way, I think that perhaps if you wish for something long enough and hard enough, it sometimes comes true.

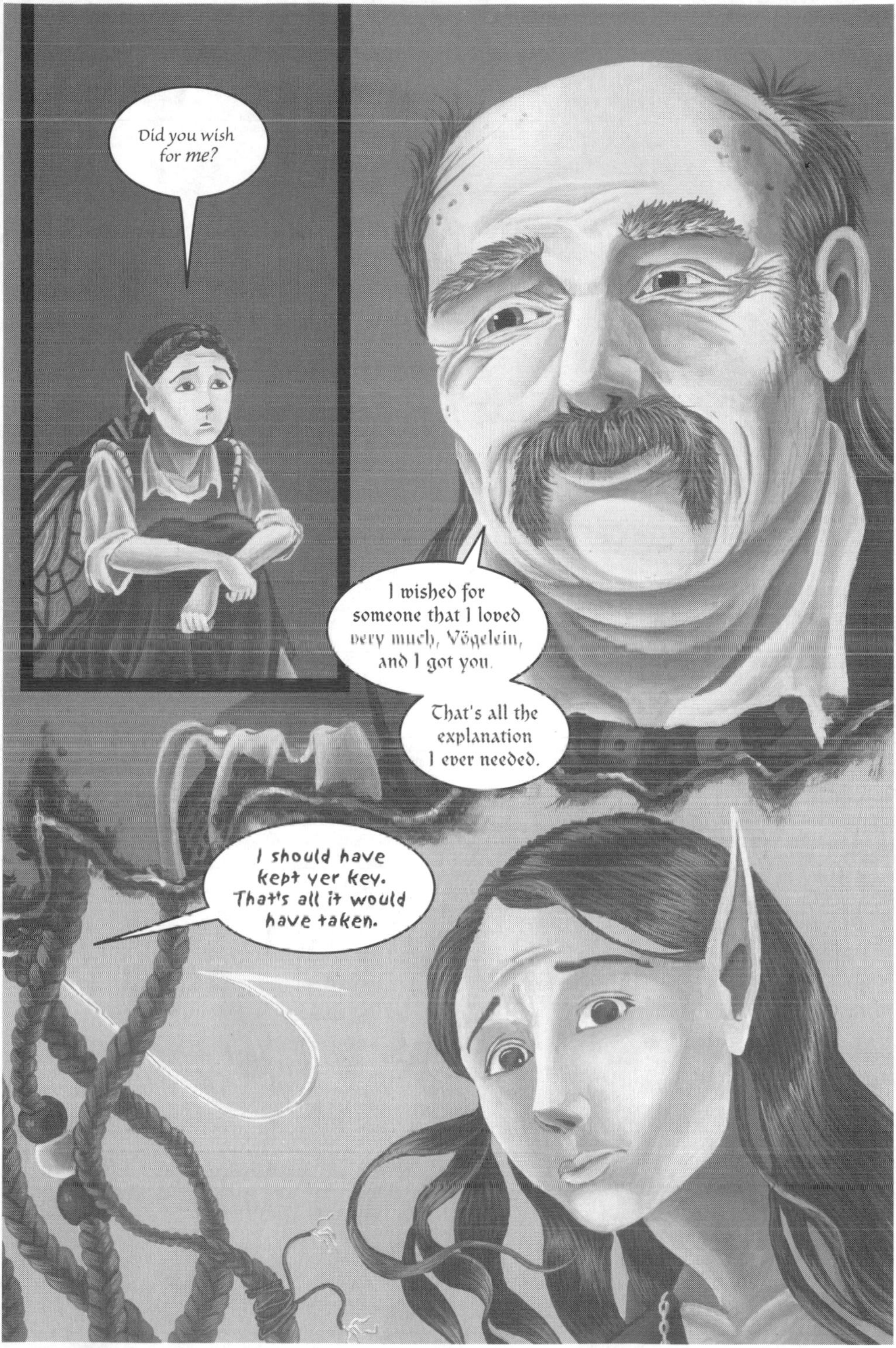

Did you wish for *me*?
I wished for someone that I loved very much, Vögelein, and I got you.
That's all the explanation I ever needed.
I should have kept yer key. That's all it would have taken.

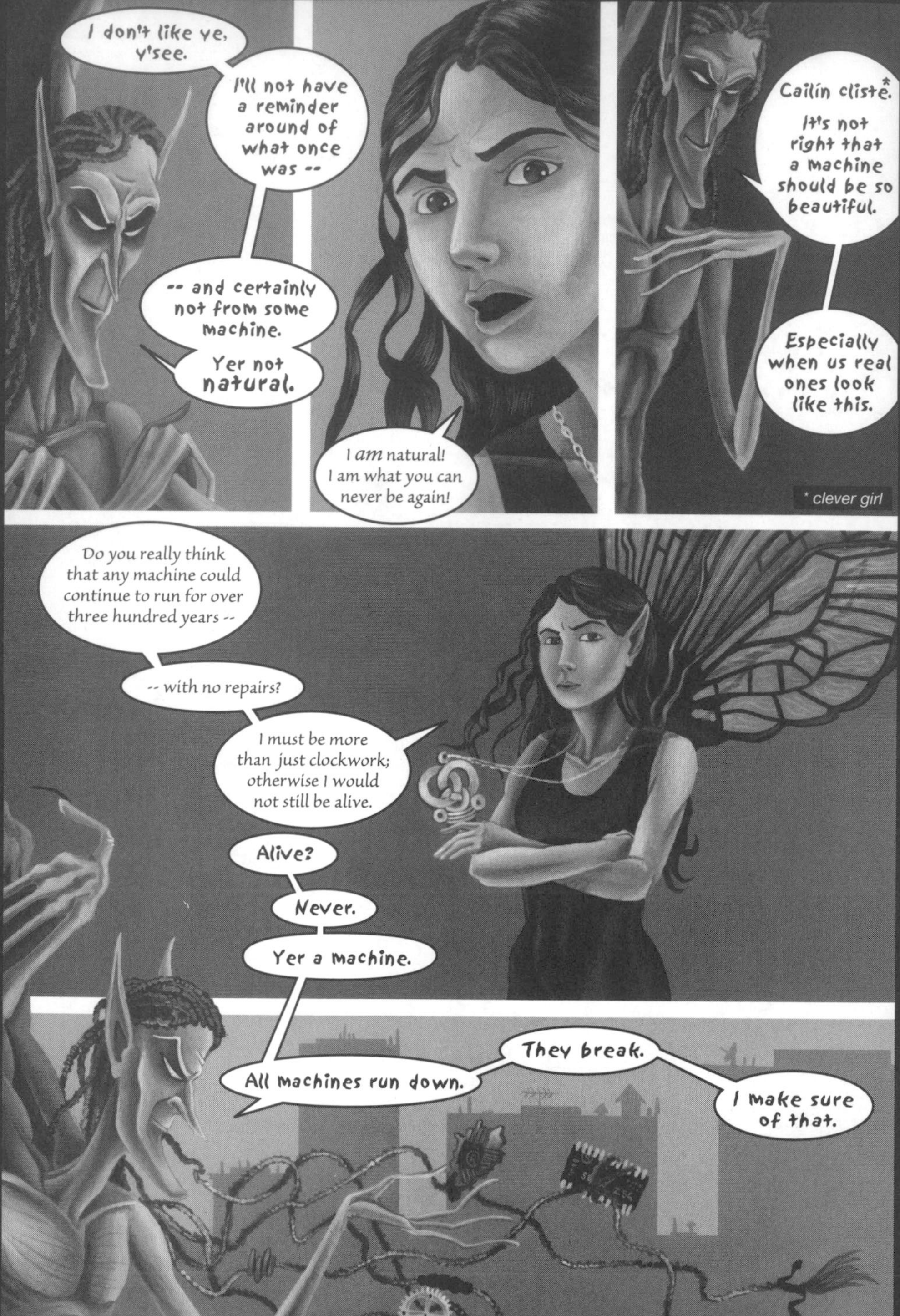
I don't like ye, y'see.
I'll not have a reminder around of what once was --
-- and certainly not from some machine.
Yer not natural.
I *am* natural! I am what you can never be again!
Cailín cliste.*
It's not right that a machine should be so beautiful.
Especially when us real ones look like this.
* clever girl
Do you really think that any machine could continue to run for over three hundred years --
-- with no repairs?
I must be more than just clockwork; otherwise I would not still be alive.
Alive?
Never.
Yer a machine.
All machines run down.
They break.
I make sure of that.

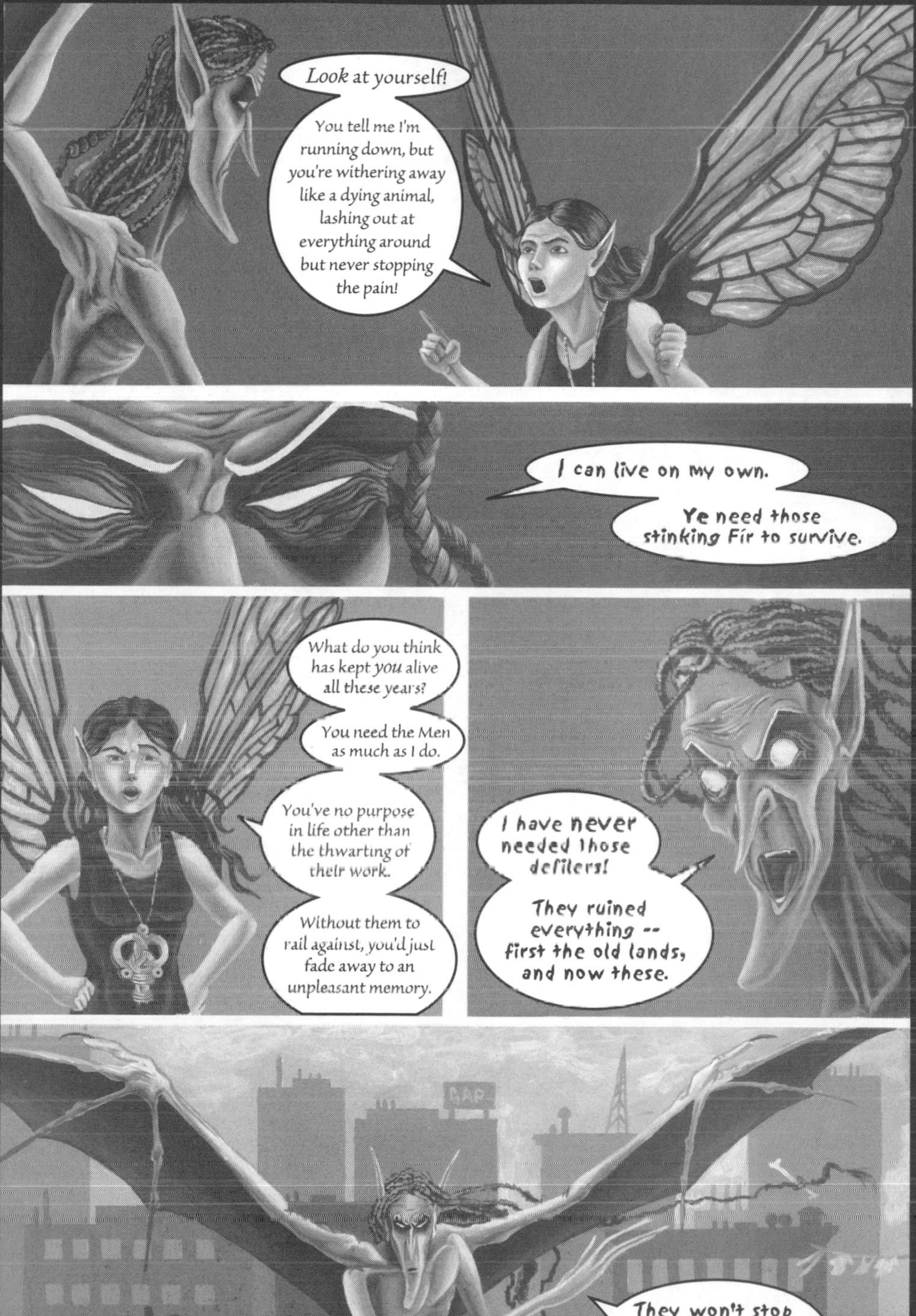
Look at yourself!
You tell me I'm running down, but you're withering away like a dying animal, lashing out at everything around but never stopping the pain!
I can live on my own.
Ye need those stinking Fír to survive.
What do you think has kept *you* alive all these years?
You need the Men as much as I do.
You've no purpose in life other than the thwarting of their work.
Without them to rail against, you'd just fade away to an unpleasant memory.
I have **never** needed those defilers!
They ruined everything -- first the old lands, and now these.
They won't stop until everything is destroyed.

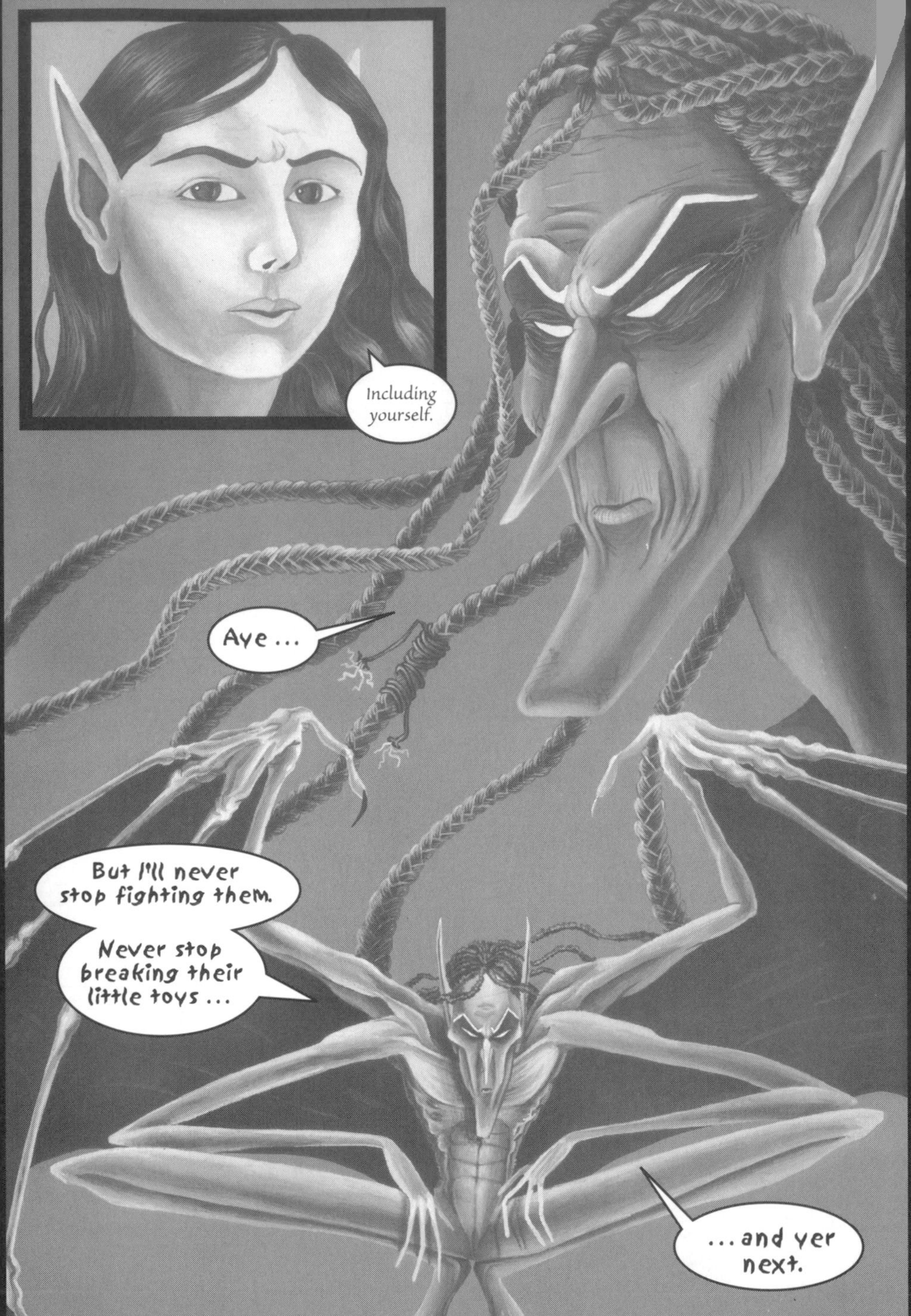

Including yourself.
Aye . . .
But I'll never stop fighting them.
Never stop breaking their little toys . . .
. . . and yer next.

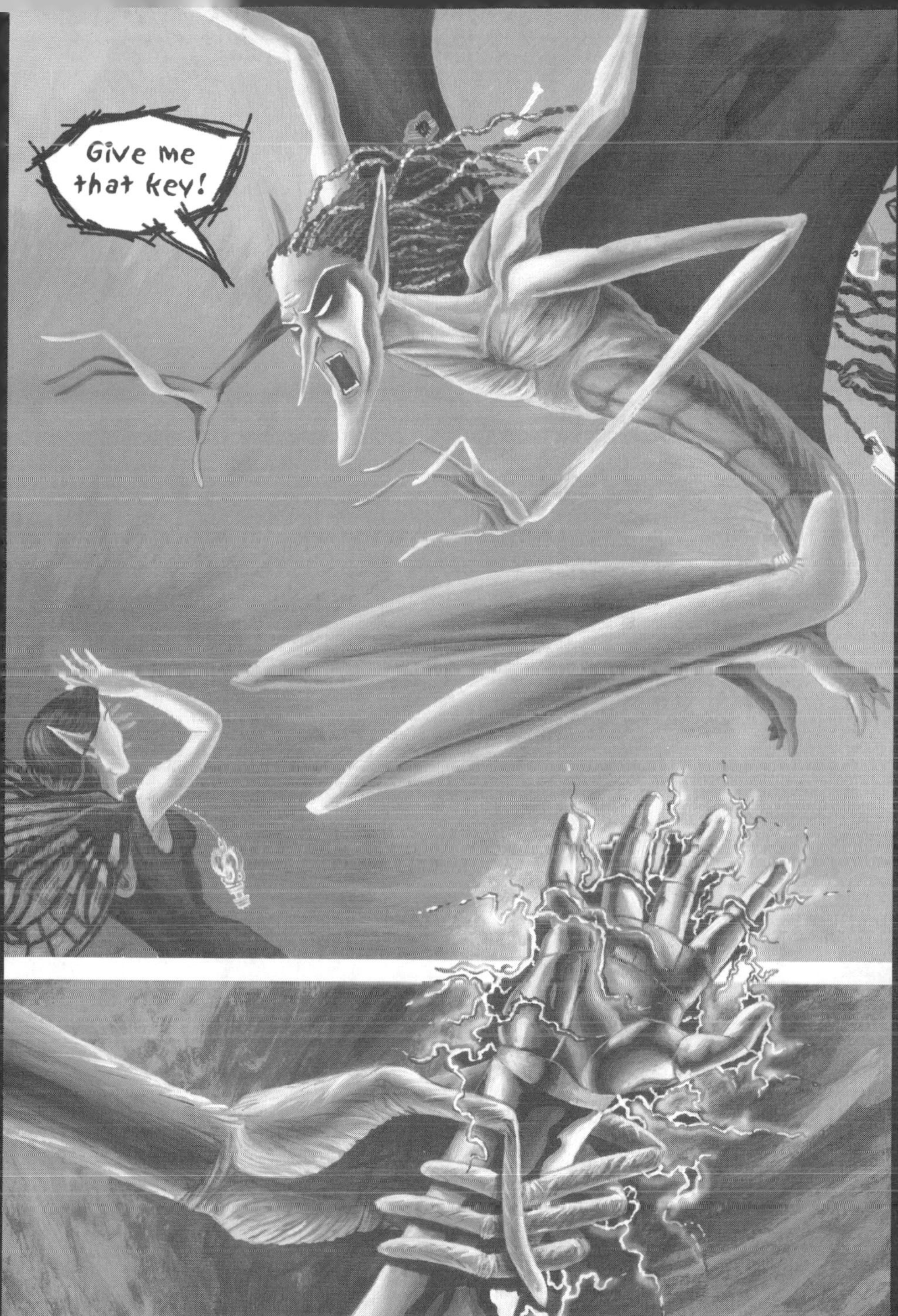
Give me that key!

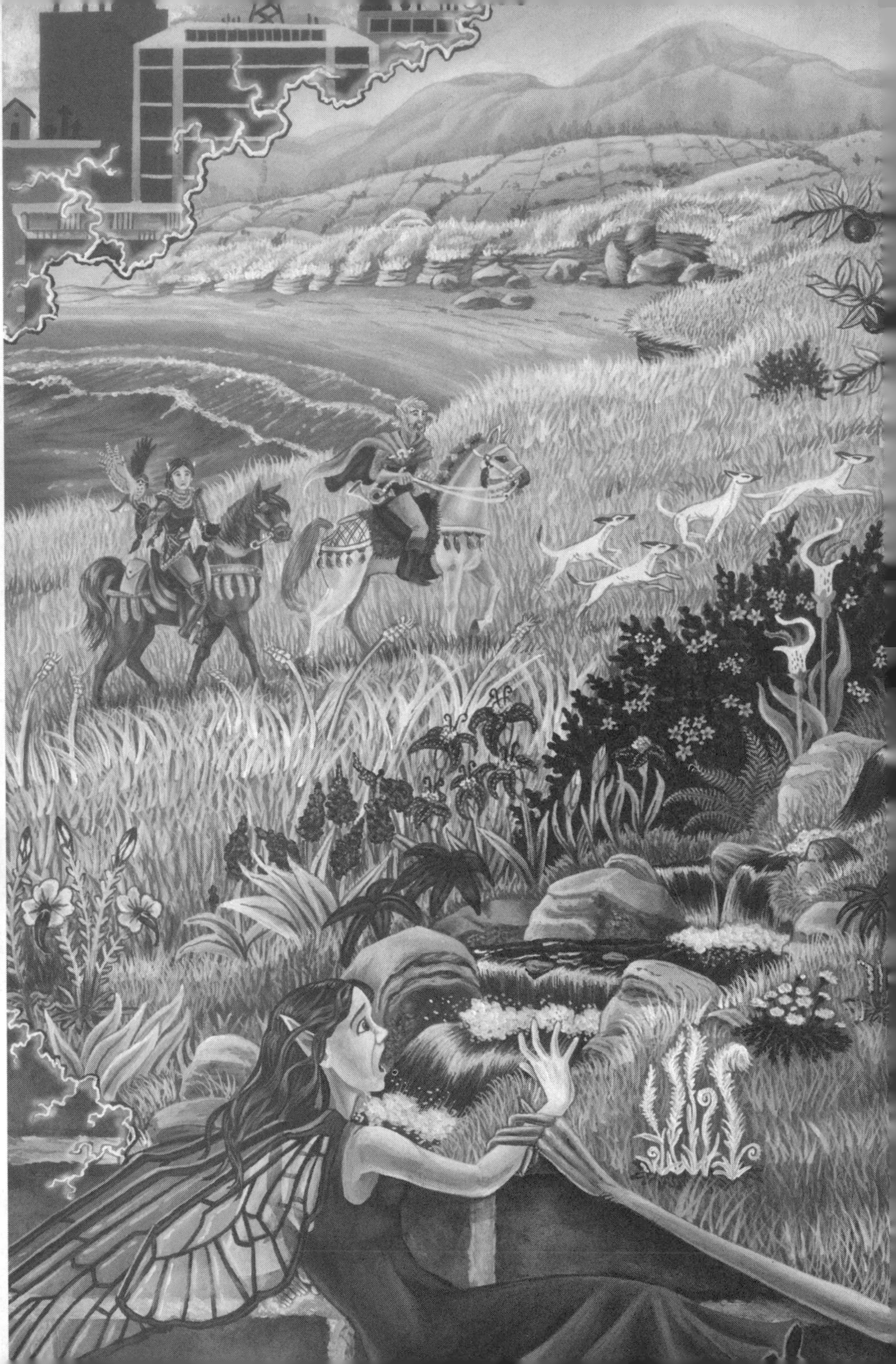

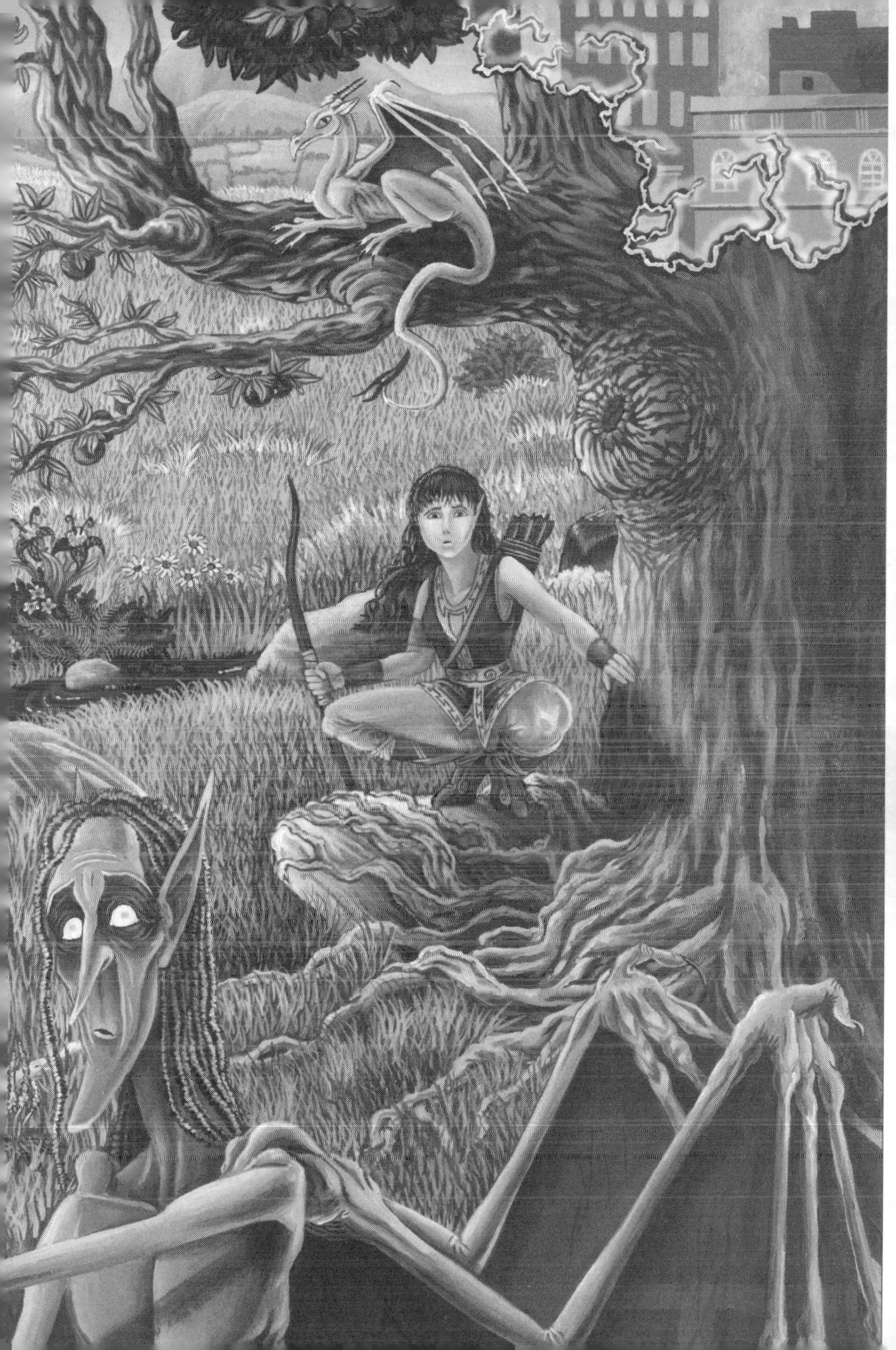

- Chapter Five -

From far, from eve and morning
 And yon twelve-winded sky,
The stuff of life to knit me
 Blew hither: here am I.

Now—for a breath I tarry
 Nor yet disperse apart—
Take my hand quick and tell me,
 What have you in your heart.

Speak now, and I will answer;
 How shall I help you, say;
Ere to the wind's twelve quarters
 I take my endless way.

-- A. E. Housman

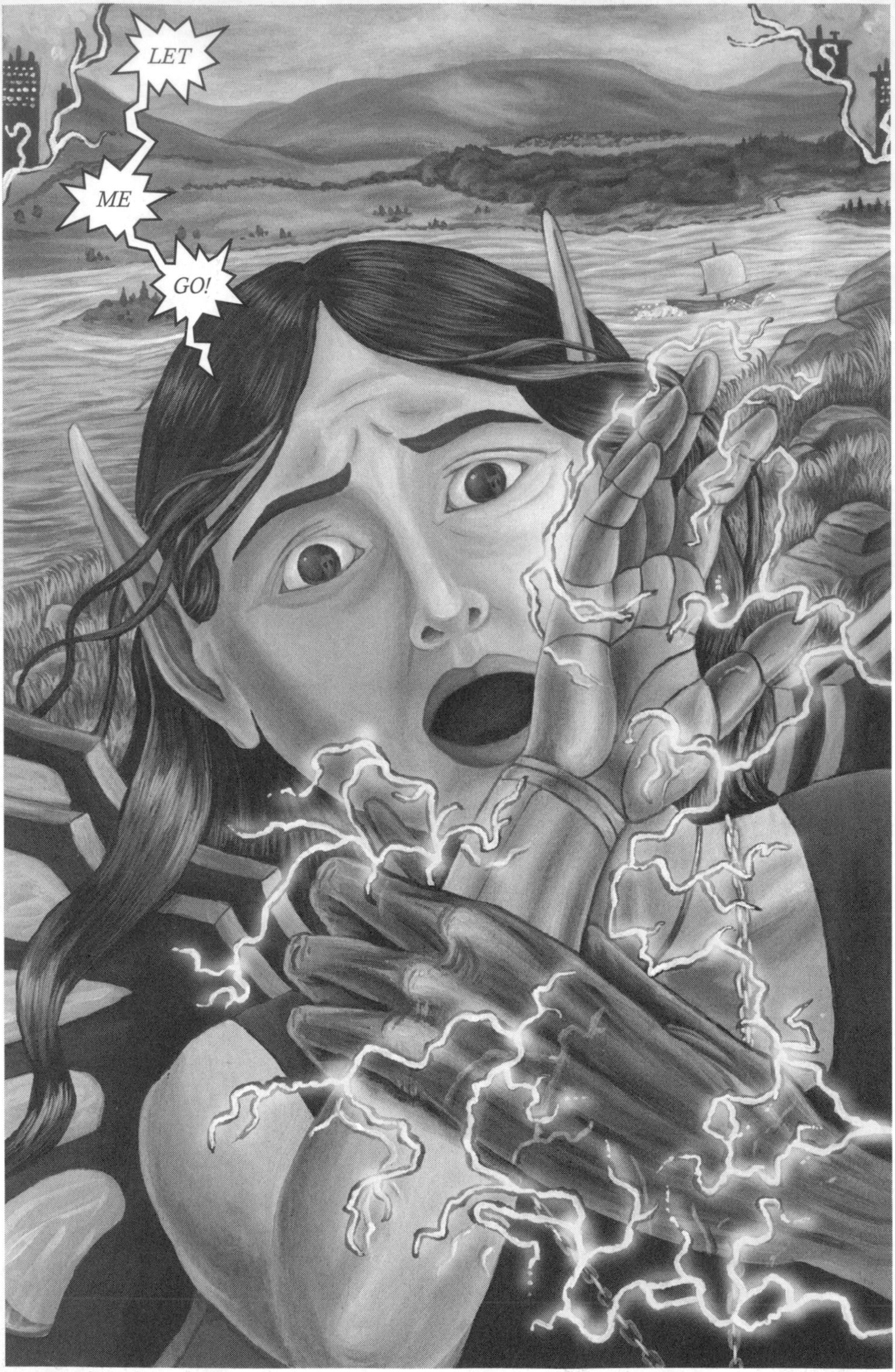
LET
ME
GO!

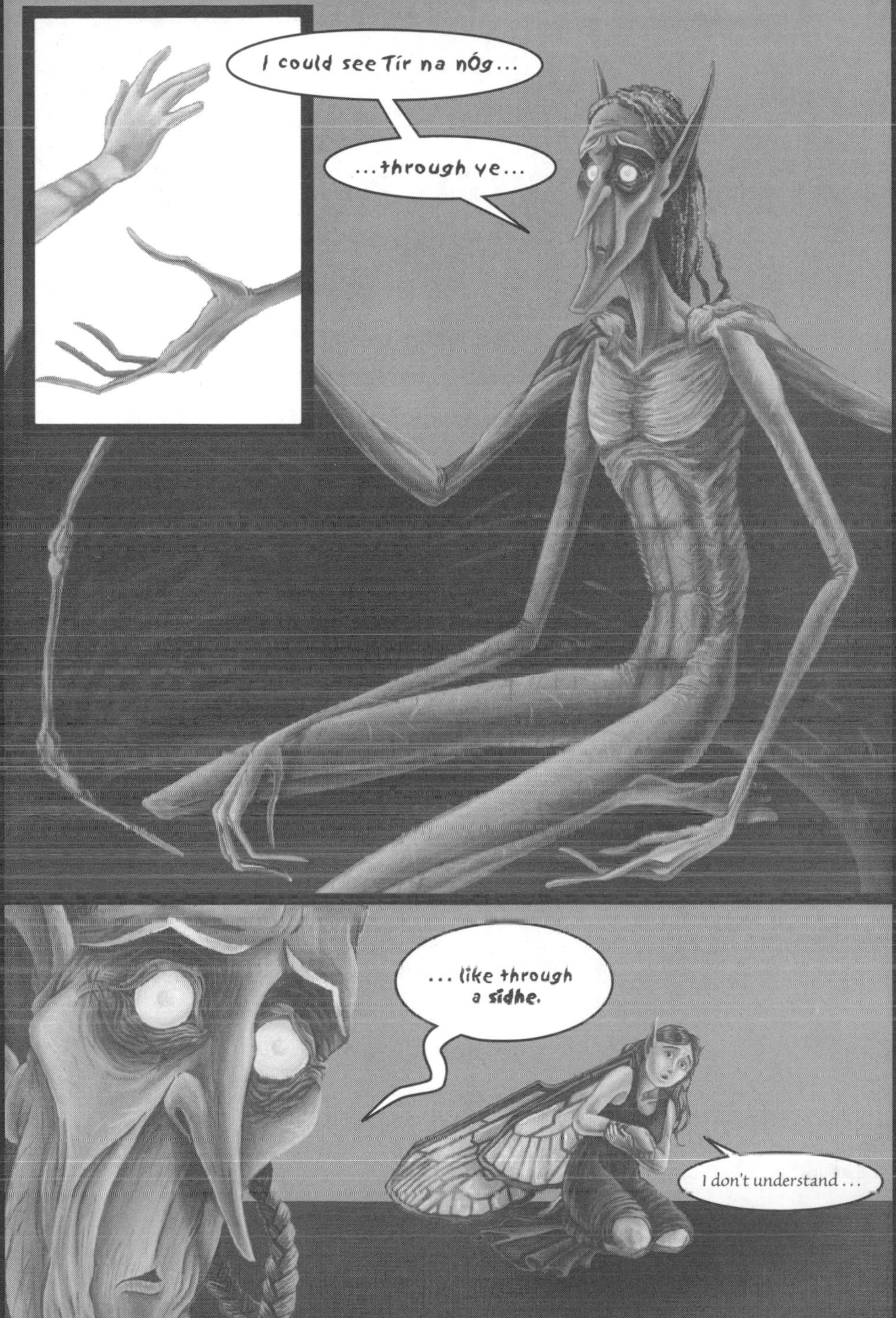
I could see Tír na nÓg...
...through ye...
... like through a **sidhe.**
I don't understand...

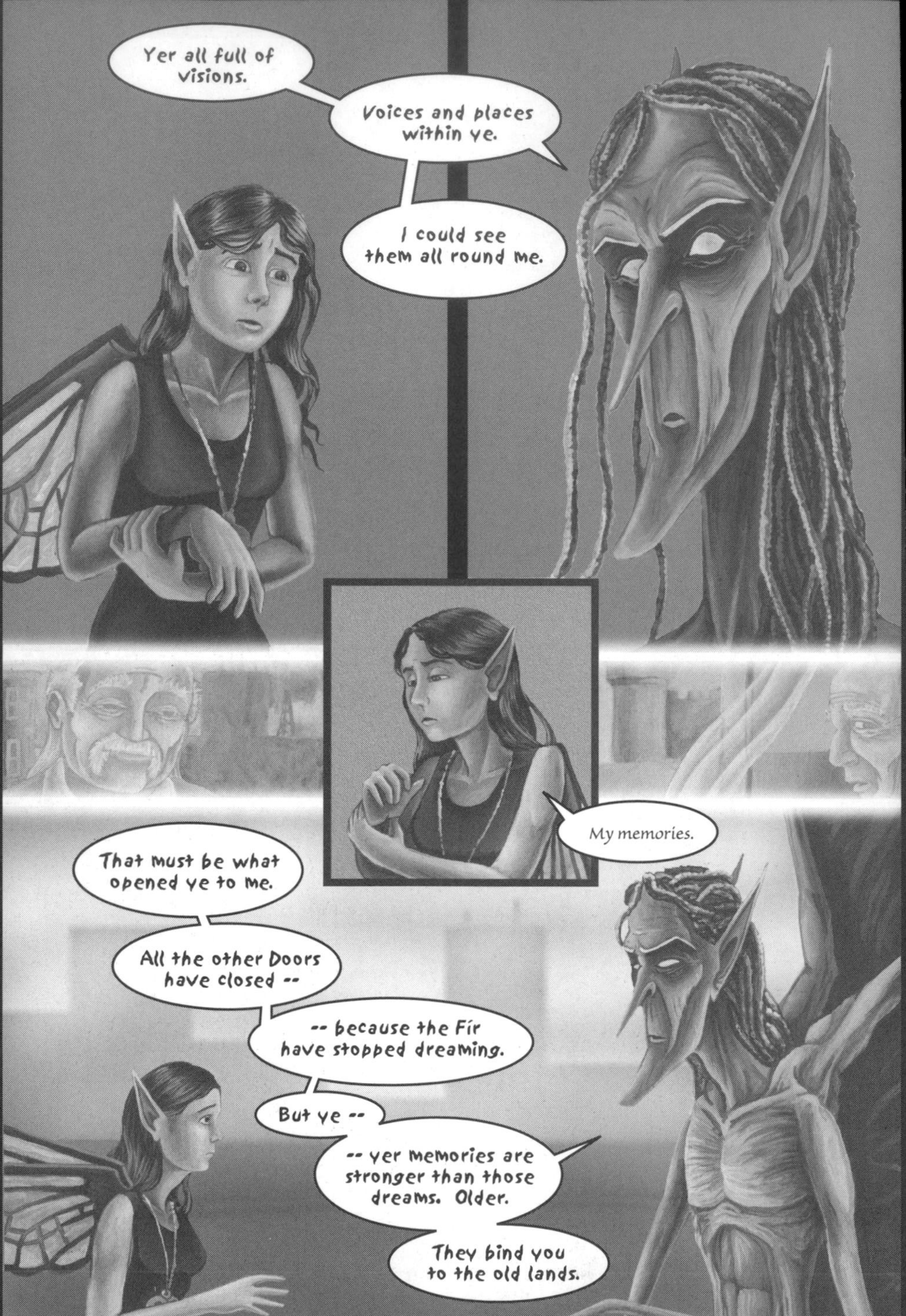

Yer all full of visions.
Voices and places within ye.
I could see them all round me.
My memories.
That must be what opened ye to me.
All the other Doors have closed --
-- because the Fir have stopped dreaming.
But ye --
-- yer memories are stronger than those dreams. Older.
They bind you to the old lands.

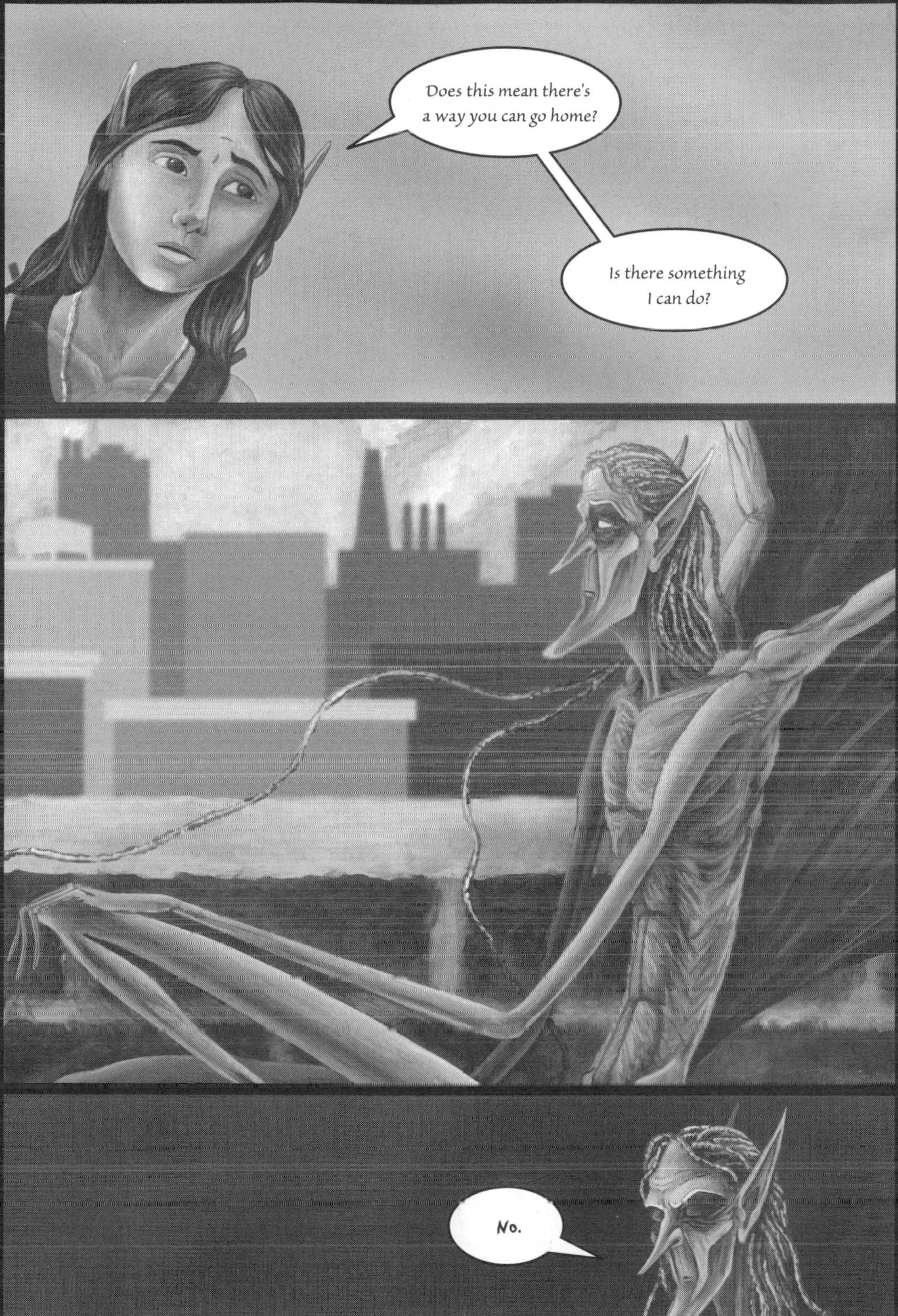
Does this mean there's a way you can go home?
Is there something I can do?
No.

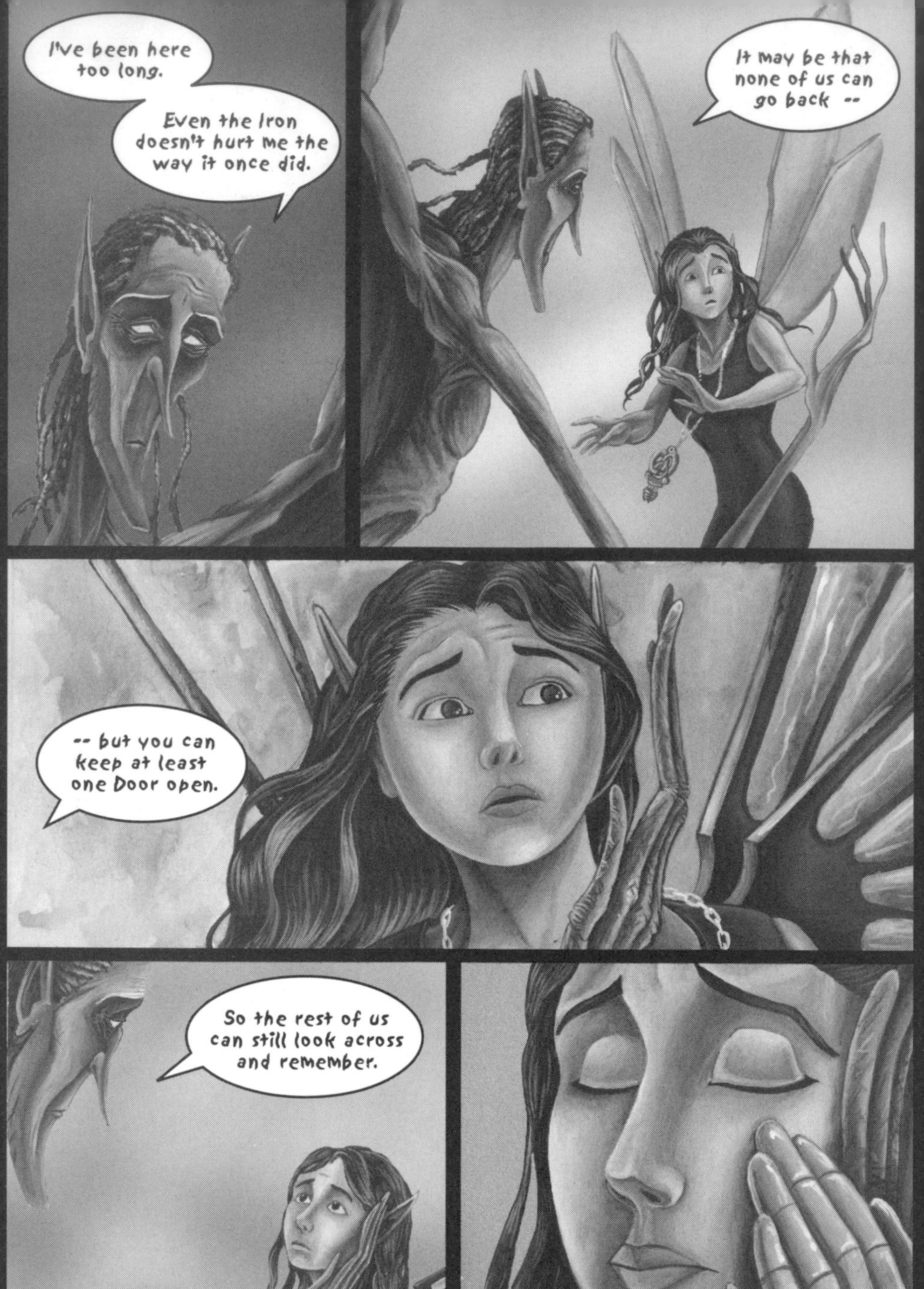
I've been here too long.
Even the Iron doesn't hurt me the way it once did.
It may be that none of us can go back --
-- but you can keep at least one Door open.
So the rest of us can still look across and remember.

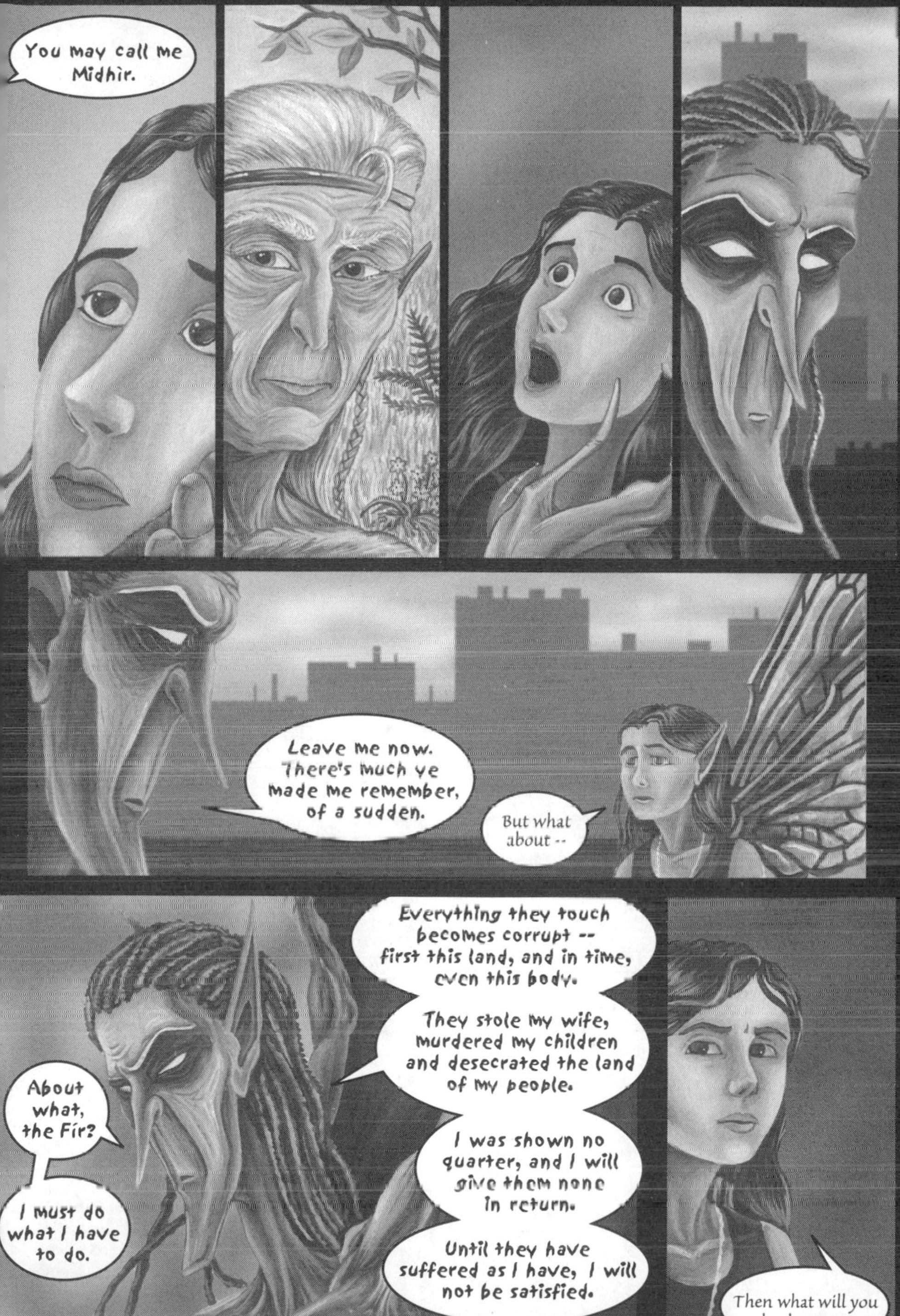

You may call me Midhir.
Leave me now. There's much ye made me remember, of a sudden.
But what about --
About what, the Fir?
I must do what I have to do.
Everything they touch becomes corrupt -- first this land, and in time, even this body.
They stole my wife, murdered my children and desecrated the land of my people.
I was shown no quarter, and I will give them none in return.
Until they have suffered as I have, I will not be satisfied.
Then what will you do about me?

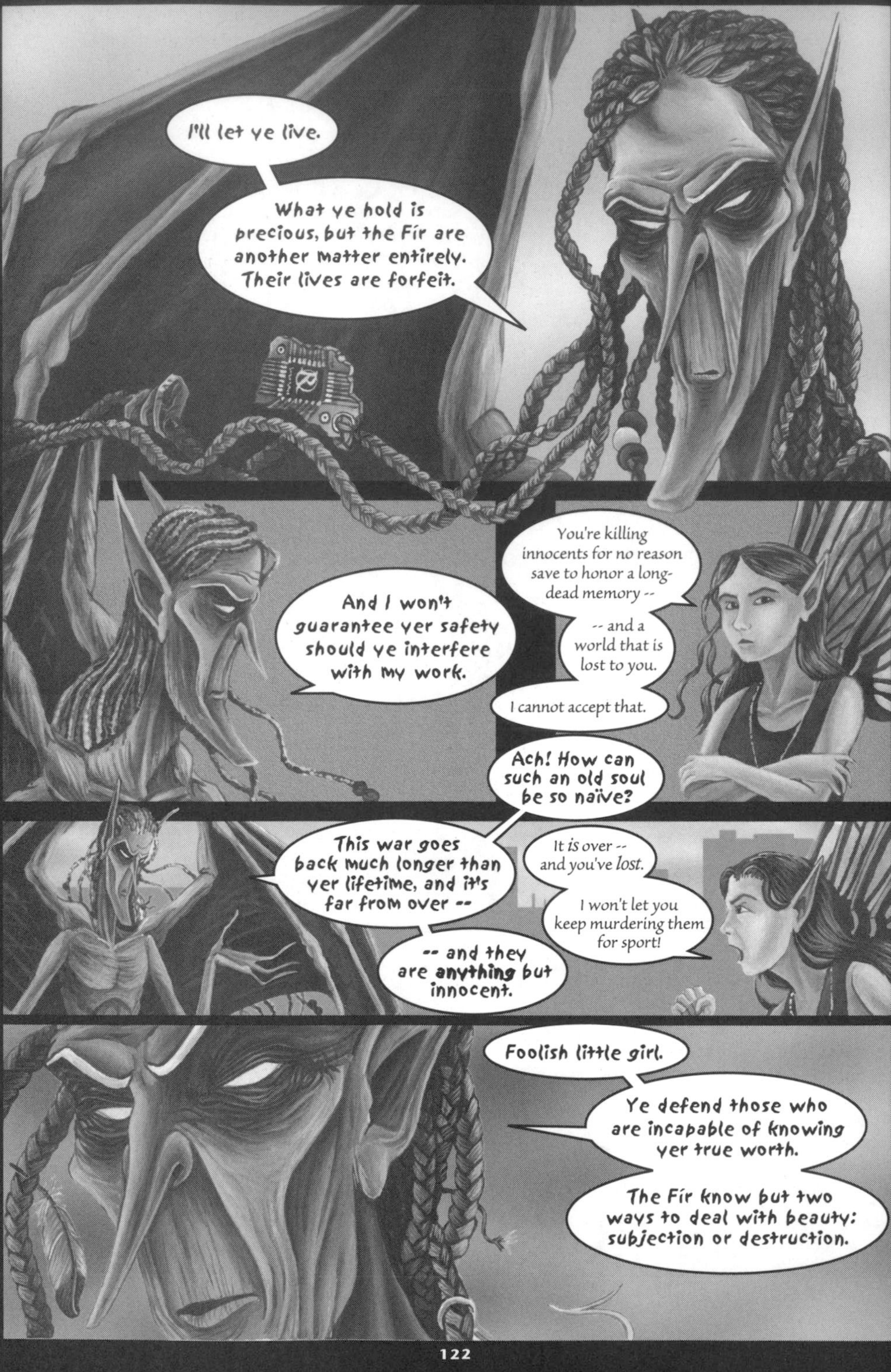

I'll let ye live.
What ye hold is precious, but the Fír are another matter entirely. Their lives are forfeit.
And I won't guarantee yer safety should ye interfere with my work.
You're killing innocents for no reason save to honor a long-dead memory --
-- and a world that is lost to you.
I cannot accept that.
Ach! How can such an old soul be so naïve?
This war goes back much longer than yer lifetime, and it's far from over --
-- and they are **anything** but innocent.
It *is* over -- and you've *lost.*
I won't let you keep murdering them for sport!
Foolish little girl.
Ye defend those who are incapable of knowing yer true worth.
The Fír know but two ways to deal with beauty: subjection or destruction.

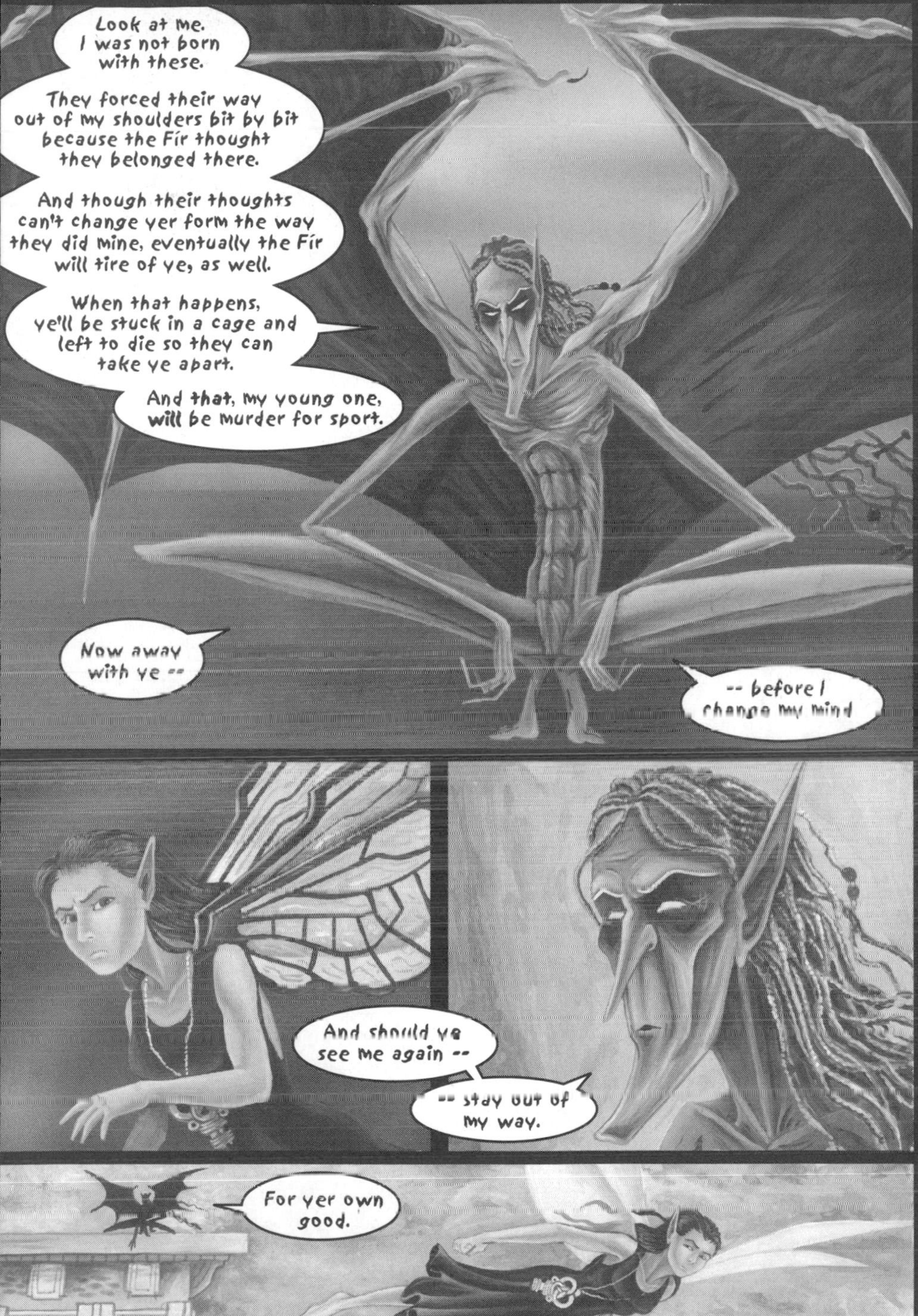
Look at me.
I was not born with these.
They forced their way out of my shoulders bit by bit because the Fír thought they belonged there.
And though their thoughts can't change yer form the way they did mine, eventually the Fír will tire of ye, as well.
When that happens, ye'll be stuck in a cage and left to die so they can take ye apart.
And that, my young one, will be murder for sport.
Now away with ye --
-- before I change my mind
And should ye see me again --
-- stay out of my way.
For yer own good.

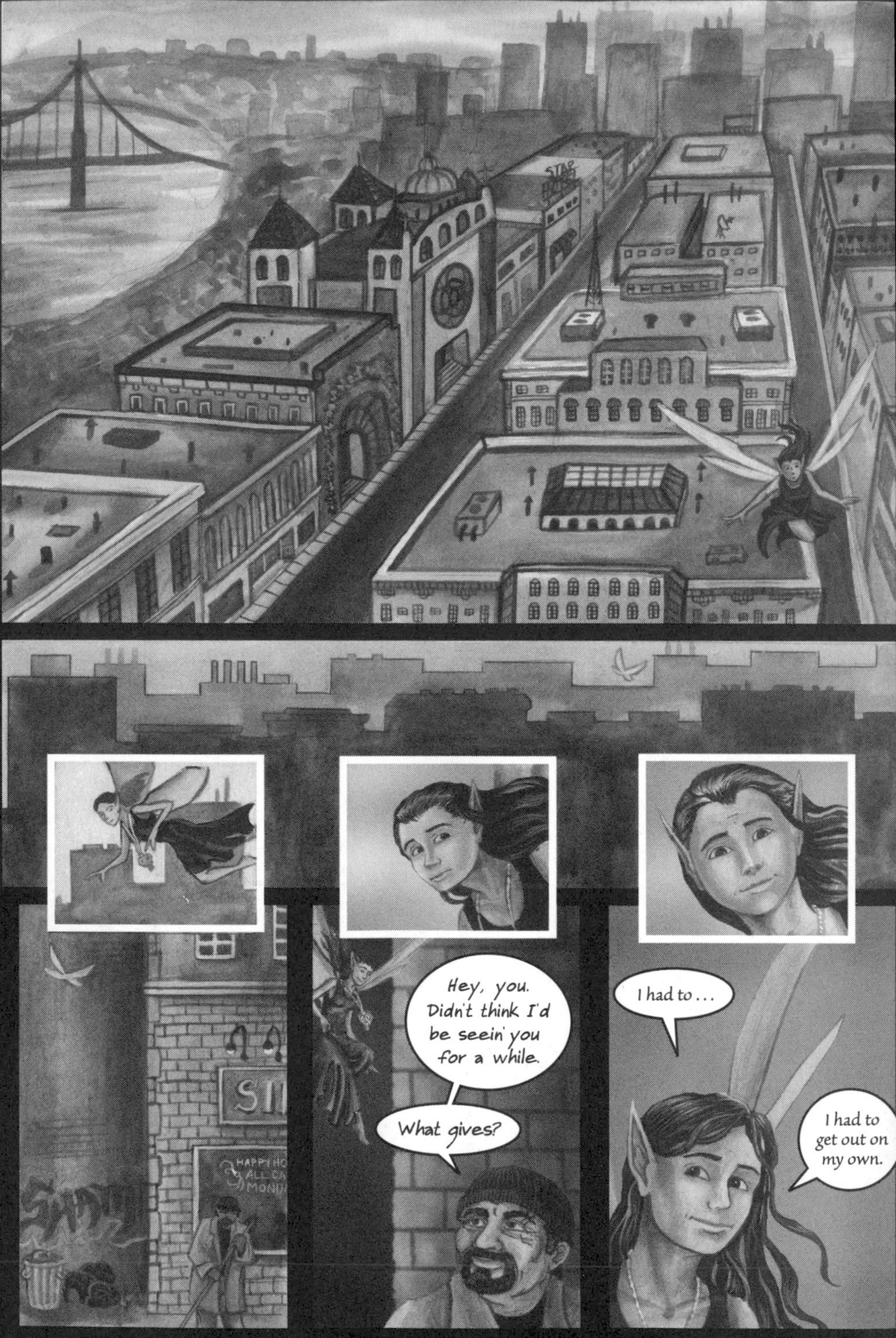
Hey, you. Didn't think I'd be seein' you for a while.
What gives?
I had to . . .
I had to get out on my own.

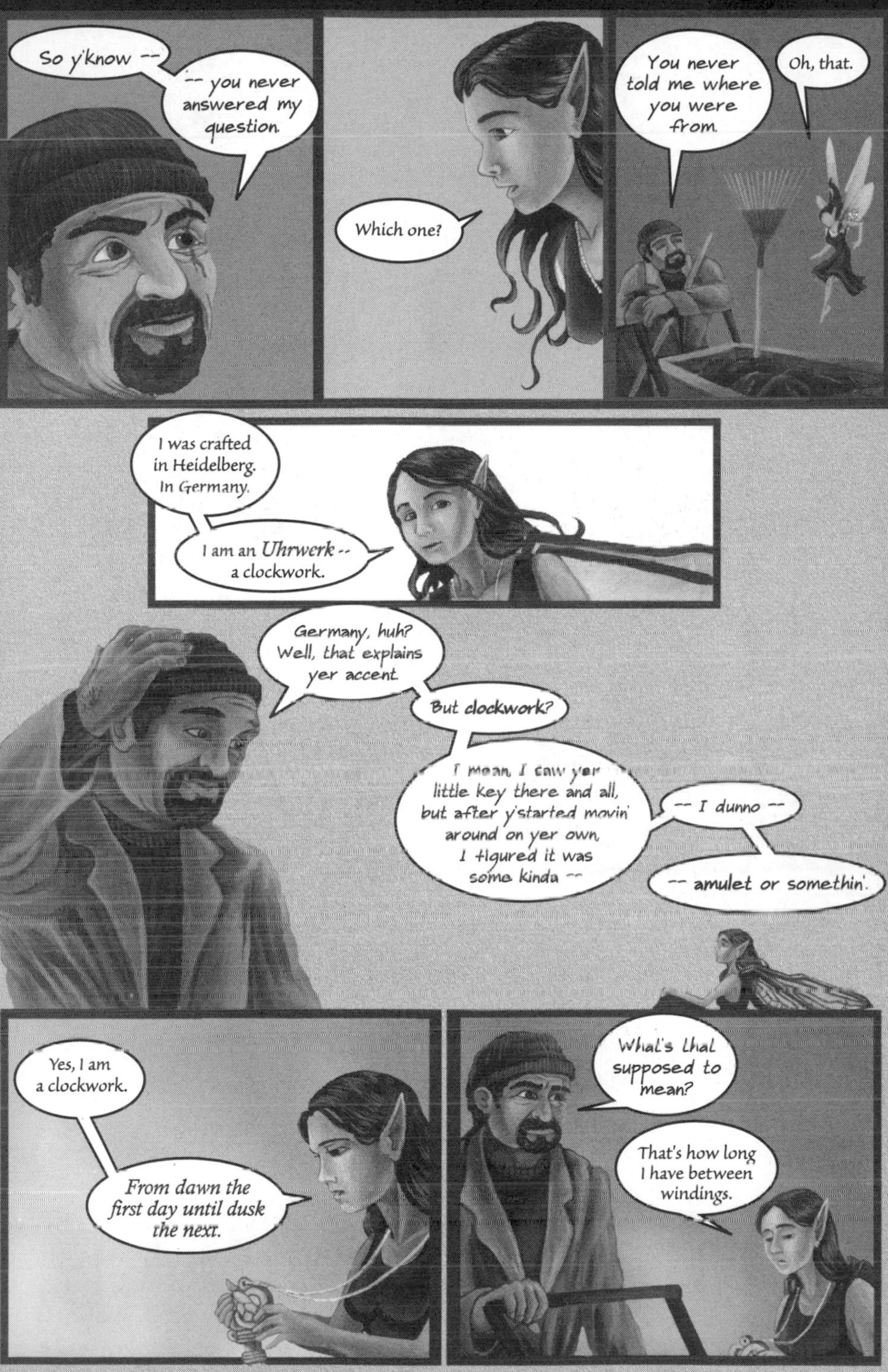
So y'know --
-- you never answered my question.
Which one?
You never told me where you were from.
Oh, that.
I was crafted in Heidelberg. In Germany.
I am an *Uhrwerk* -- a clockwork.
Germany, huh? Well, that explains yer accent.
But clockwork?
I mean, I saw yer little key there and all, but after y'started movin' around on yer own, I figured it was some kinda --
-- I dunno --
-- amulet or somethin'.
Yes, I am a clockwork.
From dawn the first day until dusk the next.
What's that supposed to mean?
That's how long I have between windings.

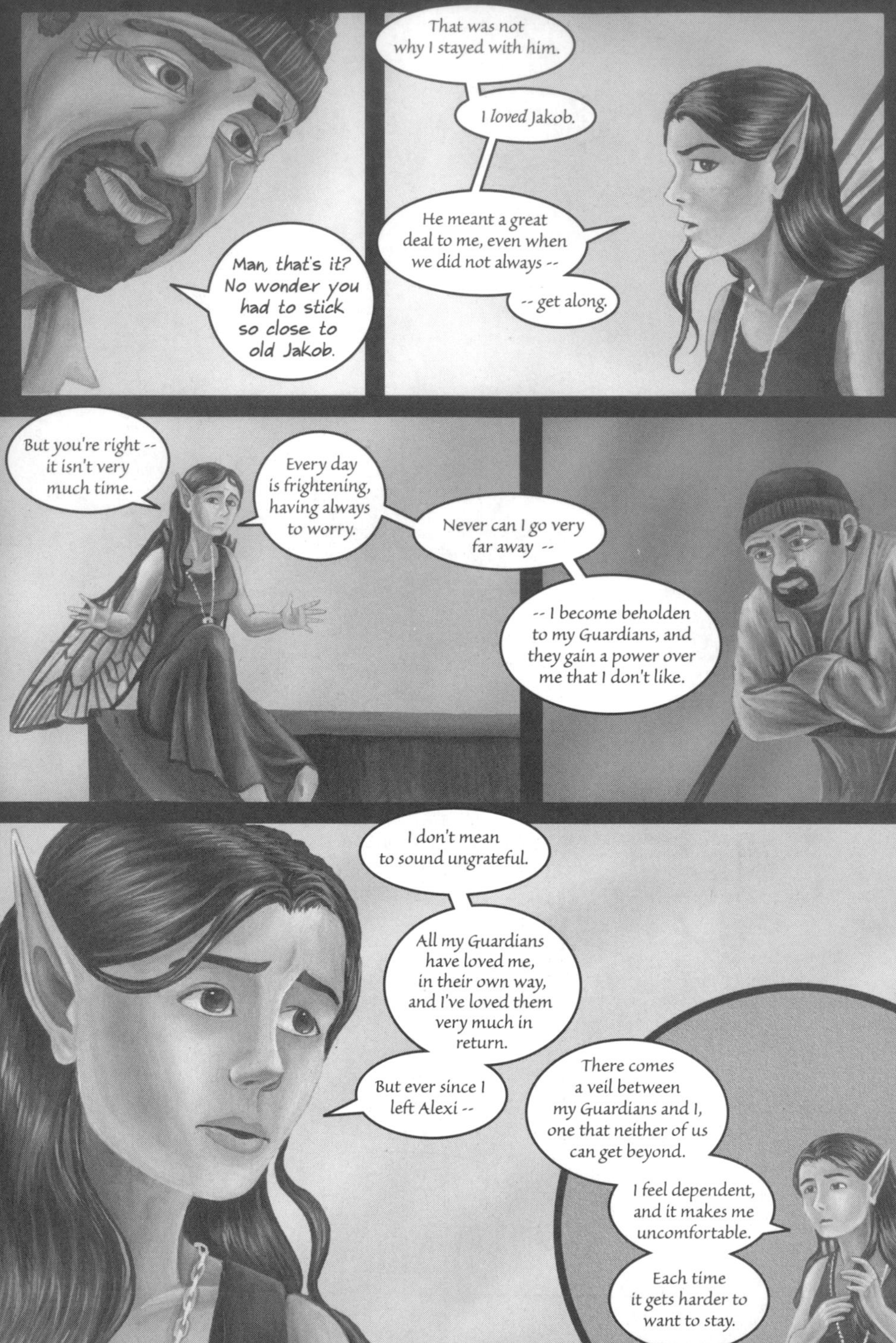
Man, that's it? No wonder you had to stick so close to old Jakob.
That was not why I stayed with him.
I *loved* Jakob.
He meant a great deal to me, even when we did not always --
-- get along.
But you're right -- it isn't very much time.
Every day is frightening, having always to worry.
Never can I go very far away --
-- I become beholden to my Guardians, and they gain a power over me that I don't like.
I don't mean to sound ungrateful.
All my Guardians have loved me, in their own way, and I've loved them very much in return.
But ever since I left Alexi --
There comes a veil between my Guardians and I, one that neither of us can get beyond.
I feel dependent, and it makes me uncomfortable.
Each time it gets harder to want to stay.

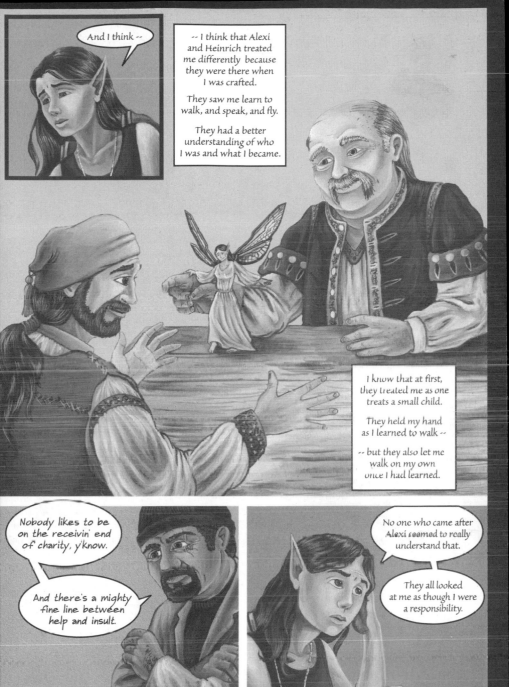

And I think --

-- I think that Alexi and Heinrich treated me differently because they were there when I was crafted.

They saw me learn to walk, and speak, and fly.

They had a better understanding of who I was and what I became.

I know that at first, they treated me as one treats a small child.

They held my hand as I learned to walk --

-- but they also let me walk on my own once I had learned.

Nobody likes to be on the receivin' end of charity, y'know.

And there's a mighty fine line between help and insult.

No one who came after Alexi seemed to really understand that.

They all looked at me as though I were a responsibility.

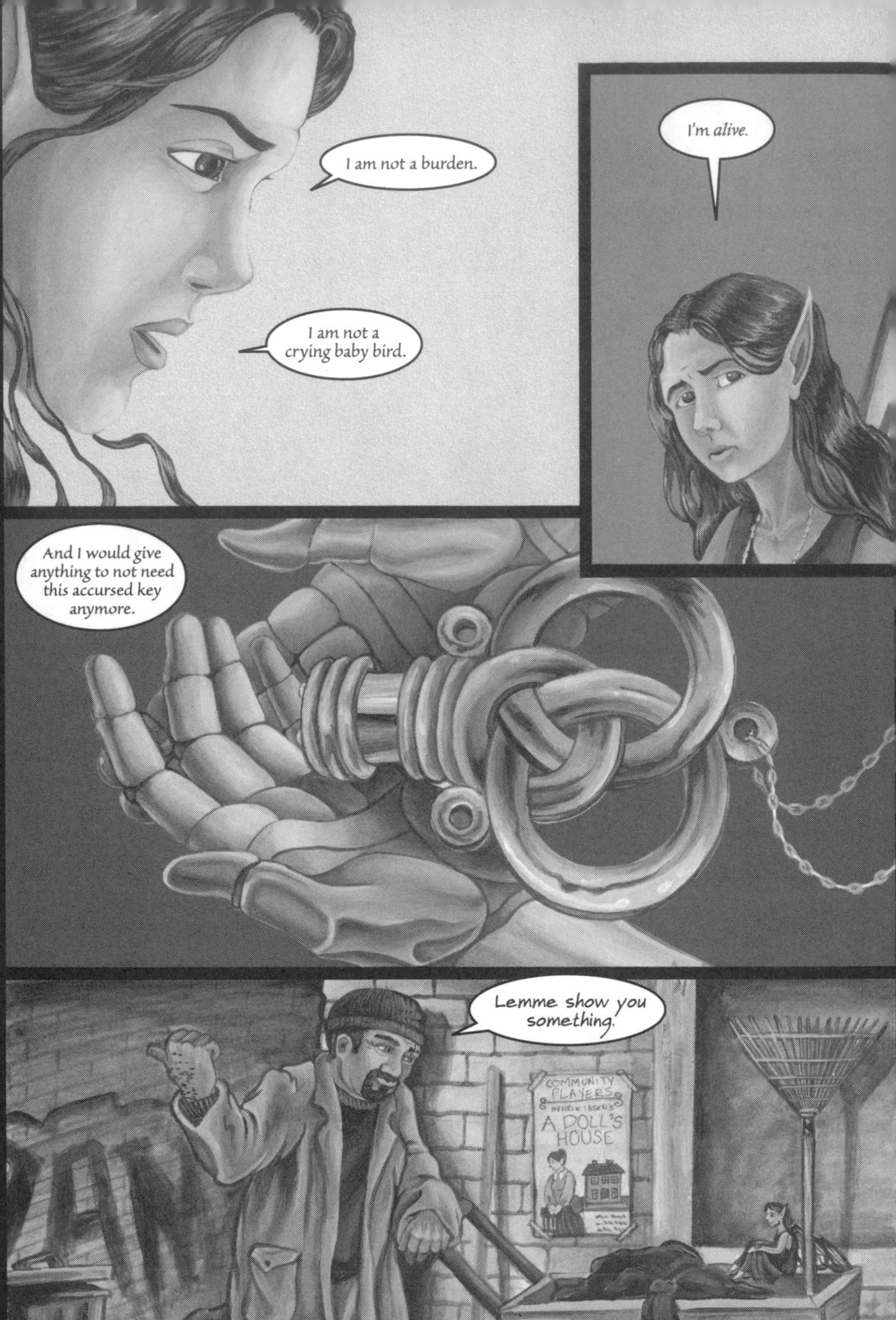
I am not a burden.
I am not a crying baby bird.
I'm *alive.*
And I would give anything to not need this accursed key anymore.
Lemme show you something.
COMMUNITY PLAYERS
HENRIK IBSEN'S
A DOLL'S HOUSE

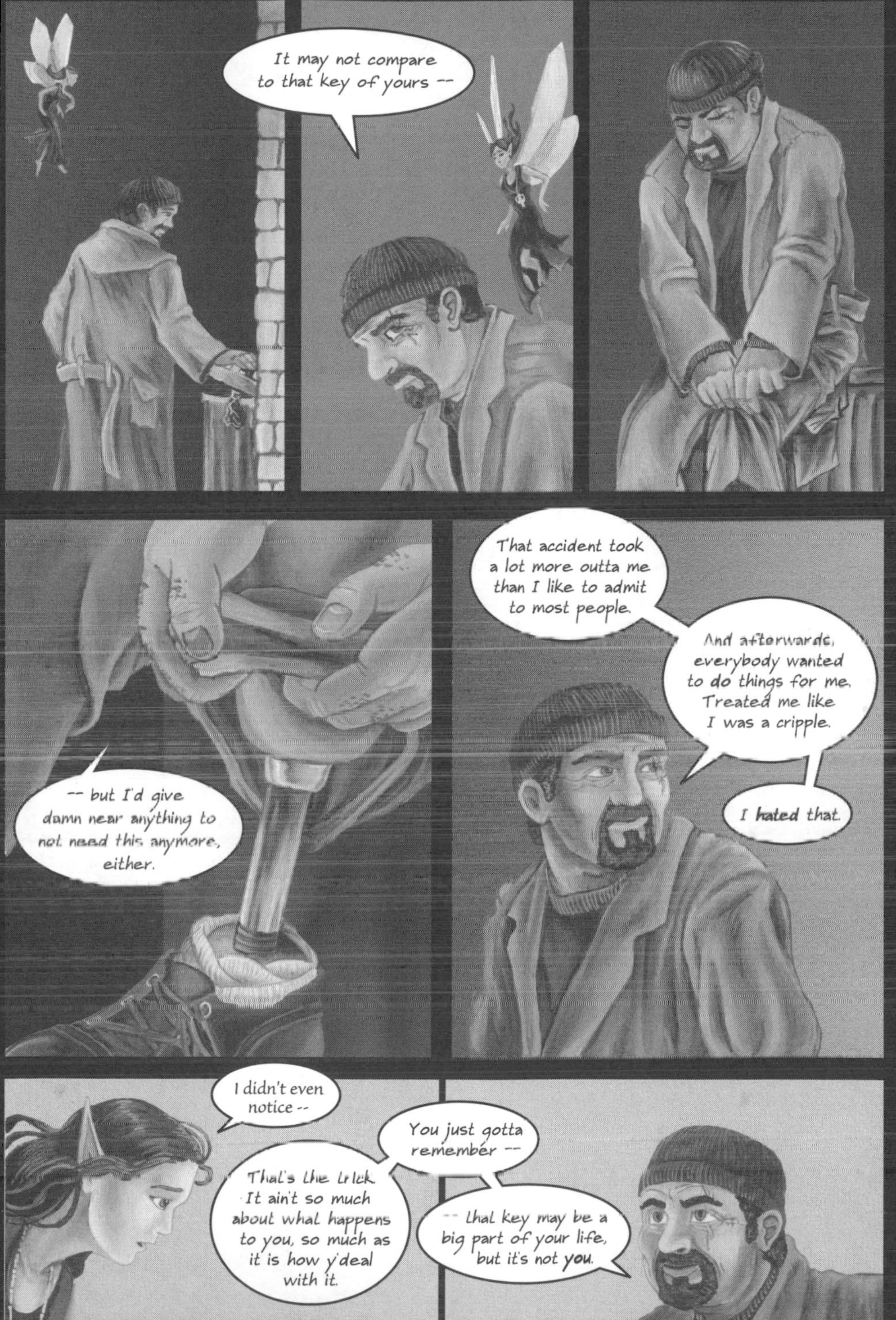
It may not compare to that key of yours --
-- but I'd give damn near anything to not need this anymore, either.
That accident took a lot more outta me than I like to admit to most people.
And afterwards, everybody wanted to do things for me. Treated me like I was a cripple.
I hated that.
I didn't even notice --
That's the trick. It ain't so much about what happens to you, so much as it is how y'deal with it.
You just gotta remember --
-- that key may be a big part of your life, but it's not you.

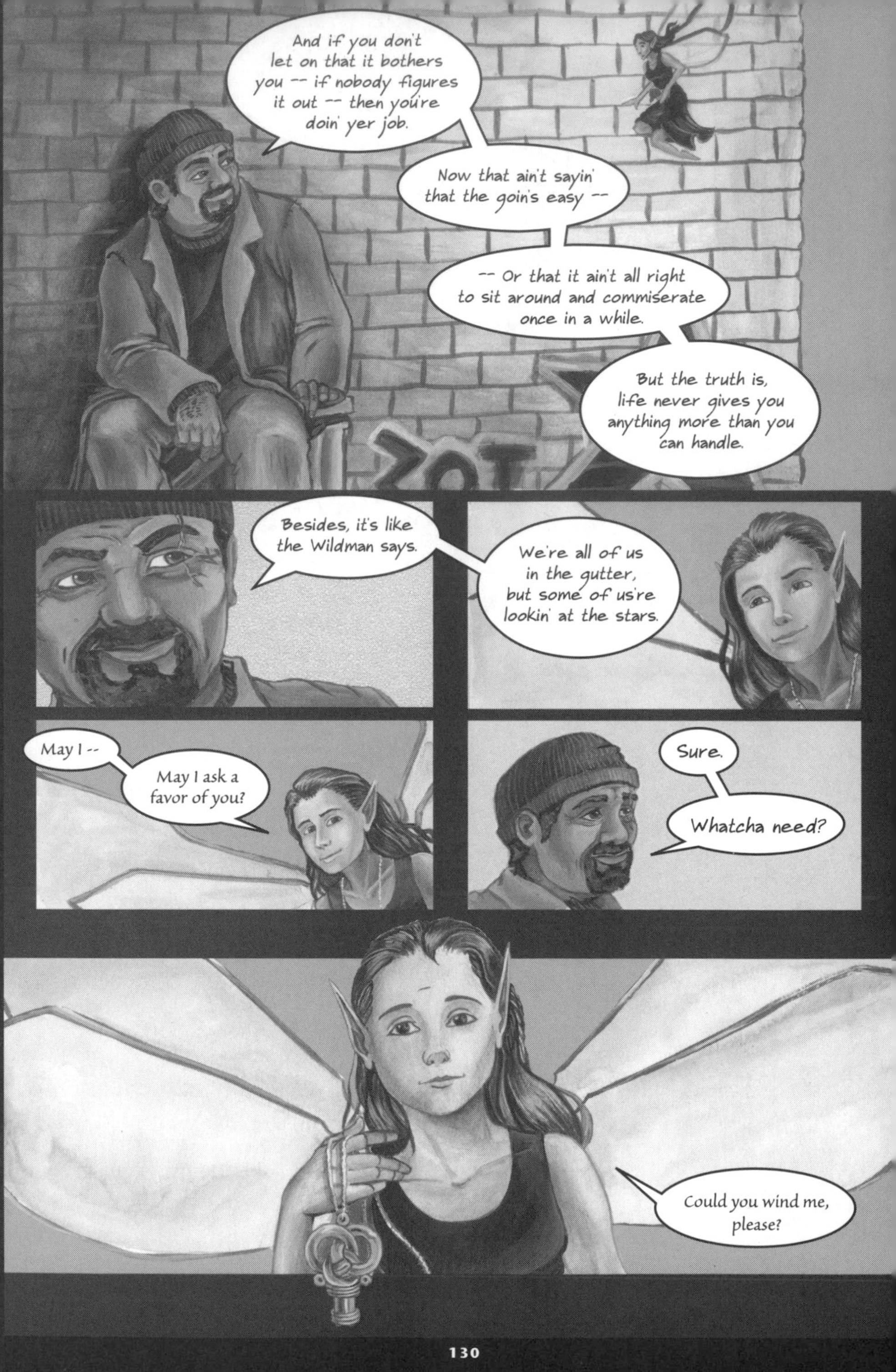
And if you don't let on that it bothers you -- if nobody figures it out -- then you're doin' yer job.
Now that ain't sayin' that the goin's easy --
-- Or that it ain't all right to sit around and commiserate once in a while.
But the truth is, life never gives you anything more than you can handle.
Besides, it's like the Wildman says.
We're all of us in the gutter, but some of us're lookin' at the stars.
May I --
May I ask a favor of you?
Sure.
Whatcha need?
Could you wind me, please?

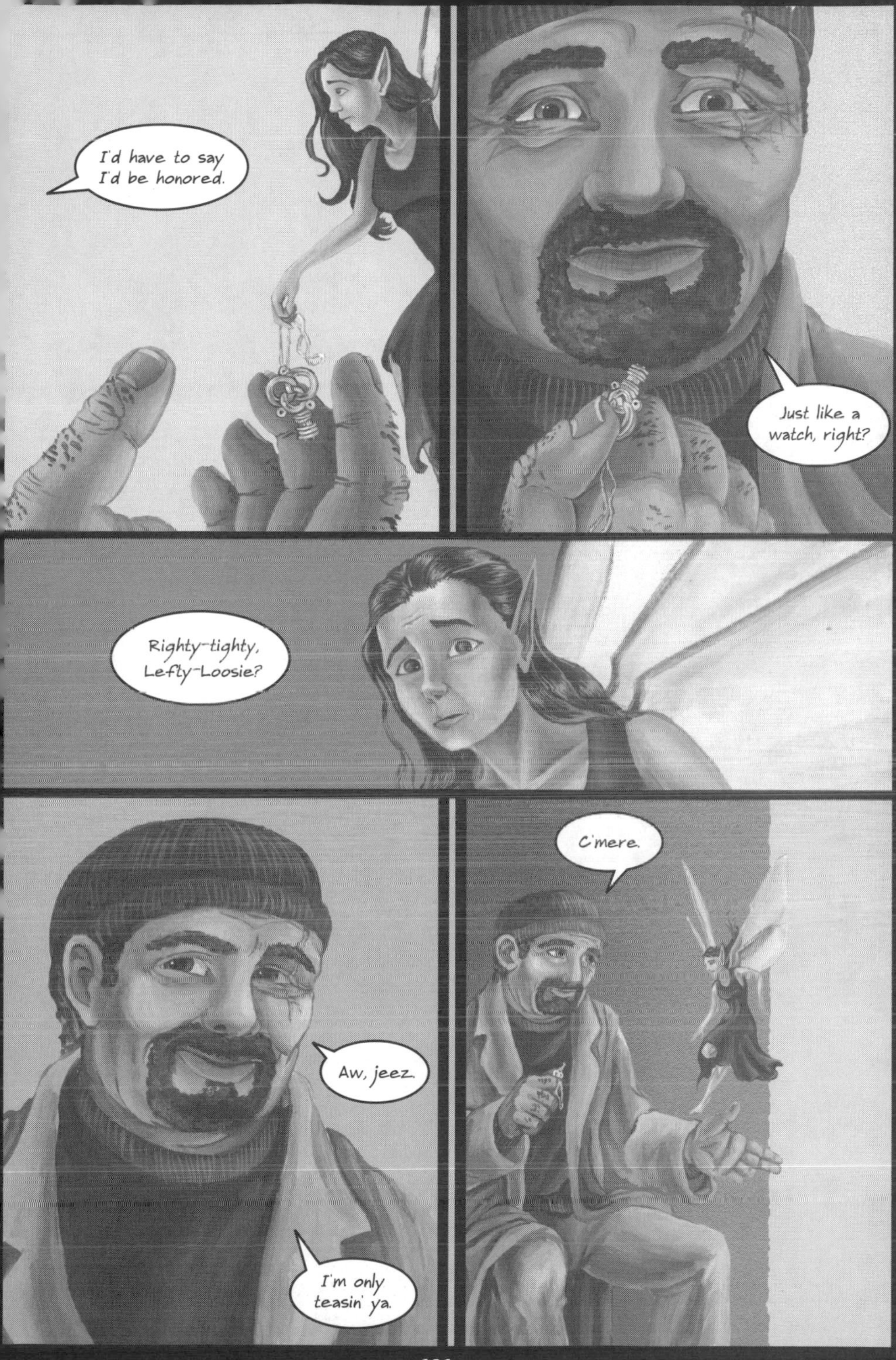
I'd have to say I'd be honored.
Just like a watch, right?
Righty-tighty, Lefty-Loosie?
Aw, jeez.
I'm only teasin' ya.
C'mere.

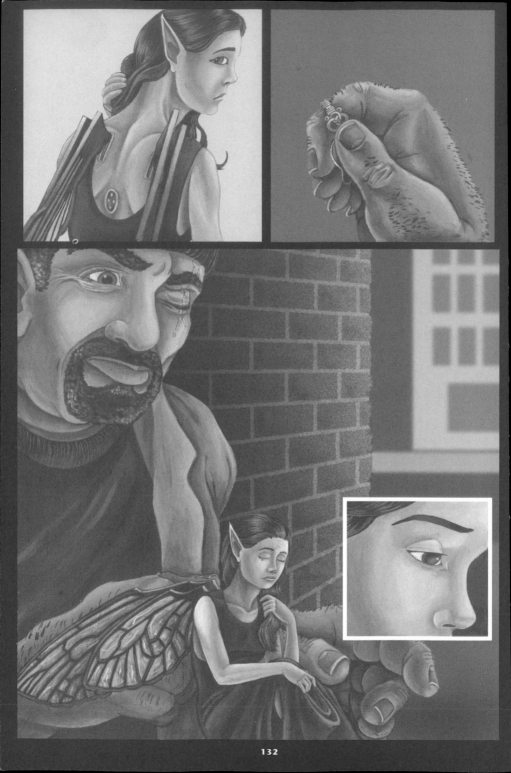

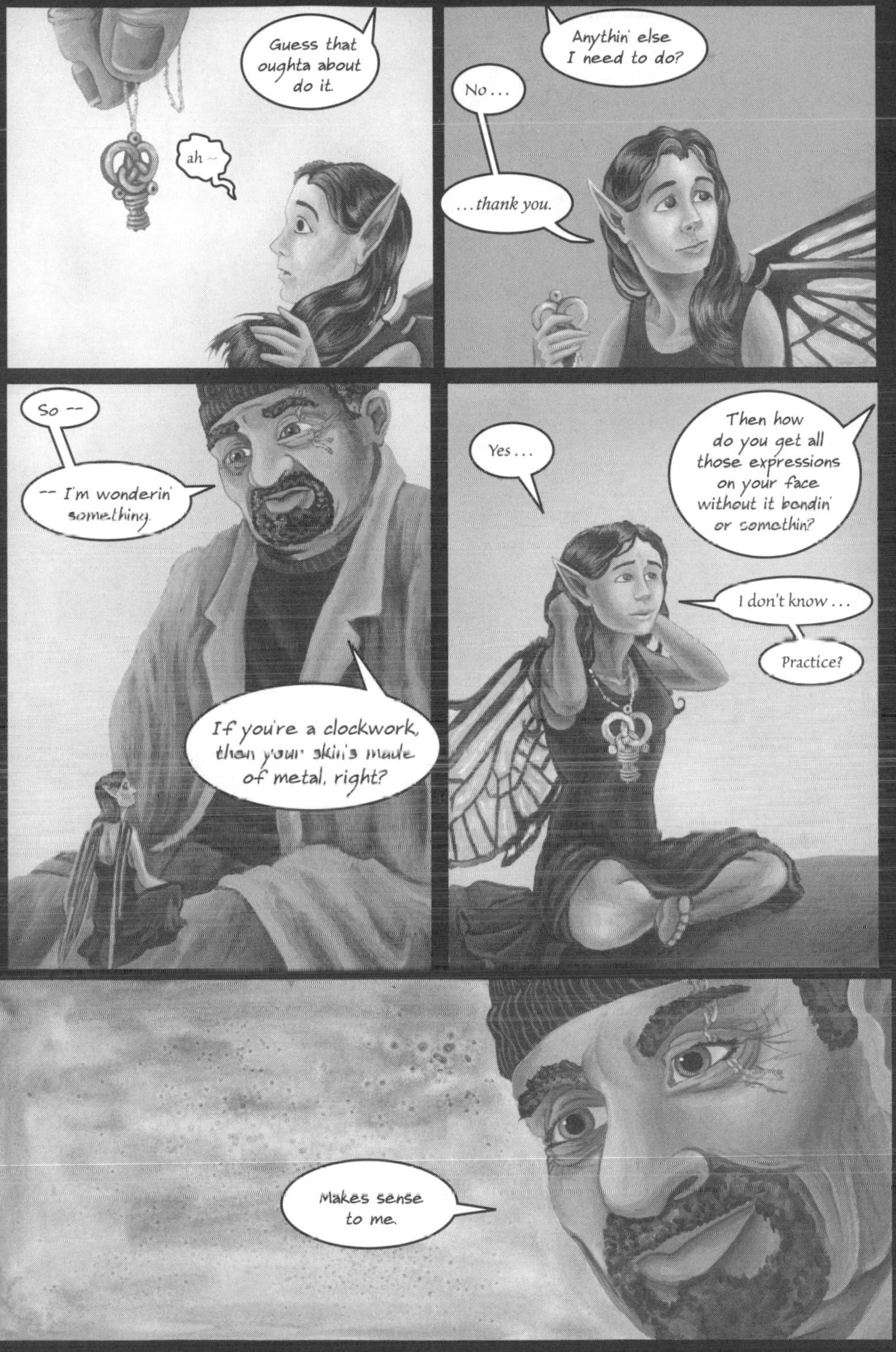
Guess that oughta about do it.
ah --
Anythin' else I need to do?
No . . .
. . . thank you.
So --
-- I'm wonderin' something.
If you're a clockwork, then your skin's made of metal, right?
Yes . . .
Then how do you get all those expressions on your face without it bendin' or somethin?
I don't know . . .
Practice?
Makes sense to me.

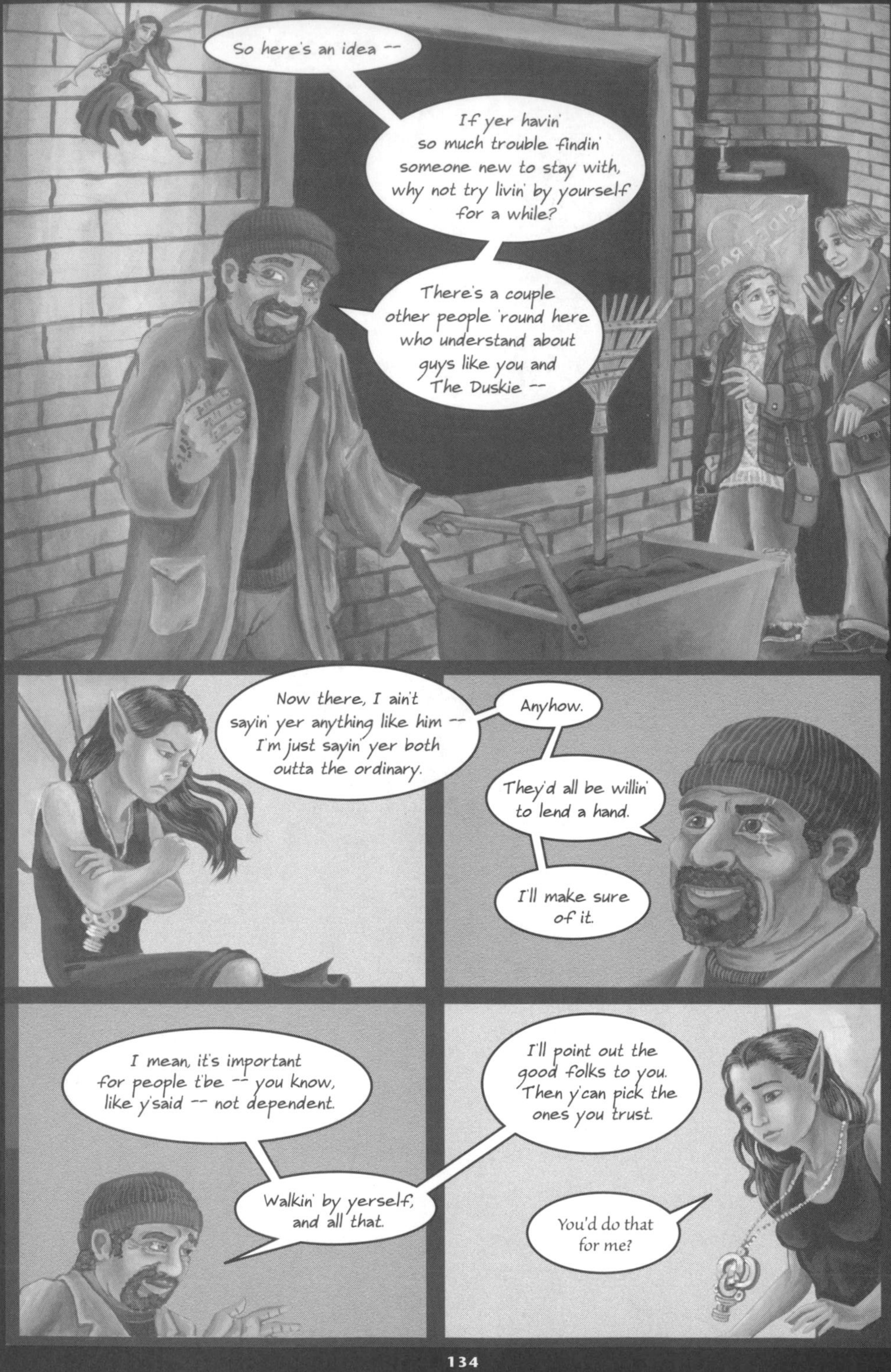
So here's an idea --
If yer havin' so much trouble findin' someone new to stay with, why not try livin' by yourself for a while?
There's a couple other people 'round here who understand about guys like you and The Duskie --
Now there, I ain't sayin' yer anything like him -- I'm just sayin' yer both outta the ordinary.
Anyhow.
They'd all be willin' to lend a hand.
I'll make sure of it.
I mean, it's important for people t'be -- you know, like y'said -- not dependent.
Walkin' by yerself, and all that.
I'll point out the good folks to you. Then y'can pick the ones you trust.
You'd do that for me?

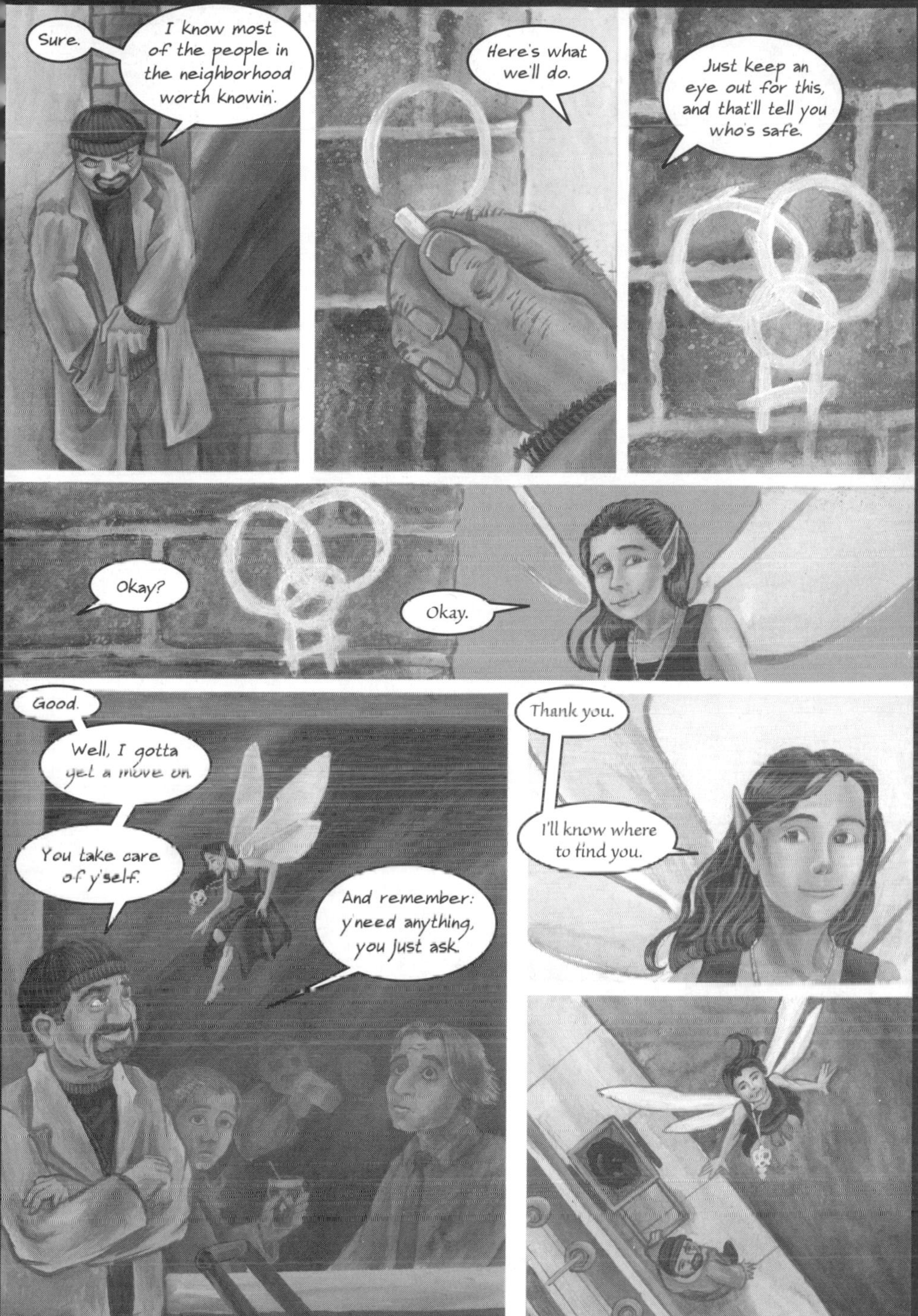
Sure.
I know most of the people in the neighborhood worth knowin'.
Here's what we'll do.
Just keep an eye out for this, and that'll tell you who's safe.
Okay?
Okay.
Good.
Well, I gotta get a move on.
You take care of y'self.
And remember: y'need anything, you just ask.
Thank you.
I'll know where to find you.

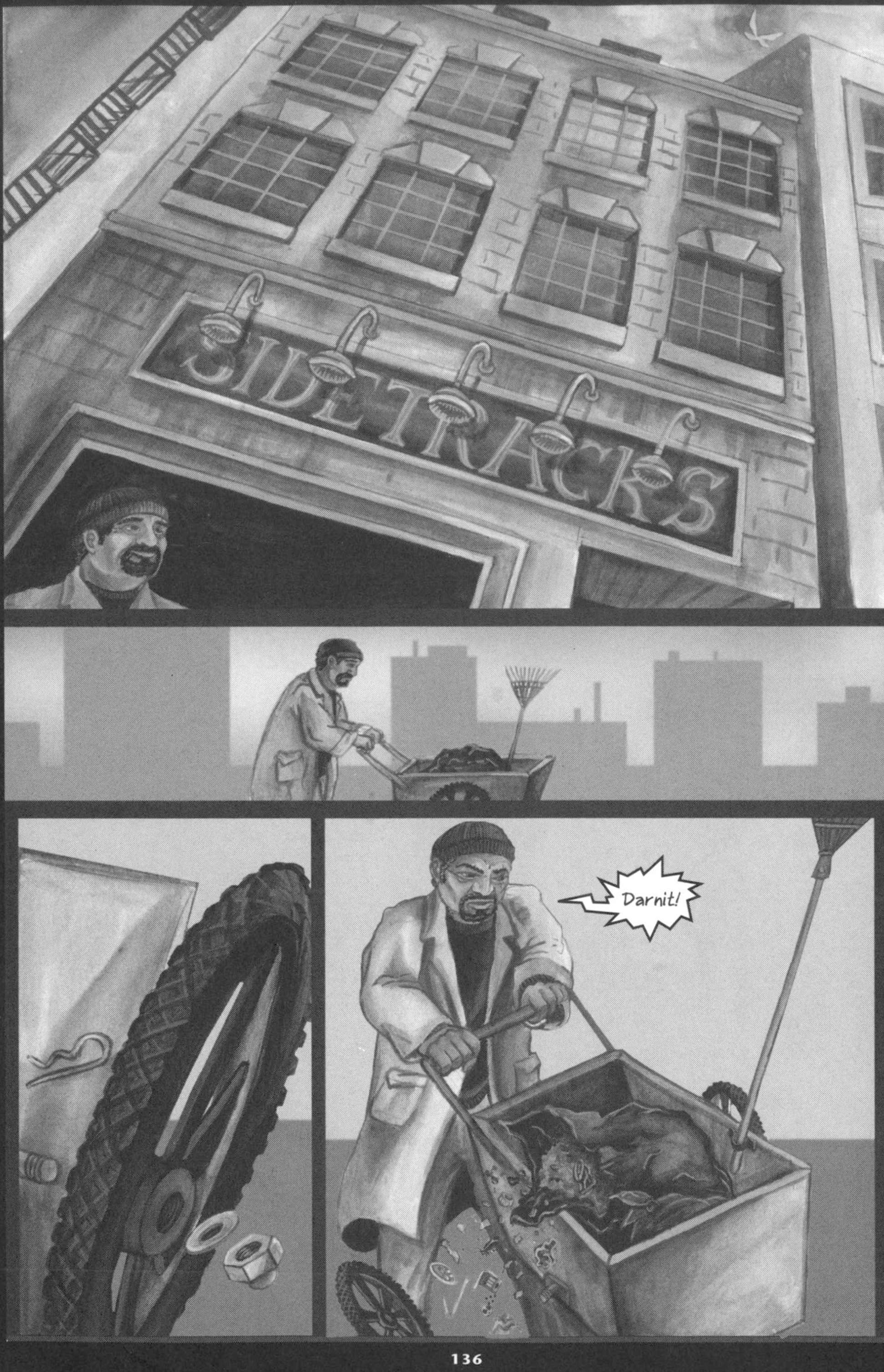

SIDETRACKS
Darnit!

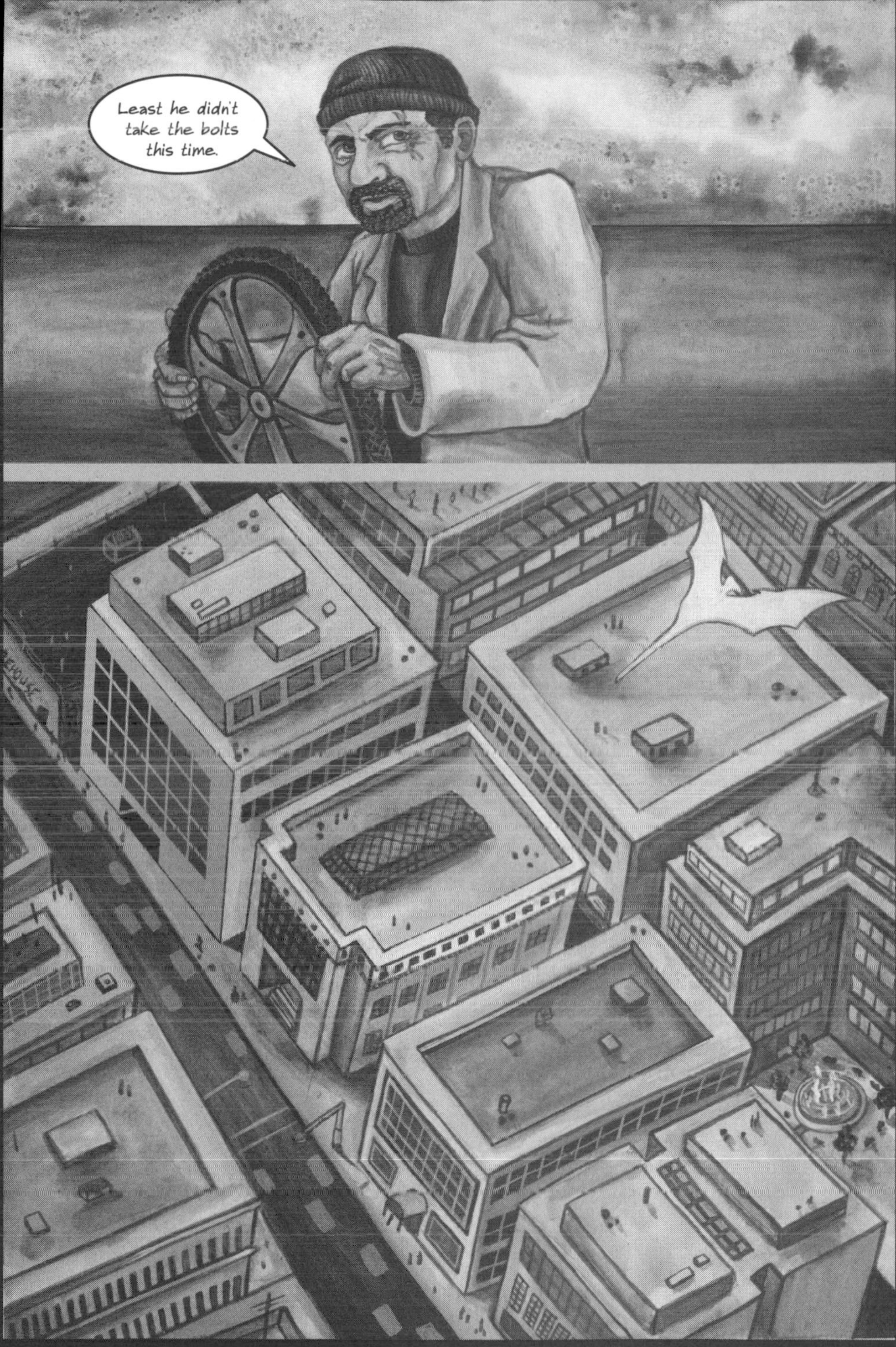
Least he didn't take the bolts this time.

The Duskie

The concrete will crack
I will be there when it does
To worship the grass

-- J.K. Berndt

Epilogue: March, 1689

Afoot and light-hearted, I take to the open road,
Healthy, free, the world before me,
The long brown path before me, leading wherever I choose.

Henceforth I ask not good-fortune—I myself am good fortune;
Henceforth I whimper no more, postpone no more, need nothing,
Strong and content, I travel the open road.

The earth—that is sufficient;
I do not want the constellations any nearer;
I know they are very well where they are;
I know they suffice for those who belong to them.

(Still here I carry my old delicious burdens;
I carry them, men and women—I carry them with me wherever I go;
I swear it is impossible for me to get rid of them;
I am fill'd with them, and I will fill them in return.)

                                   -- Walt Whitman

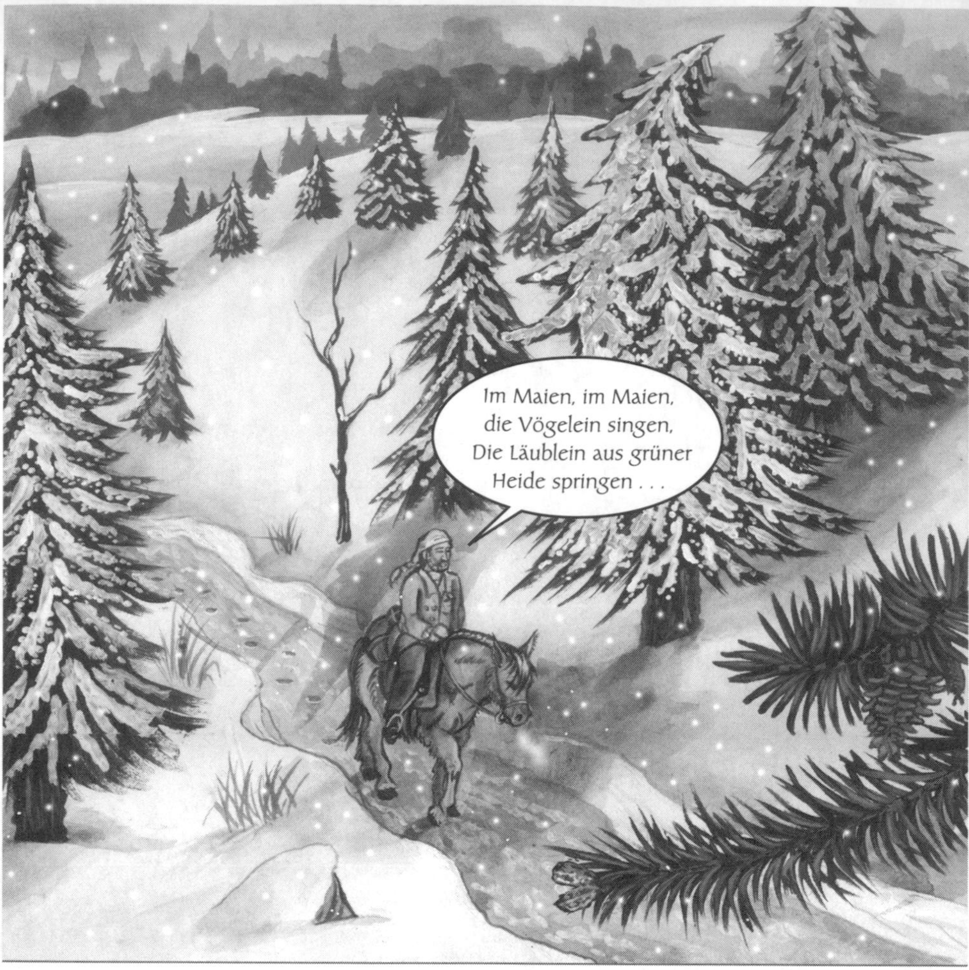
Im Maien, im Maien, die Vögelein singen, Die Läublein aus grüner Heide springen . . .

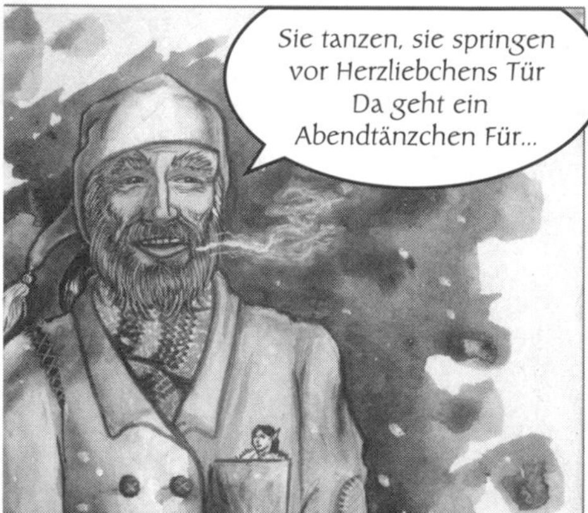
Sie tanzen, sie springen vor Herzliebchens Tür Da geht ein Abendtänzchen Für...

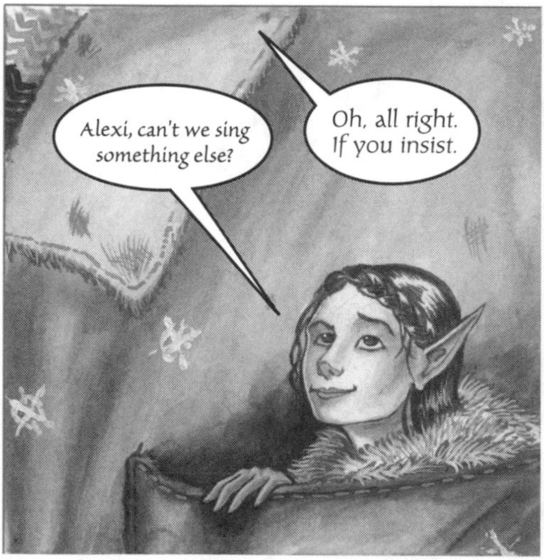
Alexi, can't we sing something else?
Oh, all right. If you insist.

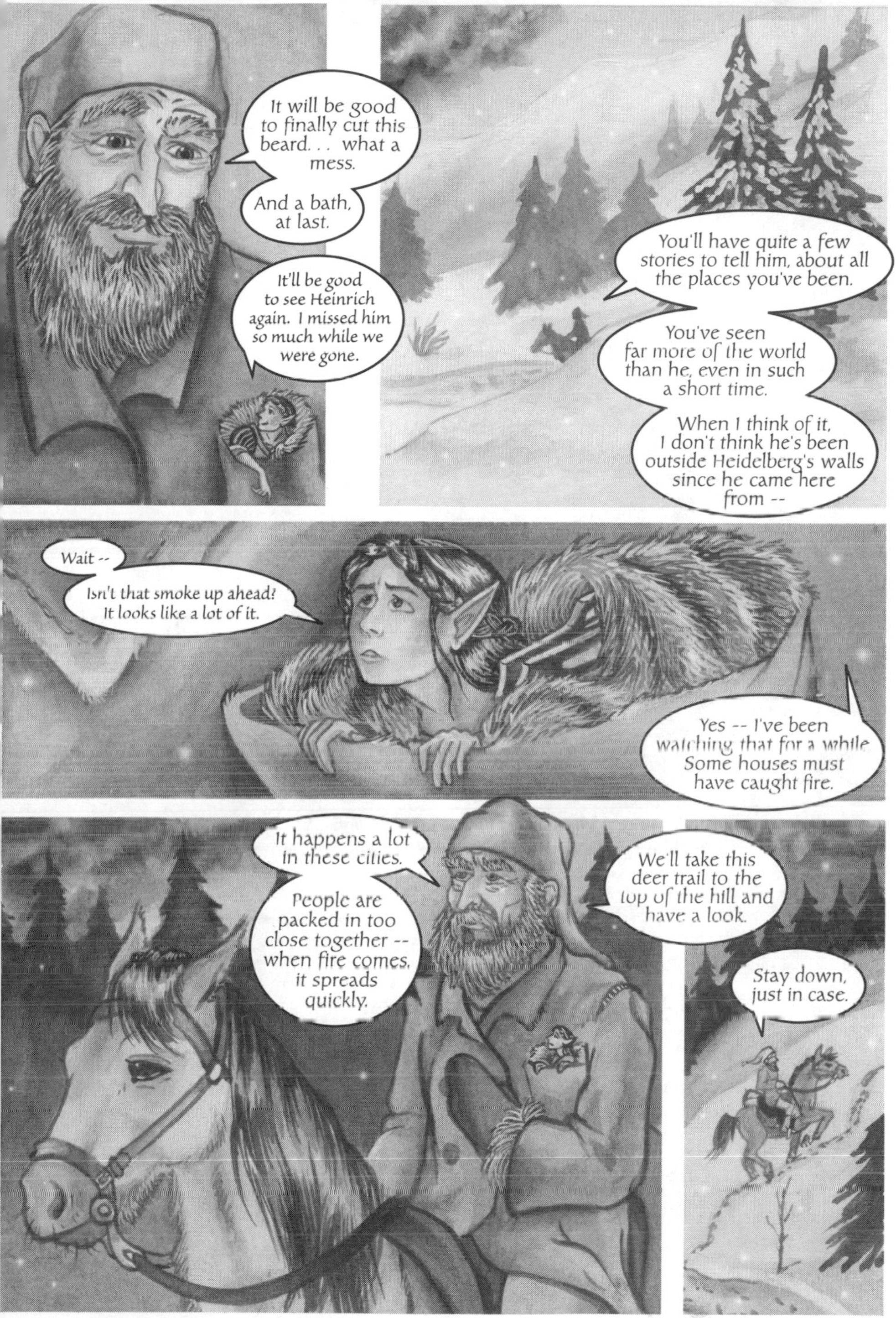
It will be good to finally cut this beard. . . what a mess.
And a bath, at last.
It'll be good to see Heinrich again. I missed him so much while we were gone.
You'll have quite a few stories to tell him, about all the places you've been.
You've seen far more of the world than he, even in such a short time.
When I think of it, I don't think he's been outside Heidelberg's walls since he came here from --
Wait --
Isn't that smoke up ahead? It looks like a lot of it.
Yes -- I've been watching that for a while. Some houses must have caught fire.
It happens a lot in these cities.
People are packed in too close together -- when fire comes, it spreads quickly.
We'll take this deer trail to the top of the hill and have a look.
Stay down, just in case.

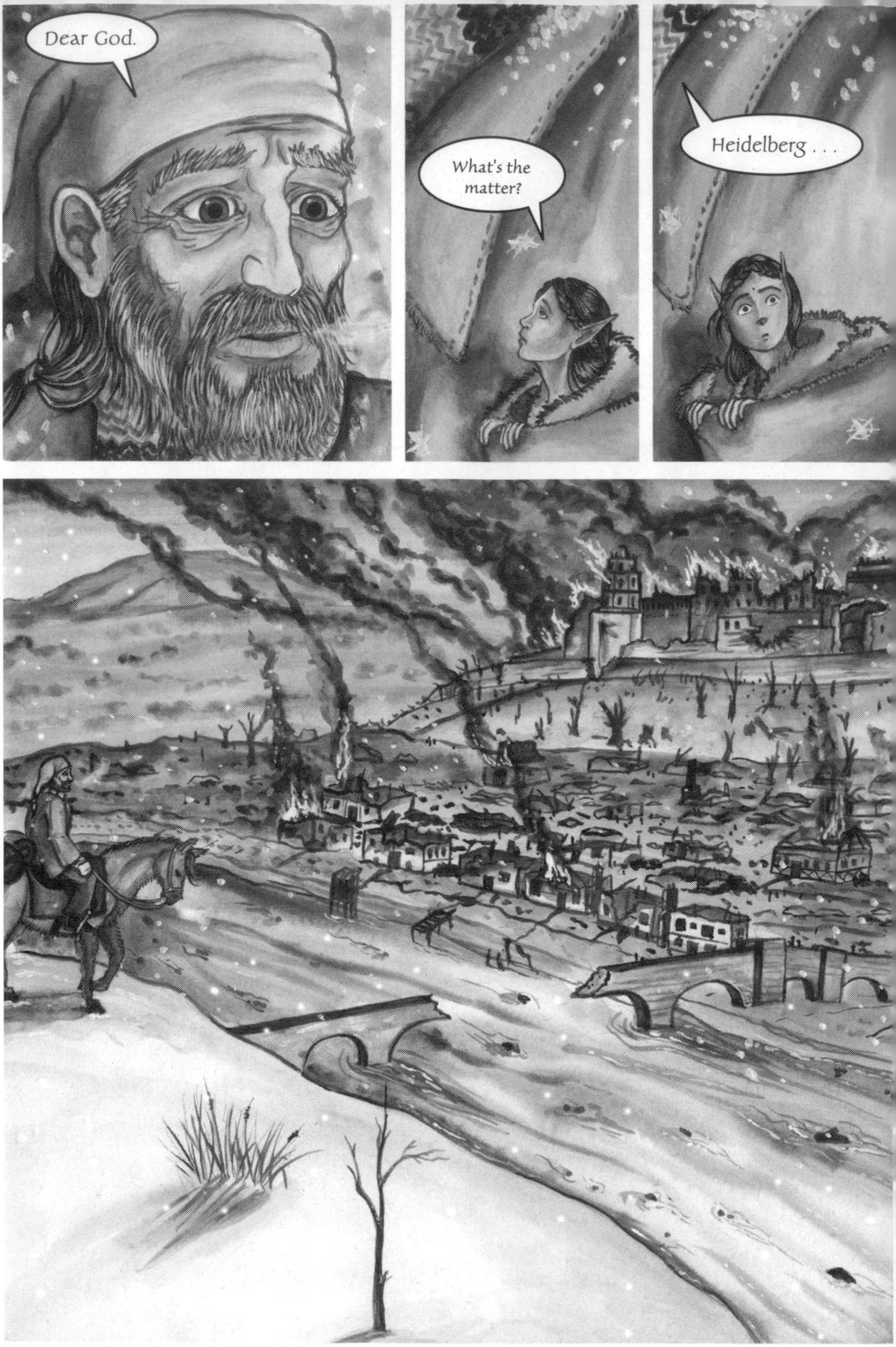

Dear God.
What's the matter?
Heidelberg . . .

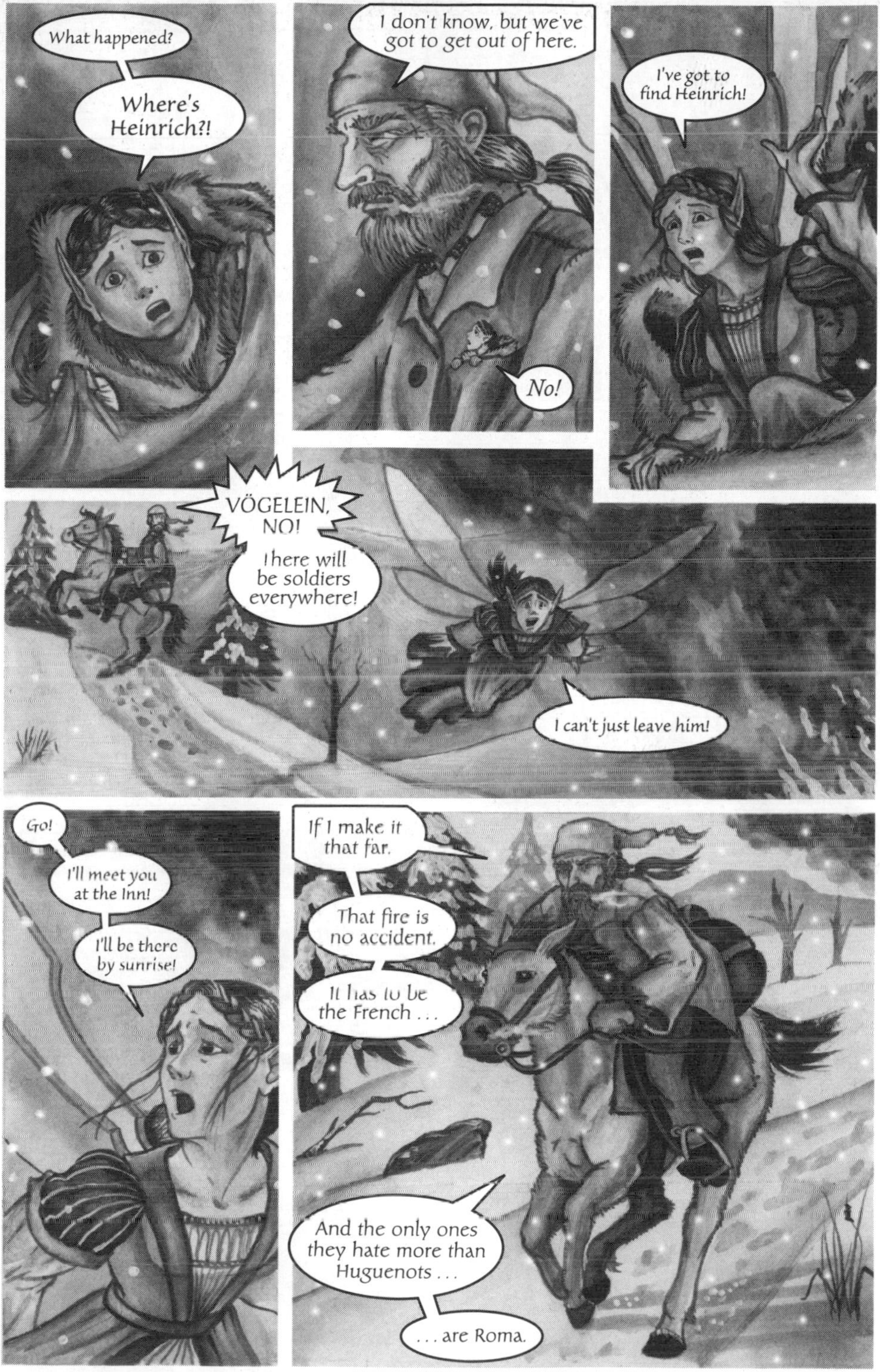

What happened?
Where's Heinrich?!
I don't know, but we've got to get out of here.
No!
I've got to find Heinrich!
VÖGELEIN, NO!
There will be soldiers everywhere!
I can't just leave him!
Go!
I'll meet you at the Inn!
I'll be there by sunrise!
If I make it that far.
That fire is no accident.
It has to be the French . . .
And the only ones they hate more than Huguenots . . .
. . . are Roma.

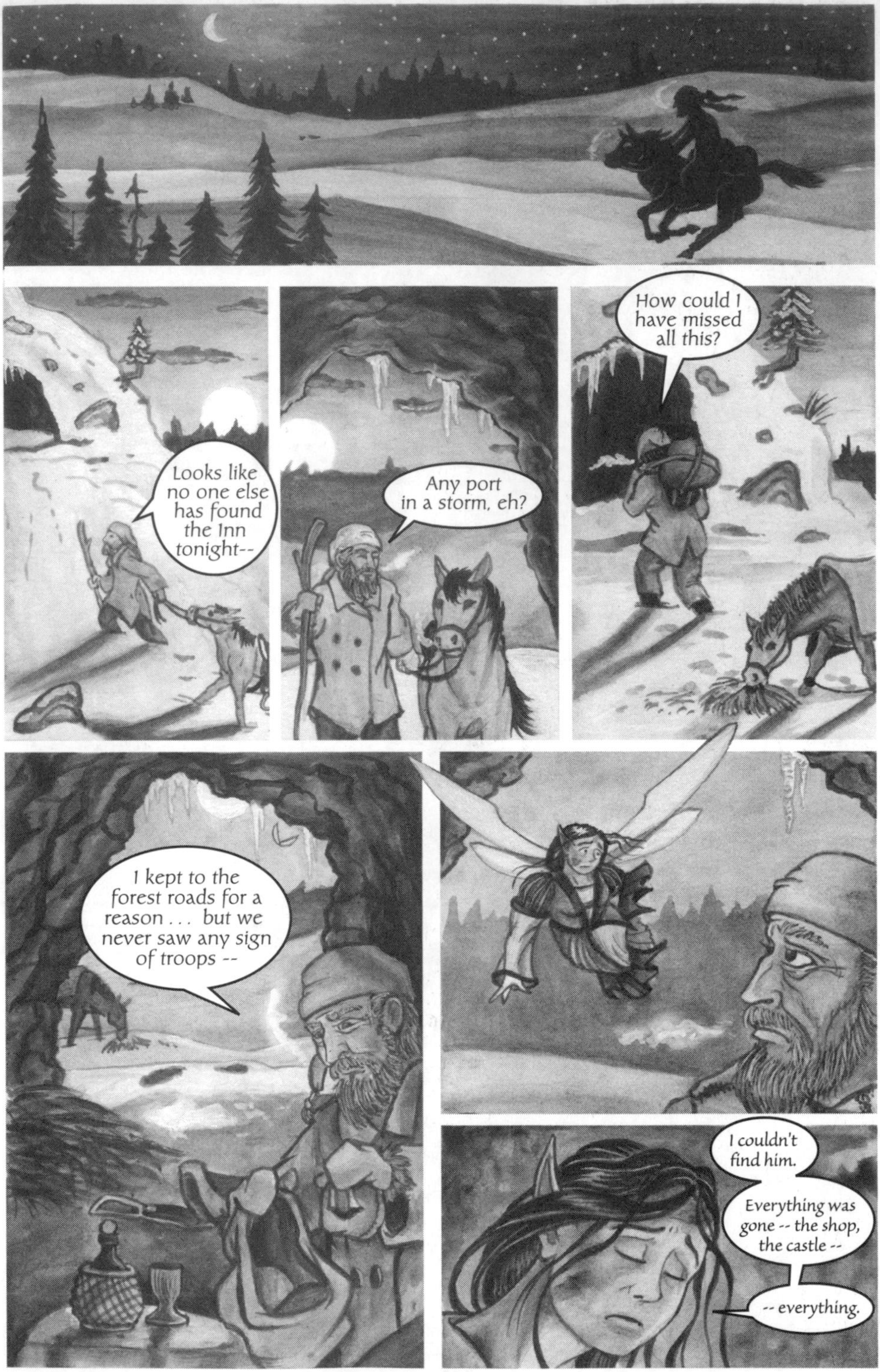
Looks like no one else has found the Inn tonight--
Any port in a storm, eh?
How could I have missed all this?
I kept to the forest roads for a reason . . . but we never saw any sign of troops --
I couldn't find him.
Everything was gone -- the shop, the castle --
-- everything.

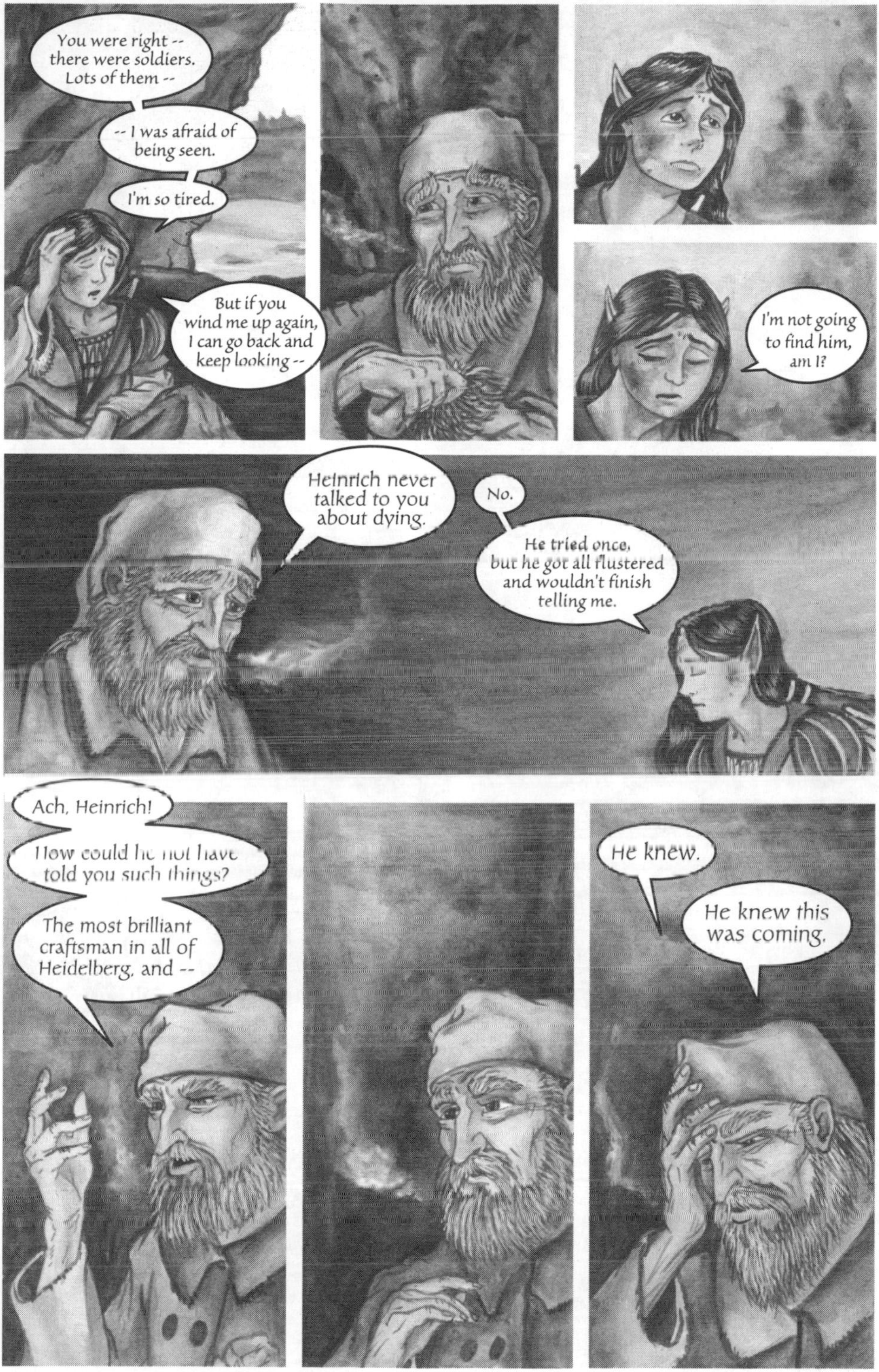
You were right -- there were soldiers. Lots of them --
-- I was afraid of being seen.
I'm so tired.
But if you wind me up again, I can go back and keep looking --
I'm not going to find him, am I?
Heinrich never talked to you about dying.
No.
He tried once, but he got all flustered and wouldn't finish telling me.
Ach, Heinrich!
How could he not have told you such things?
The most brilliant craftsman in all of Heidelberg, and --
He knew.
He knew this was coming.

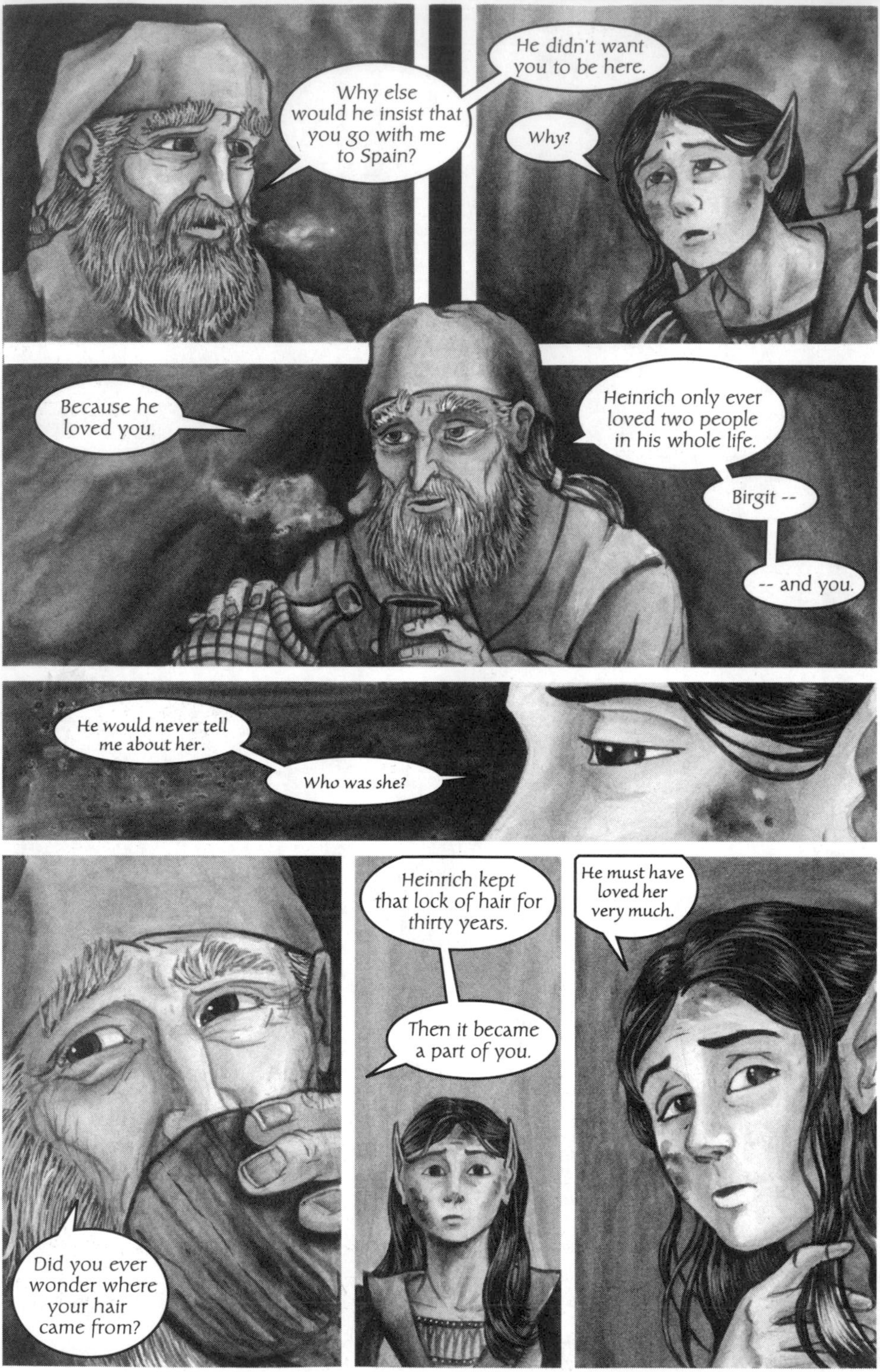
Why else would he insist that you go with me to Spain?
He didn't want you to be here.
Why?
Because he loved you.
Heinrich only ever loved two people in his whole life.
Birgit --
-- and you.
He would never tell me about her.
Who was she?
Did you ever wonder where your hair came from?
Heinrich kept that lock of hair for thirty years.
Then it became a part of you.
He must have loved her very much.

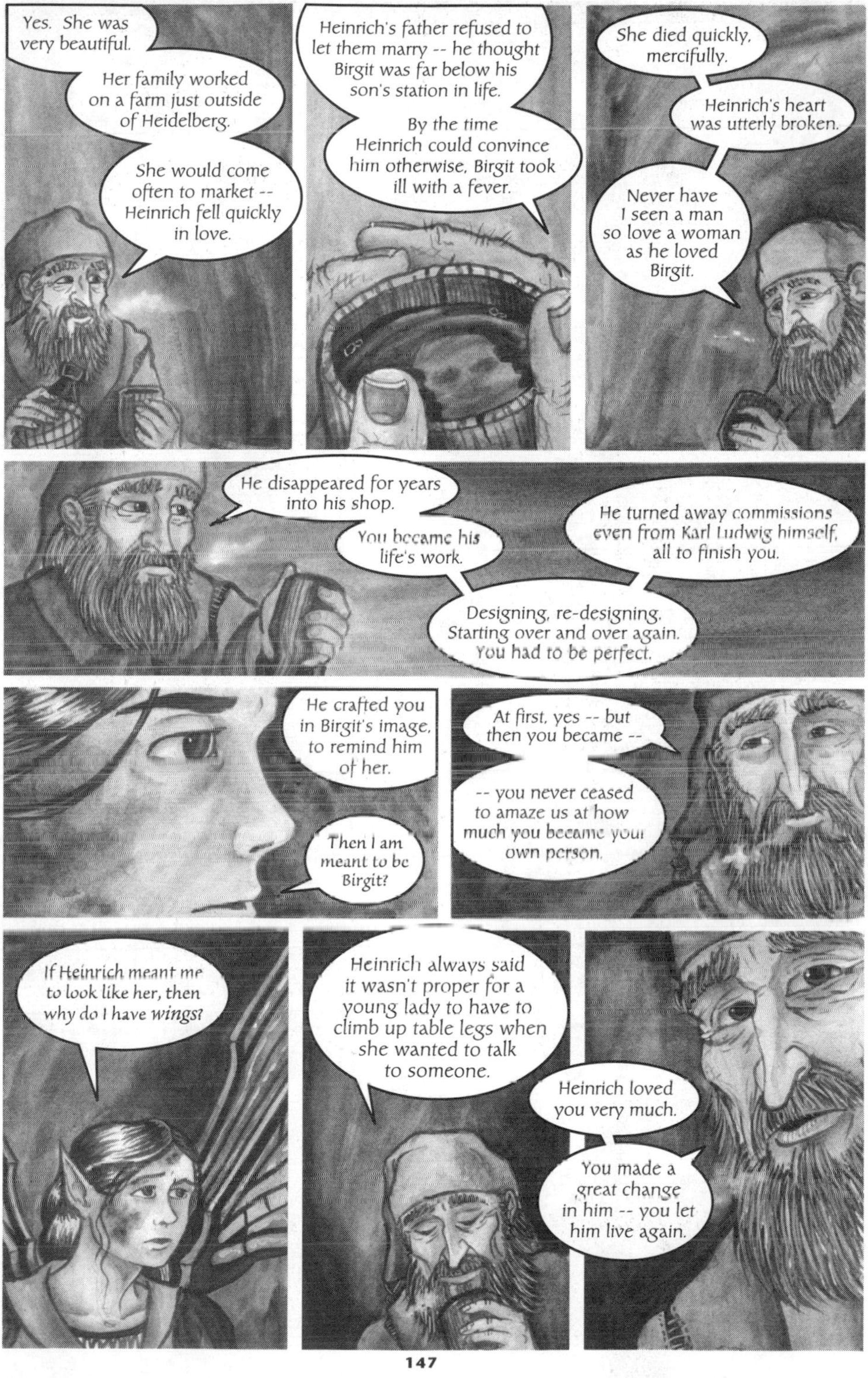
Yes. She was very beautiful.
Her family worked on a farm just outside of Heidelberg.
She would come often to market -- Heinrich fell quickly in love.
Heinrich's father refused to let them marry -- he thought Birgit was far below his son's station in life.
By the time Heinrich could convince him otherwise, Birgit took ill with a fever.
She died quickly, mercifully.
Heinrich's heart was utterly broken.
Never have I seen a man so love a woman as he loved Birgit.
He disappeared for years into his shop.
You became his life's work.
He turned away commissions even from Karl Ludwig himself, all to finish you.
Designing, re-designing. Starting over and over again. You had to be perfect.
He crafted you in Birgit's image, to remind him of her.
Then I am meant to be Birgit?
At first, yes -- but then you became --
-- you never ceased to amaze us at how much you became your own person.
If Heinrich meant me to look like her, then why do I have *wings?*
Heinrich always said it wasn't proper for a young lady to have to climb up table legs when she wanted to talk to someone.
Heinrich loved you very much.
You made a great change in him -- you let him live again.

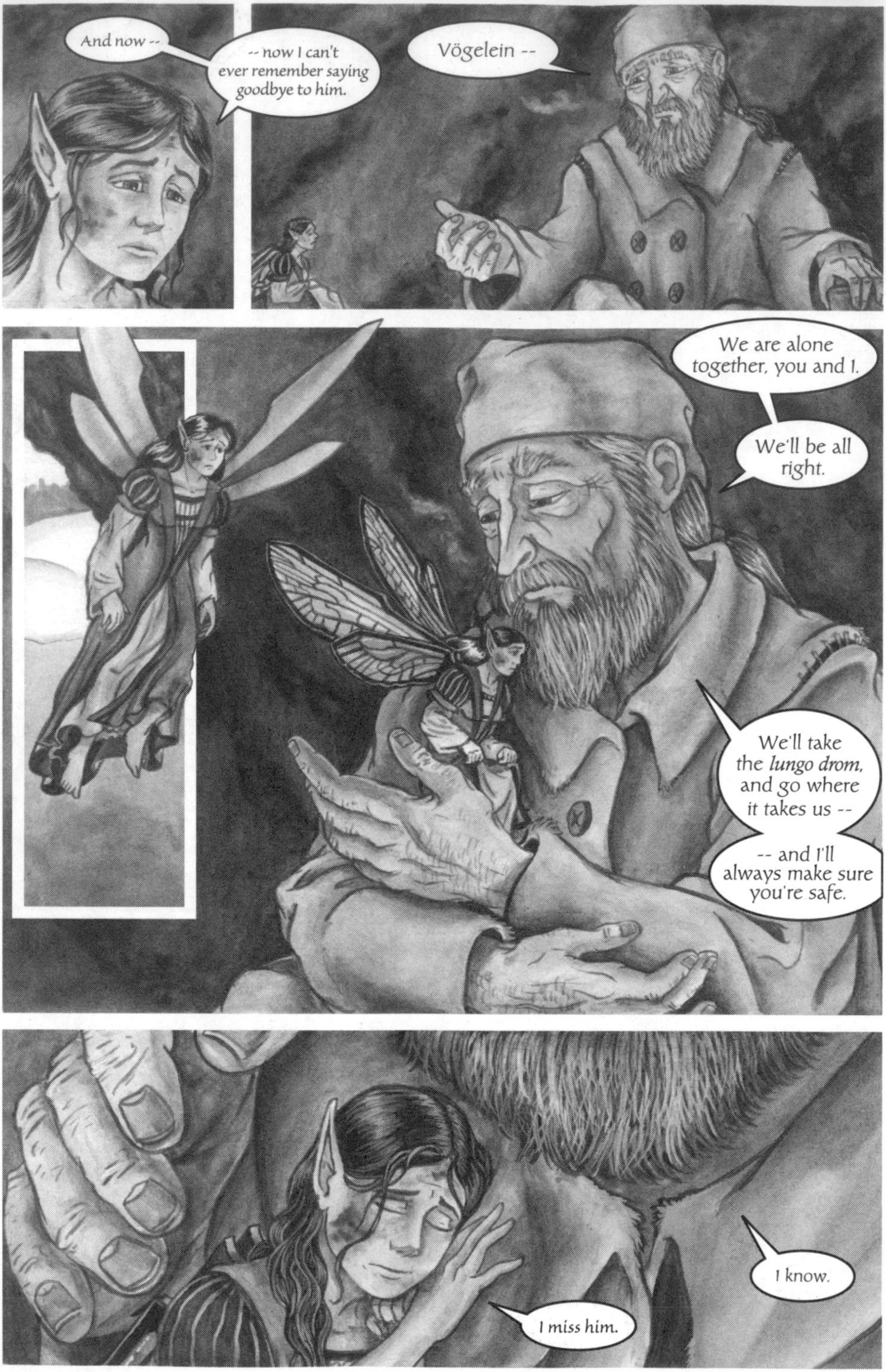

And now --
-- now I can't ever remember saying goodbye to him.
Vögelein --
We are alone together, you and I.
We'll be all right.
We'll take the *lungo drom,* and go where it takes us --
-- and I'll always make sure you're safe.
I miss him.
I know.

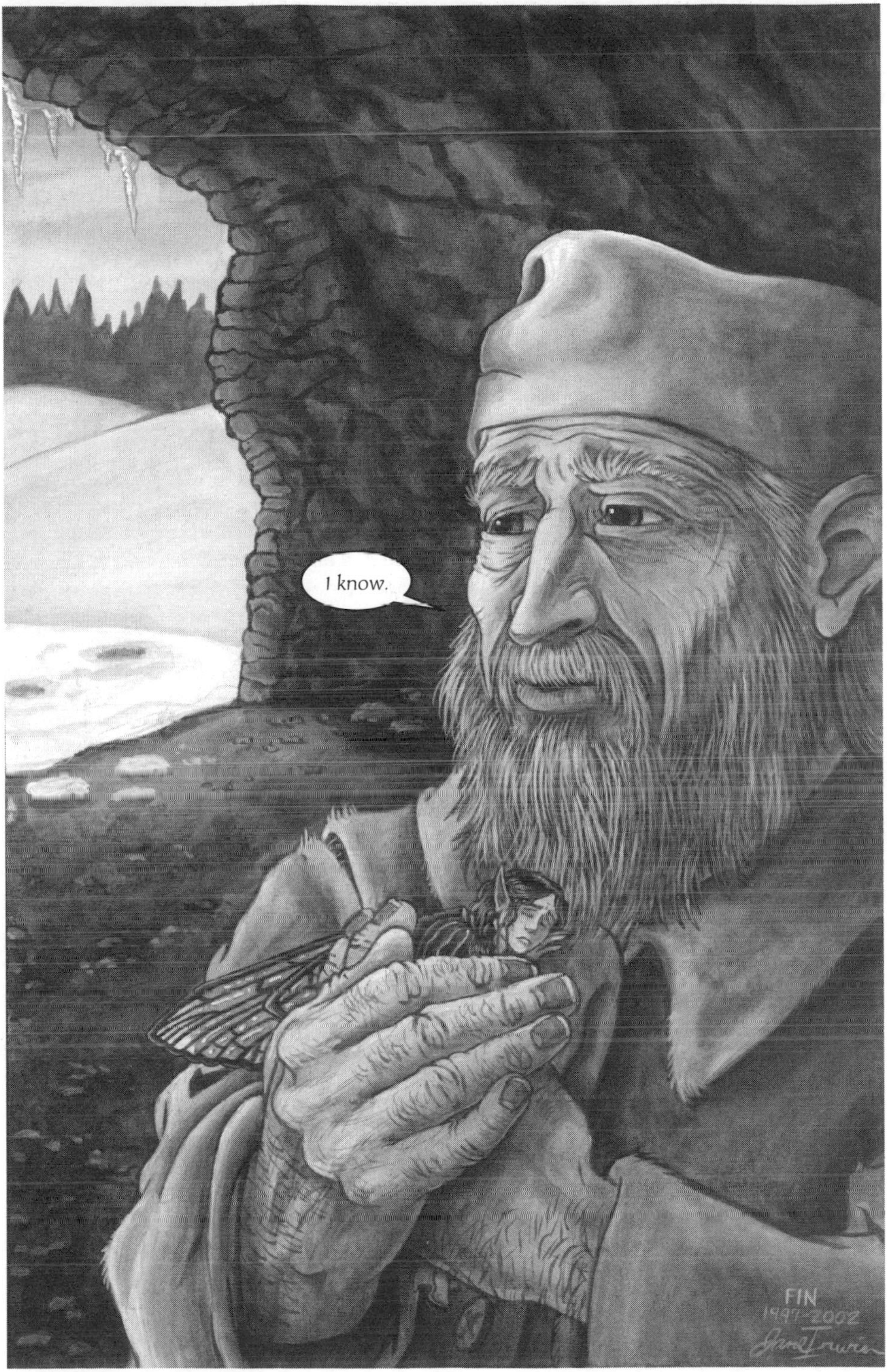
I know.
FIN
1997-2002

ENDNOTES

Page 12, Vögelein in flight: When Vögelein's flying, her wings go "clear" to indicate they're moving rapidly. It's a kind of visual shorthand for the hummingbird-like movements her wings go through to keep her aloft.

Page 15, Vögelein in front of the Church: Since Vögelein is a clockwork, she eventually runs out of power and needs to be wound again. As she winds down, her least critical functions shut down first, to conserve energy (though, in this scene, Vögelein would probably argue about her wings being less than critical...); first her wings stop, then her legs, then her arms, and finally, she shuts completely down until she is wound again.

Page 18, Why can't Vögelein wind herself? Ever try scratching right between your shoulderblades? Seriously, even if she could reach around her wings, she couldn't wind herself anyway. Think about when you wind a clock: for the second or so it takes you to rotate the key in the winding mechanism, the clock stops. It'd be like operating on your own heart while it was beating.

The next question that everyone asks is "If Heinrich were such a genius, why didn't he just make another machine that would wind her?" Here's an analogy: Let's say you were in a horrible car accident and wound up a quadriplegic but still had all your mental facilities. If someone told you that you could have a robot in your home to impersonally shovel food into your mouth, would you take it? Or would you rather have a caring human being on the other end of the spoon?

I talked to my friend Russ about this. He's an Occupational Therapist and has actually tried these machines, so he can tell his patients what he thinks of them. He said he'd use one if it could help him be more independent, but he woudn't like it much. I, on the other hand, have spent a long time helping take care of an eldery relative who needed help to eat, and the thoughts of her (or me, for that matter) needing to use a machine like that are darn near unbearable.

Vögelein "grew up" with Heinrich's kind hand at her back, and saw it as just something that needs to be done every day, like eating or sleeping. While she's grown much more fiercely independent with the passage of time, she's still holding on to her "humanity" with a fairly tenuous grasp -- to draw attention to the fact that she's a machine by the daily presence of another machine to "service" her would only make matters worse. Sure, Heinrich could have made a winding machine for Vögelein, but she was repulsed at the thought of it. Others might want their independence at any cost, but Vögelein prefers a touch of humanity in her life.

Page 29, Why does the rain make Vögelein miserable? Around the time when Heinrich was working as an apprentice (c. 1630), scientists were dabbling with static electricity in earnest. Heinrich designed Vögelein's wings with panels of mica and frames coated in gold leaf to help conduct the "kleinblitzen", as he called them. As Vögelein's wings fan the air, they work up quite a charge. She prefers dresses made of silk for the same reason.

Heinrich was an amazing watchmaker, but even he couldn't make clockwork small enough to move Vögelein's fingers precisely, so he made her fingers from tiny hinged tubes, coated them in gold leaf, and relied on static electricity to move them. Since she was meant to be a dancing automaton, she didn't have to pick things up or do fine movements with her hands, but Heinrich thought it would be nice to have her fingers individually jointed so they would move more naturally.

When it turned out that Vögelein was more than just a beautiful masterpiece, she was able to control her fingers on her own -- but the static electricity still has quite an effect on her mood. On days when there's a lot of moisture in the air, it's harder to conduct electricity, and Vögelein feels mopey, sluggish and sad. Dry days make her feel hyperactive and excited -- not unlike having too many cups of coffee.

Page 30, "Guthrie's Garbage": Go listen to "Alice's Restaurant".

Page 31, A bath of spirits: Heinrich is pouring her a bath of hot alcohol. It won't hurt her clockworks the way water or oil would, and as it evaporates, it will take some of the moisture with it. In this same era, riflemen in the field knew to pour boiling alcohol down the barrels of their muskets to prevent them from rusting, and Heinrich is using the same logic here.

Page 33, "From dawn the first day until dusk the next": In the mid 17th century, when Heinrich was crafting Vögelein, typical watches had only one hand – an hour hand, because the average pocketwatch was only accurate to about 15 minutes per day. If you were lucky, a watch could stay wound for twenty-four hours; though the technology was improving rapidly, that was about the limit. The fact that Vögelein can go for thirty-six hours without winding down is yet another testament to Heinrich's brilliance as a watchmaker.

When they lived together, Heinrich insisted that she be wound every day, preferably twenty-four hours or less from the last time

she was wound. Letting a watch wind all the way down is not particularly good for it, not to mention the fact that Heinrich had no idea what might happen to Vögelein if she *did* wind completely down, and didn't want to find out the hard way.

Vögelein has two mainsprings, (one for her head, arms and wings; the second for her legs). both of which are driven by the same fusee, so that both of them can be wound with the same key.

Considering that many 17th century watchmakers still used boar's bristles in their watches to help regulate the movement of the balance wheel, saying that Heinrich was a man ahead of his time is a bit of an understatement. While he was crafting Vögelein, most other clockmakers were still trying to figure out the finer points of pendulums, and the average "pocketwatch" was about the size of a coffee saucer.

Page 40, "What manner of manitou... are you?" "Manitou" is a Native American word meaning "little mystery" and translates roughly to "Fairy". The Duskie isn't from America, originally, so he uses the word for his kind that he thinks Vögelein will understand -- he assumes she's a native.

Page 42, top panel: Before any of you horologists start jumping on me, I know this gear is drawn incorrectly. Very early on in their studies, watchmakers and clockmakers realized that gear teeth couldn't be exactly square, or they wouldn't mesh right. Instead, they have to slope downward, like rows of tiny flattopped mountains.

The square teeth indicate not only that the gear must be very very old, but that the storyteller was ignorant of this fact when she painted this panel.

Fír: The Irish gaelic word for "men". Depending where you go in Ireland, it's pronounced "Far", "Fir" or "Feer". For our purposes, it's pronounced "Feer". You may recognize it from the term "Fír Bolg" or "Men of the Bolg", whom the Tuatha de Dannan defeated in the Second Battle of Moytura.

Tuatha de Dannan or "Children of Danu" were a race that ruled ancient Ireland for a time. They are sometimes referred to as Faerie-folk, other times as gods and goddesses of Ireland. I strongly recommend reading *Gods and Fighting Men* by Lady Gregory for a good primer on Irish Mythology.

Tír na nÓg: Translated as "Land of the Young", this is the place where the rest of the Tuatha de Dannan have retreated, according to the Duskie. Depending on which version of the mythology you're reading, this place is sometimes also known as Avalon, the Island of Apples.

Page 43, "Daghda's Bones!" The Daghda, or "Good God" is the patron deity of the Celtic pantheon, the Gaelic Zeus. Daghda was a fierce warrior, but preferred to win his battles through astounding feats of eating and drinking, challenging opponents that he could eat entire pits of porridge -- and won.

Page 54, Sidhe: In Irish gaelic, his word means "Hill". After losing enough battles to the humans that were slowly taking over their homeland, the Tuatha de Dannan moved beneath the hollow hills, which thereafter became their namesakes, hence banshee means "Woman of the Hill".

Page 70, "Fish Oil": Whale oil, but back then, people thought whales were fishes. Vögelein knows better, but still refers to it as "fish oil" because that's what Heinrich called it.

Page 88, "Was mich nicht . . ." It took me three hours of crawling around in the U of M Grad Library stacks to find that quote in its original German.

Page 97, Music: The music the Duskie is hearing is Franz Schubert's 1815 setting of the Goethe poem "Wanderers Nachtleid," the same poem that served as the frontspiece of chapter one. Also remember: there's iron in magnetic tape.

Page 101, Heinrich's machine: That's a wheel-cutting engine.

This clever machine allowed watchmakers to make perfect gears back in a day when everything had to be fashioned by hand. It's set up like a hand-powered record player, with the record being a plate inscribed with circles of different diameters. Each circle is marked with precise, equidistant "stops", like little divots, around the perimeter -- a wider circle would have more stops, a smaller circle, fewer.

When you wanted to cut a new watch gear, you'd figure out how many teeth the gear needed, then select the circle with the same number of stops. You'd place the "arm" of the "record player" into the first stop on the groove of the proper circle. Then you'd fasten the blank (the uncut gear) into the little vise at the top of the machine (the bit that looks like a wing-nut) so that it lay parallel with the lower plate.

A turn of the lower hand crank would rotate both the metal plate and the blank, like the record and spindle on a turntable, until the arm found the next stop. Then you'd turn the upper crank, which drove a vertical cutting wheel that carefully ground out the first space between the teeth on the gear. Another turn of the lower crank would advance the plate and blank to the precise spot where the next space would be cut, and so on, all the way round the gear. The bigger the circle, the more teeth on the gear.

Sound tedious? Now you know why watches cost so much in those days.

Historically speaking, the earliest known wheel cutting engines date to about 1675, which puts Heinrich about fifteen years ahead of his time. In those days, scientists made a lot of parallel discoveries (and a reclusive genius like Heinrich would not have made his findings public) so it's not inconceivable that he could have created his own wheel cutter to make his work easier.

What's that thing on Heinrich's head? Heinrich, like most people, is losing his vision in his old age. He fashioned this contraption to help him see the tiny tools of his trade.

If they seem a little weird and experimental, that's because they were. Bear in mind that this scene takes place sometime around 1673, when Antony van Leeuwenhoek, the Dutch scientist largely credited with the invention of the modern microscope, was just learning to grind lenses. Dozens of other scientists, including Robert Hooke in England, were experimenting with compound lenses, but microscopes as we know them would not be readily available for another thirty to fifty years.

Aren't Heinrich's clothes a little . . . ragged for a watchmaker? Yes. If anyone's paying attention, they're also about fifty years out of style. Heinrich was a bit of a curmudgeon, and never saw the logic of spending money on things as frivolous as clothes when he could be pouring it into his master work, Vögelein. The fashions of the time -- huge ruffed collars, lace sleeves, and the overpowering style of the Sun King, Louis XIV -- were revolting to him, and impractical in the shop.

Most of what you'll see Heinrich wearing throughout the series are his father's old fineries -- they had been saved for good use and were still in fine shape, so Heinrich wore them for everyday clothes.

Page 117: Sidhe Vögelein is a *sidhe*, but she

isn't a *sidhe*. She has become a *sidhe* (Doorway) -- but was not born a true *sidhe* (Faerie) like the Duskie.

When Heinrich was crafting Vögelein, he was wishing so hard and working with such genius and genuine love that something on the other side took notice. When he wound Vögelein for the first time, a little bit of Faerie slipped across -- and hasn't left yet. That bit is roughly equivalent to a human soul, and allows Vögelein to have emotions, memories and facial expressions, despite her metal form. As it crossed over, it created a tiny bridge between this world and Faerie.

Bodies of all kinds have their limitations, and when a body begins to fail, the soul's tenuous grip on the body fails with it. When Vögelein winds down, she essentially dies, and her bit of Faerie drifts away, losing its connection to her body. If she is wound up again quickly enough, it may be called back to her, but not without a price -- the longer she remains unwound, the more memories she loses.

As long as that part of Faerie stays within her, that tiny link to the realms beyond will remain intact. That link, and not Heinrich's mastery, is what keeps her body more or less immortal. No matter how well a watch is made, after three hundred years of daily use its gears would be worn to nubs. The part of Faerie within Vögelein allows her to continue living without internal repairs, only needing to be wound each day to stay alive.

But isn't Vögelein German? I thought Faerie was Irish or British. Faerie is not limited to one culture. Rather, it is like a crowd beholding an angel; each person sees her own culture's holy one.

I thought Vögelein had parts made of steel. Don't Faeries hate Iron? Yes, on both counts. Perhaps it's only Faerie bodies that are harmed by Iron; perhaps the ties that bind Vögelein to Faerie are strong enough to overcome that ancient poison; perhaps that's why she must still be wound every day rather than becoming truly immortal. Who knows? That's why they call it magic.

Page 123, Wings: Faerie that live in the water often have webbed toes and fingers. Faerie that live in the woods often have hair and skin the color of the forest. How would Faerie look after they lived through the Industrial Revolution, choking down coal smoke and filthy water for hundreds of years?

Midhìr, in addition to the influence of his environment, is also subject to the collective consciousness of the humans that surround him. Our beliefs and stories have changed the myth of the Faerie from the tall, graceful kings that ruled the land before our arrival to tiny, fluttering mischief-makers -- and as our Faerie tales change, so do the Faerie themselves.

Page 140, Alexi's song:
Thanks to Donna Barr, I finally have a full translation for this old German Folksong:

In May, in May
The little birds are singing,
The fresh young sprouts are pushing up
   out of the green heath
They dance, they hop
before my darling's door.
There is dancing in the evening...

Page 142, Heidelberg: In 1689, King Louis XIV laid waste to Heidelberg over a claim to the Palatinate. Karl Ludwig, the Elector of the Palatinate, of which Heidelberg was a part at that time, had married his daughter Liselotte to Philip of Orleans (the brother to King Louis XIV), to forge an uneasy pact between the two nations. Karl Ludwig passed away, and when his successor died with no heir, Philip and Louis made a claim to the throne of the Palatinate through Liselotte. French troops began marching in October of

1688, and laid waste to most of the Palatinate, burning and pillaging as they marched on Heidelberg. A coalition of other countries was formed to hold Louis' expansionist forces in check, and the incident became known as the War of the Grand Alliance, or War of the League of Augsburg.

Page 143, Huguenots: The Edict of Nantes, originally passed in 1598 by French king Henri IV, granted the Huguenots (French Protestants) equal rights with Catholics. When Louis XIV revoked the Edict in 1685, thousands of Huguenots were murdered at the hands of their countrymen. Thousands more fled in a mass exodus, most going to Great Britain and Germany.

Alexi wasn't joking about Louis XIV hating Roma. This quote is taken from the Patrin website, a site containing excellent historic and current information on the Roma: "1682: Louis XIV reiterates his previous policy: [Roma are given] punishment for being "Bohemian". Men are sentenced to the galleys for life on the first offence. Women's heads are shaved and children are sent to the poor house. For a second offense, women are branded and banished." Such punishment, just for being a Rom in France. Please visit the Patrin website at www.patrin.com. It is an indispensable resource.

Page 149, "Lungo drom": This is a Romanichal term meaning "long road".

─────────────────

Notes on Ezrael: Ezrael is based upon a very real person. His name is Ezell, and he's a very important part of the community I lived in for over 9 years.

Ezell is one of the most wonderful people you'll ever hope to meet. He's an elderly black man, always dressed in a stocking cap cocked at a rumpled, sagging angle and pushing a black plastic wheelbarrow full of tools, collected trash and mulch. He's always, always smiling. Everyone that passes gets a cheerfully shouted "Howyadoin?!" or "A-men!" He's sweet, gentle and always glad to see you, no matter who you are. He's also what my grandmother would call 'a bit touched'. But that's okay -- because his city, and its care and maintenance, have become his life -- that's what he cares for, and he does a darn good job of it.

Ezell's a constant, never changing. His good nature and disarming smile are irrisitable in a place where a lot of people either ignore what goes on around them or participate in its destruction. He embodies the good parts of the city where I lived, reminds us that there are still people who care about how the streets around here look. I'd hate to think how bad the downtown blocks would get if he ever quit.

When I designed the character of Ezrael, I originally intended to base him directly on Ezell, but the character grew and put different demands on his role, so I decided to change his name and his looks a bit, to distance him from the real person.

I went to rename him, enlisting the help of a thick book of Angel names that a friend of mine loaned to me. Out of curiosity, I flipped to the "E" pages. There, staring back at me, was the name "Ezrael". That particular angel has a lot of responsibilities, but they vary depending on who you ask.

Directly translated from the Hebrew, it means "The Help of God." I've seen reference to him in Muslim lore as one of the angels who has found Allah, along with Michael and Gabriel. The Apocalypse of Peter, one of the Apocryphal books of the Bible found in caves in Cairo and Ethiopia, states Ezrael is the angel of wrath, and it was he that took the lost souls "and cast them into a place of darkness, even the hell of men..." Another reference I've read (and

can't remember) listed him as the savior of lost souls right before the end of the Apocalypse.

In any event, Ezrael the Angel was pretty important, and so, that became the character's name. The names are close, but not (strangely enough) related -- and besides, it's always a good idea to put The Help of God on the side of your protagonist.

Notes on Alexi: When I sat down to write this book, I knew I wanted to include a character that was a Gypsy. I had some vague idea of Gypsy culture, but I also knew how badly they'd been stereotyped throughout history -- so I bought a bunch of books, especially those by Dr. Ian Hancock, and started reading. I was immediately taken aback by the depth and breadth of Romani culture and history -- and by my own unwitting prejudice and ignorance.

There is no one type of "Gypsy", as they have spread themselves out over the world and have been assimilated to varying degrees by whatever local culture surrounds them. As a general rule they call themselves Roma, but that may differ from one family to the next.

The Roma have suffered indignities throughout history on parallel and scale with the Jews and Native Americans. As late as 1850 they were being bought and sold in Eastern Europe as slaves; there were times in the 17th century when they were hunted in Austrian forests like rats, with a bounty paid for each Romani head brought in. At one time or another, leaders of nearly every country in Europe issued orders to shoot or hang Roma on sight -- lighter punishments included whipping and scarifying by branding or removal of ears or noses. A second offender -- someone who was seen bearing one of these scars -- could be hanged immediately, without trial or recourse.

Almost as bad as their treatment in the past is the treatment leveled at the Roma today. The Romani people still suffer under prejudice, sometimes being denied even the most basic human rights of shelter and citizenship, even if they no longer practice a nomadic lifestyle, simply because they are of Romani blood. In lesser prejudices, we think nothing of saying "I've been Gypped", or "We'll sell you to the Gypsies if you don't behave." These statements are racial slurs, and most don't even realize it. What would public reaction be to statements like those if you replaced "Gypsy" with "Jew"?

Today, scholars like Dr. Ian Hancock are working hard to destroy the stereotype surrounding Romani culture, and to return the dignity and poise that this proud people deserves. Many of his articles, including his definitive book, *The Pariah Syndrome*, are available online in their entirety at www.patrin.com. Please have a read through some of them -- they're fascinating, sobering, and necessary reading for anyone who wants to learn more about the Roma. Another excellent book, recommended on the Patrin site, is *The Gypsies* by Angus Fraser.

As I did more writing about the character of Alexi, I knew I wanted him to be a loner -- moving from one society, one city to another, trying his best to just get by, but never quite fitting in anywhere. Though many Roma were "tinkers," coppersmiths, goldwashers, horsetrainers or entertainers, I chose to make Alexi a trader and a networker; someone who knew the value of everything and could trade for anything. On Heinrich's payroll, he could move freely and quickly, getting out of town before trouble could find him.

My goal was to never paint Alexi as a thief or scoundrel, but rather to break that mold and show the struggles he would have gone through to simply make a living -- just trying to get from town to town in one piece would have been a difficult task all by itself.

PRONUNCIATION GUIDE

Vögelein: VEU-gul-ein, but the German "V" is softer than the hard, American "V", so it comes out more like PFEU-gul-ine. When you say it fast, it sounds like Pfeu-Geline. I won't be offended, though, if you say "Vogue-el-ine". She's an immigrant, after all, and that's how the Americanized version of her name would be pronounced.

Her name means "Little Bird" in German; Vögel means "bird" and -ein is a diminutive.

Midhìr: Pronounced ME-eer, or MY-tir, depending on who you ask. A fairly authoritative source, Knud Mariboe's *The Encyclopedia of the Celts*, lists it as "mi'yâr", and that's how I choose to say his name. His epithet in many stories is "Midhir the Proud", and his name is also commonly spelled "Midir" and "Mider".

Tír na nÓg: TCHEER na noh. It's an Irish gaelic term meaning "The Land of the Young".

Sidhe: SHEE. An Irish gaelic word meaning "Hill", it can also be used when referring to a member of the Fair Folk.

Tuatha de Dannan: Again, Irish gaelic pronunciations sometimes vary from dialect to dialect. Most will agree on either TOOTHA day DANnan or TOO-ah-tha day DANnan. This term means "Children of Danu", and refers to the legendary race who once inhabited Ireland, thought to be the offspring of the Goddess of the moon.

Daghda : DAHG-da. The chief god in Irish Mythology, god of earth and fertility.

Fír: The Irish gaelic word for "men", pronounced "Far", "Fir" or "Feer". In this story, I pronounce it "Feer".

Ezrael: EZZ-ray-ell. Someone more familiar with Hebrew might pronounce it Ez-rah-EL.

PINUP GALLERY

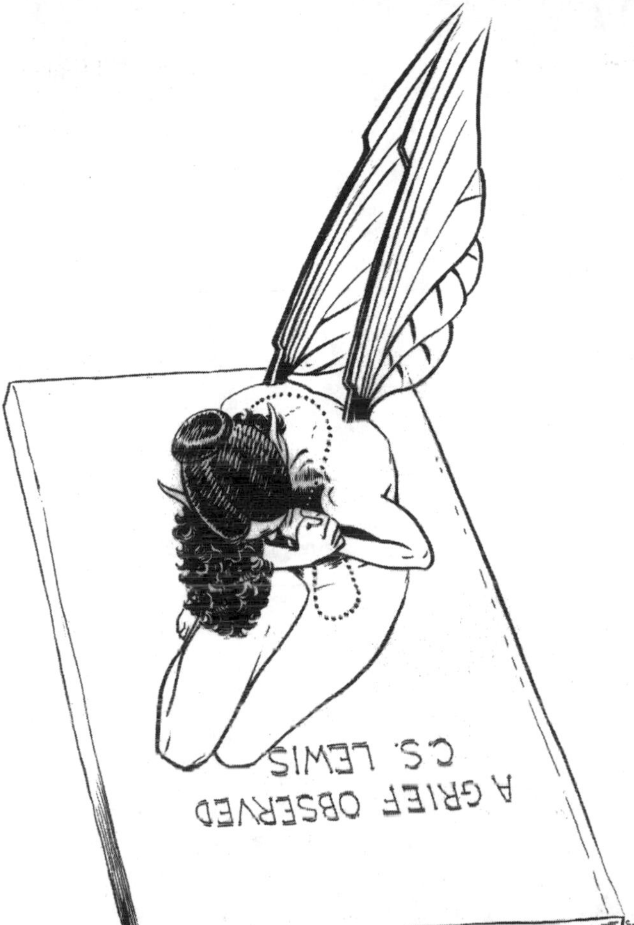
A GRIEF OBSERVED
C.S. LEWIS

Carla Speed McNeil is the creator, writer and illustrator of ***Finder***, a comic series that has been nominated for numerous Eisner Awards. She is currently working with accomplished writer Greg Rucka on a three-issue story arc of ***Queen and Country***, published by Oni Press. You can read more about ***Finder*** at Carla's website, www.lightspeedpress.com, and about ***Queen and Country*** at www.onipress.com.

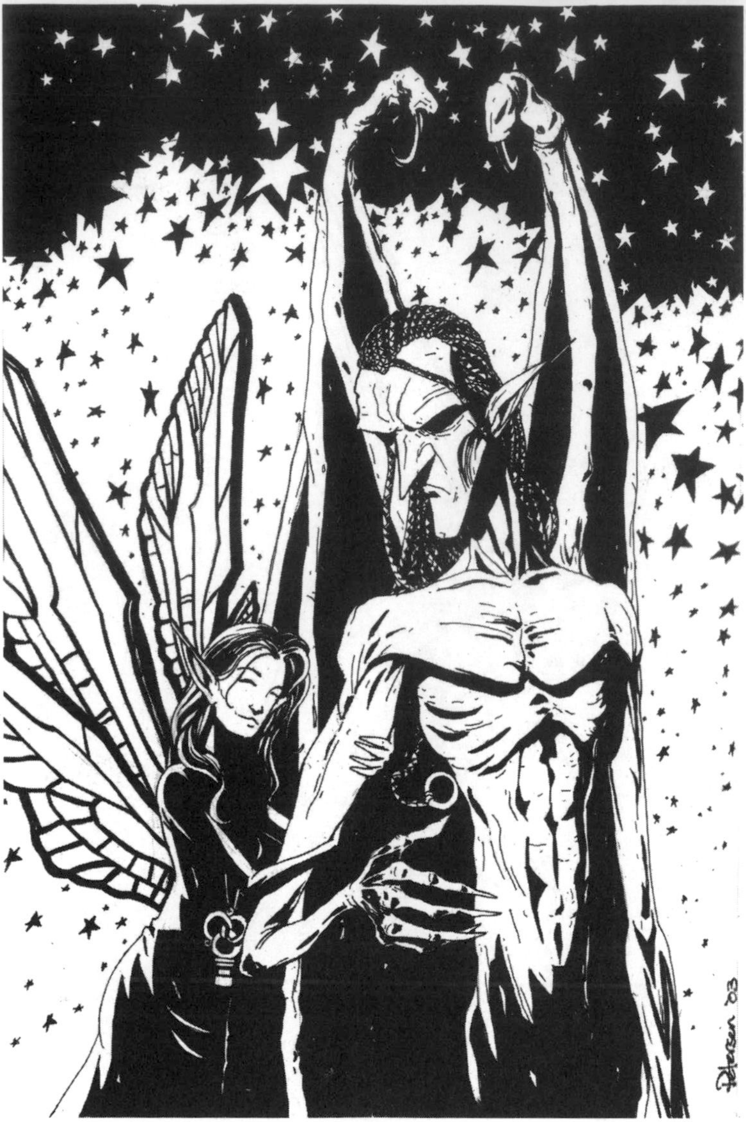
Petersen '03

David E. Petersen was born on July 4th of 1977. His artistic career soon followed. A steady diet of 80's cartoons, comic books from all ages, and tree climbing fed his imagination and is what still inspires his work today.

You can visit David's website at www.davidpetersen.net.

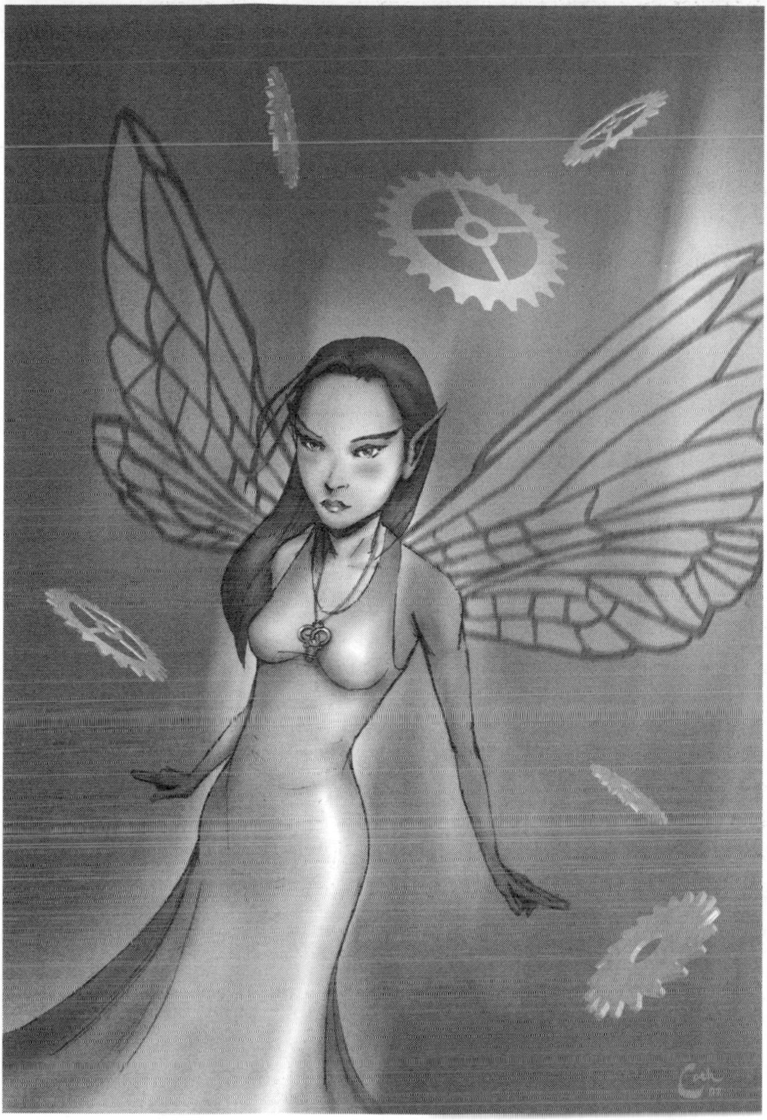

Matt Cash is a freelance artist living in Ypsilanti, Michigan. He is a graduate of Eastern Michigan University where he studied art and literature. He is the creator of ***Jen Electric***, an online comic available from his website www.crowboy.com.

Matt likes to ink with a sable brush and is influenced by the works of David Mack, Jamie Hernandez, Frank Miller, Chris Bachalo, and Mike Allred. Besides drawing, Matt enjoys writing, 3D animation, digital painting, and web design.

He is part of the independent film production company Evil Genius Entertainment. Their first feature, director John Vincent's horror film ***Witchunter*** is available from their website, www.evilgeniusentertainment.com.

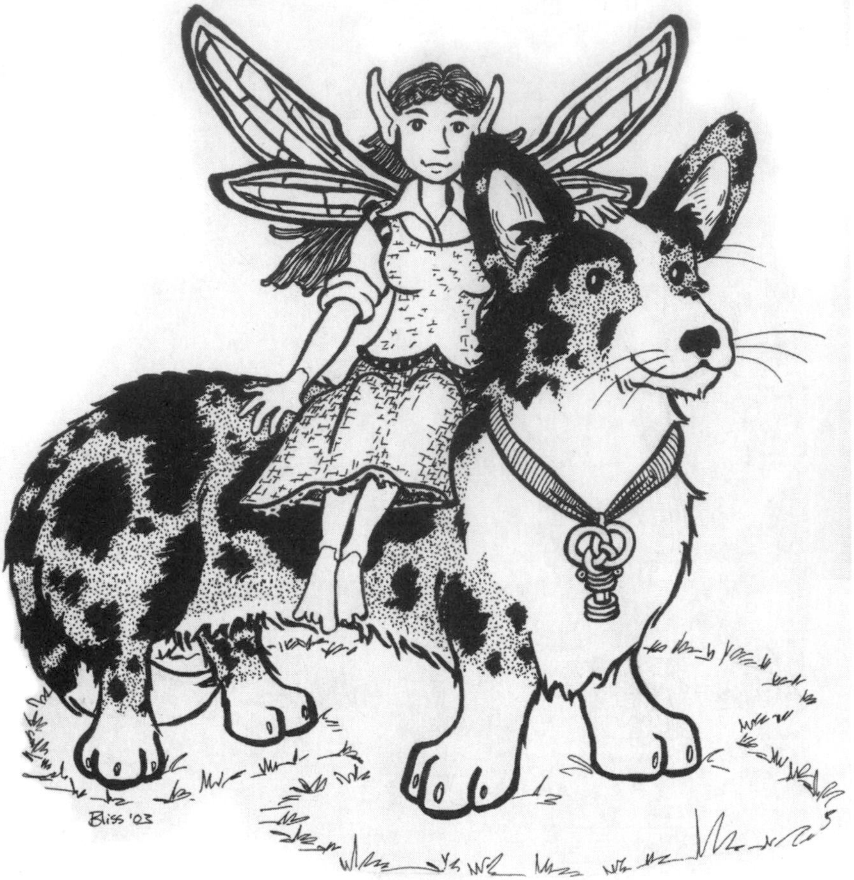
BLISS '03

Pam Bliss has been making comics of all sizes in Northwest Indiana since 1989. Her cartoon stories range from kid's adventures, to tales of time travel, to celebrations of the absurdity of everyday life, and, of course, dog stories. She is also the author of the popular essay series ***Hopelessly Lost but Making Good Time***, which combines philosophy with comics how-to. Her current project is something new for her: a graphic novel of spooky romance called ***Fox Acre***. Send an SASE to PO Box 304,Valparaiso, IN 46384 for a catalog and sample minicomic, or visit www.paradisevalleycomics.com on the web.

Tom Beland was working at a Napa Valley newspaper as a cartoonist and staff artist -- until he visited Disneyworld on assignment and met his future wife, Lily Garcia, at a bus stop. He took the story of their first meeting and subsequent courtship and turned it into the Eisner Award-nominated *True Story, Swear To God.*

Currently, Tom lives with Lily in her native San Juan, Puerto Rico and persues his dream of being a full-time comic artist. *True Story, Swear To God* is available through AiT/Planet Lar Publishing at <u>www.ait-planetlar.com</u> and -- very soon -- through Tom's own website at <u>www.tombeland.com.</u>

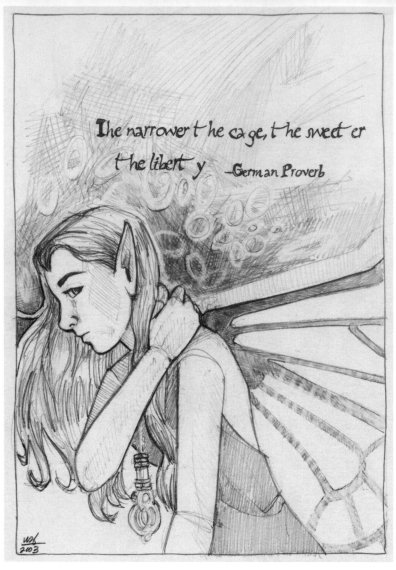

The narrower the cage, the sweeter the liberty —German Proverb

Wendi Strang-Frost is currently drawing *Johnny Public: OUT OF THE WILDERNESS*, (www.johnny-public.com), a minicomic serial story that is on its sixth of eight chapters. She's been experimenting with sequential art for over ten years and is probably best known for ElfQuest's *Wavedancers*. She lives in rural Michigan in a turn-of-the century house with her writer-husband, (auther of *Johnny Public*), and three neurotic cats. She can't really imagine doing anything else.

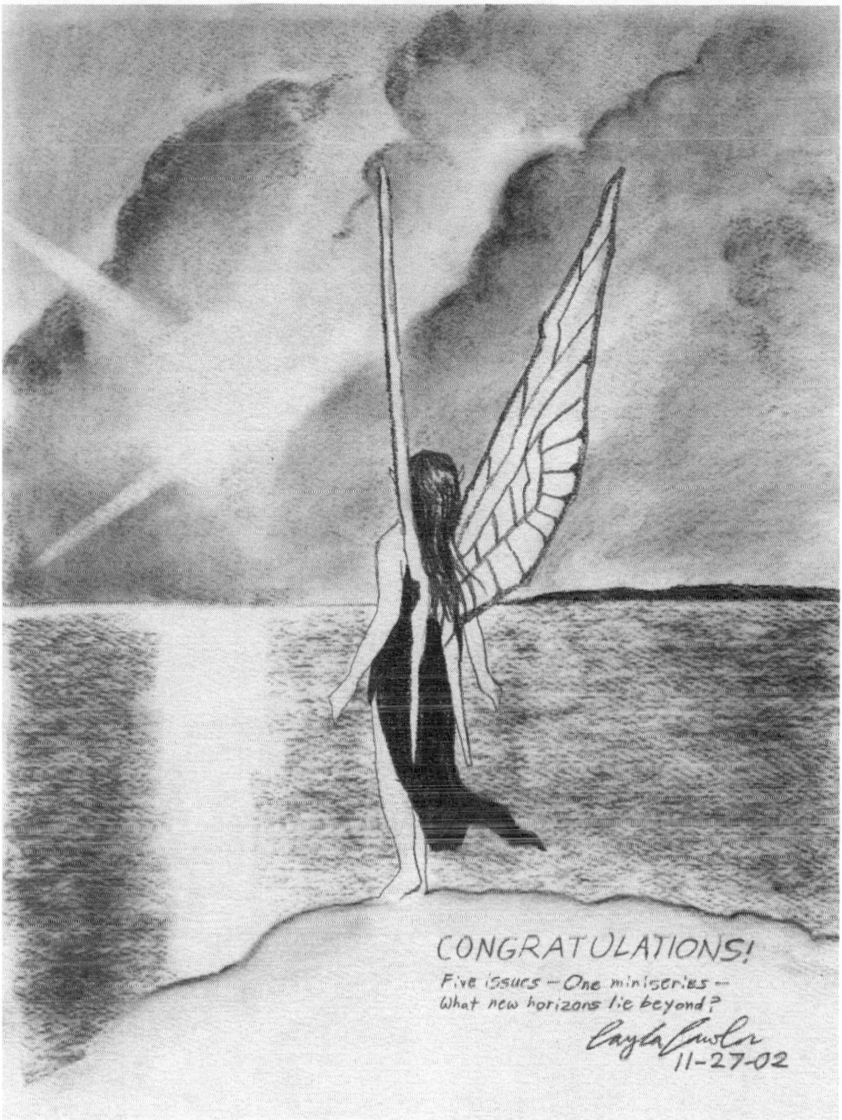
CONGRATULATIONS!
Five issues – One miniseries –
What new horizons lie beyond?
11-27-02

As an Alaskan comics fan, **Layla Lawlor** searched in vain for comics with an Arctic setting. So she set out to create her own. In the far-north fantasy world of ***Raven's Children***, trickster gods fly through the skies on ravens' wings, and tribes of dogsled-riding warriors roam the snowy mountains of their homeland. With an empire invading from the south and war looming on the horizon, the fate of the northern people lies with three individuals -- an outcast, a dishonored southern nobleman, and a tribal chieftain. . . each of them more interested in their own vendettas than in being heroes. Please visit Layla's website at www.ravenschildren.com.

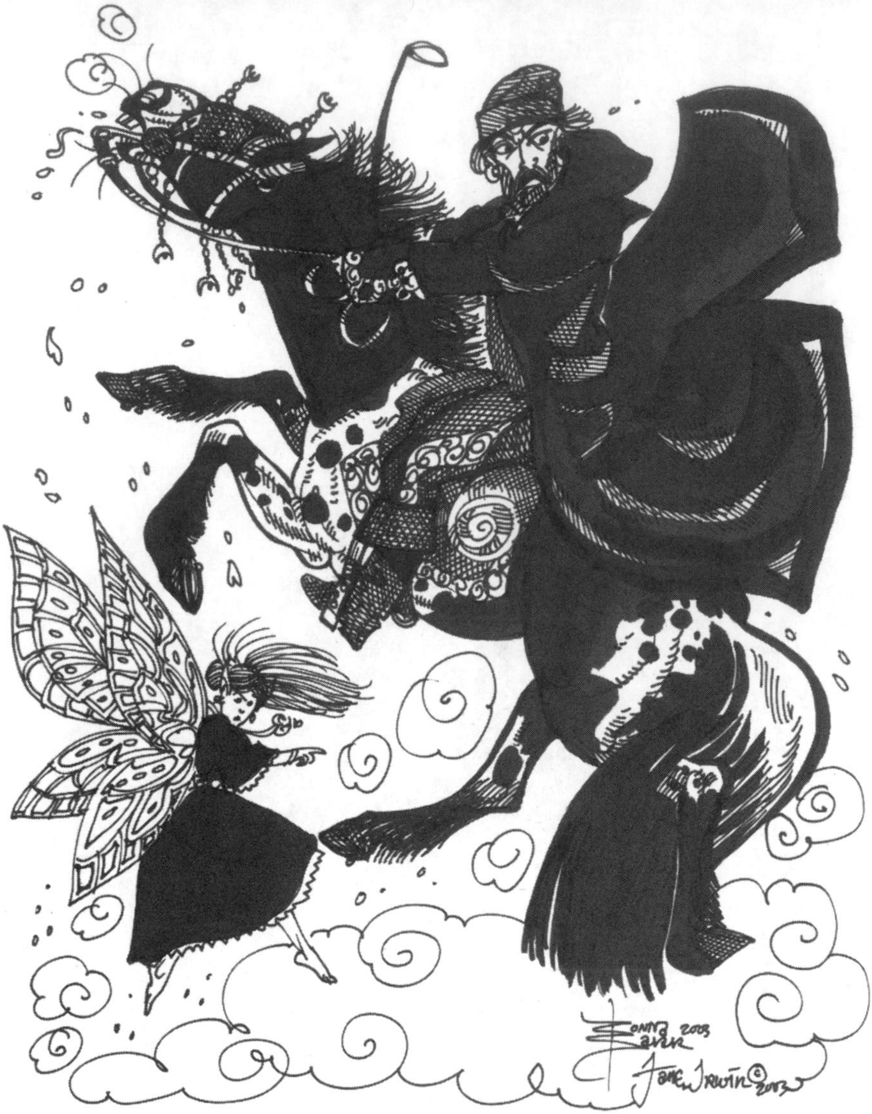

Donna Barr began drawing in 1954, writing in 1963, was published in 1986, and began publishing in 1996. She has a loyal, eager world-wide audience for her critically-acclaimed and much-awarded books and series, including ***The Desert Peach***, ***STINZ***, ***Hader and The Colonel***, and ***Bosom Enemies***.

Her website is <u>www.stinz.com</u>. Donna's webcomics are available at <u>www.moderntales.com</u> and <u>www.girlamatic.com</u>. ***The Grandmothers' Hive*** (1982) is her first full-color print-on-demand book, available through her website.

BATTLE FAERIE

VÖGELEIN

"While the essence of this book has always been very caring and human, I noticed that Jane never shied away from letting it be known that Vögelein is a machine, a construct made of metal and "powered" by a mainspring and static electricity. This was what prompted me to take my pinup in this direction: an homage to *Battle Angel Alita*, one of my all-time favorite manga series. Alita is a machine like Vögelein, yet it is her need of love and human emotion that make her interesting to me, same as Vögelein. I've done my best to "Manga-sizer" this vision of "V", seeing her through the lens of Japanese comic styles."

Paul Sizer is a graphic designer by day, and the creator, writer and artist of the comic book *Little White Mouse* all the rest of the time. You can visit Paul's website at www.littlewhitemouse.com

MEET THE MODELS

When I was in college, I had a lot of great friends who were into theatre and role-playing games, and most of us were hams in one way or another. Being an artist, I always had a camera at the ready, and over time accumulated five shoeboxes full of photos of my friends dressed in silly clothes and taking goofy action poses -- Renaissance dresses, chainmail, cloaks, Halloween costumes, or just mugging for the camera.

When the time came round for me to actually start painting Vögelein, I called up my friends one at a time and asked them to run through scenes from the script for me so I could use them for photo reference. As they were all excellent sports, they all agreed (have I mentioned what great friends they are?) and the pictures below became the book you're holding now.

First off, here's Jeff Berndt. Together, we came up with the idea for Vögelein, and Jeff helped write the initial script and big chunks of the first three issues.

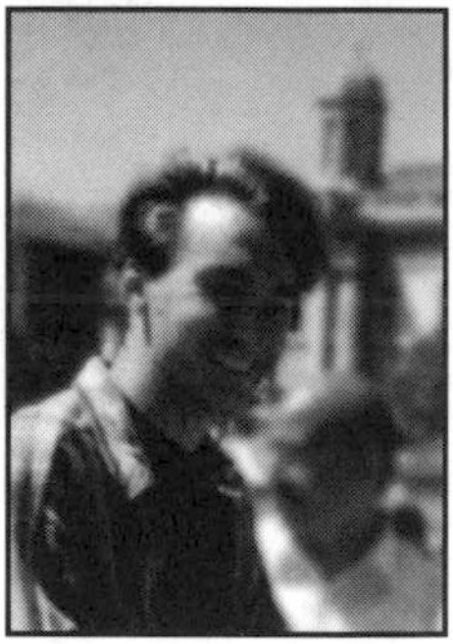

Jeff likes community theatre, Revolutionary War reenactments, playing and listening to Irish music and spending time with his wife, Melissa, and their beautiful new son, Alex.

I really couldn't have done this project without Jeff's help, and now his and Melissa's continuing support.

Plus, I get to be Alex's honorary Auntie.

Next, meet Jason Winkler. Jason's another old college buddy of mine -- he and Jeff used to live around the corner from each other (literally) in an apartment building.

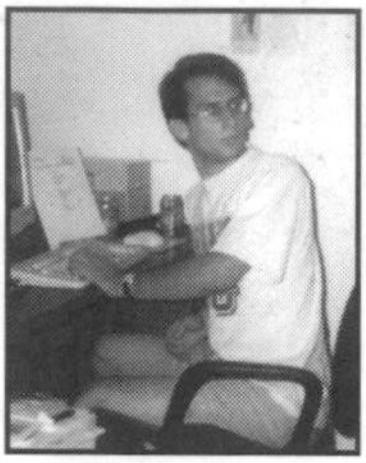

Jason was one of my most intuitive models I handed him a slip of paper with some stick figures drawn on it and said "Do this."

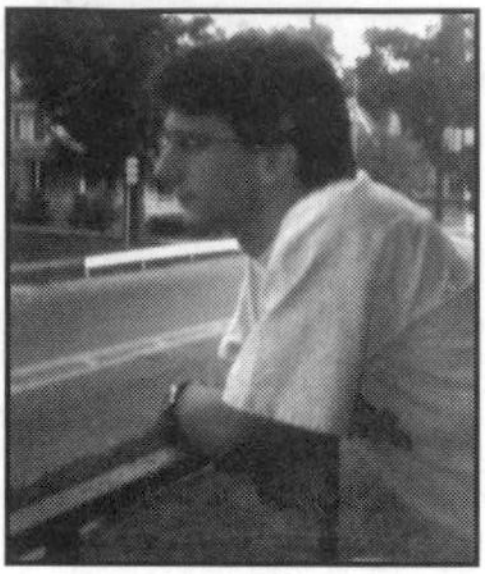

He did -- and acted out the sequences with more grace and interpretation than I could have ever directed him to.

Now Jason's settled down in Syracuse, New York, with his lovely and talented wife, Dr. Amanda Eubanks-Winkler. Amanda also provided invaluable editing assistance on the book.

This is Russ Ellis. In addition to being one of the kindest and most open-hearted people I know, Russ has also fashioned a name for himself in our group of friends as the man who can fix anything.

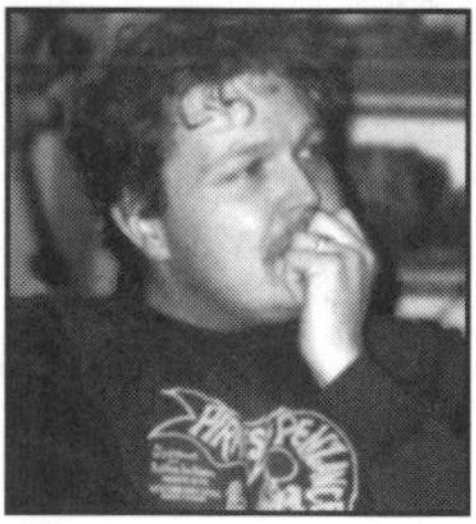

His feats include building a generator that used moldy potatoes for fuel and could run a VCR, and constructing a working telephone from spare wires and a Pepsi can.

Is it any wonder he became the model for Heinrich?

Next we have Craig, the model for Alexi. Seen here wearing the infamous "Sta-oopid hat", Craig was a wonderful sport and put up with several separate photoshoots to get the poses I needed.

Craig's good humor and near-endless optimism made him an ideal choice for Alexi, not to mention a wonderful friend throughout the years.

Here we have "Scary" Mike Zawacki, who was a body model for the character of

Ezrael and other occasional characters. Mike is an artist in his own right, working in collage, photography, and makes some of the most powerful found-object sculpture I've ever seen, including the "Hand Of Turing," a powerful talisman for computer geeks.

In addition to his art, Mike's very involved in moviemaking, and had a major role in bringing the new indie film *WitchHunter* to the screen. He's also working on at least three scripts that he plans to pursue on his own. You can find out more about Scary's film work at www.evilgeniusentertainment.com.

Allow me to introduce you to Dagny Hanner. When these pictures were taken, sometime in 1998, Dagny had just joined up with our group of friends. Her new boyfriend, Scary Mike said, "Hey, Jane's doing this comic book and she needs to take some body model photos of me. Ya wanna come?" To her credit, Dagny, who hardly knew me

at the time, threw on her unitard and spent an afternoon good-naturedly jumping around my yard. She became the new body model for Vögelein -- replacing me because she's way more graceful than I am.

Proving that art does imitate life, the

picture below inspired the scene you read earlier in the book. It was such a lovely photo that I had to paint it, even though it hadn't been in the script originally. Dagny just walked past the window, and the shot literally came into focus.

And finally - this is Sol Foster, who has been my "warehousing agent" for the entire run of the comic. Though he doesn't actually appear in the book, he gets a big thank you for letting me fill up his spare

bedroom with boxes and boxes of back issues.

Acknowledgements

Work on *Vögelein* began in 1997, and in the years between now and then, I've received an unbelievable amount of help from many, many people. Grateful acknowledgements to:

Jeff Berndt, for endless cups of tea and buckets of Chinese food, three-legged poetry races, pictures of downtown Heidlerberg, Jedi Mind Tricks, hitchhiking, coattailing and Duck Turning. Couldn't have done it without you, Jeff. Don't forget that.

Mark "M'Oak" Oakley, who gave *Vögelein* an enormous push-start by printing the entire first issue in the back of *Thieves and Kings* #36. You can get copies of this superb comic at www.iboxpublishing.com. I strongly encourage you to read this book!

Steve Benedict, whose capable brush aided many a tedious background panel in issues three and four.

All my Editors and Proofreaders: "Scary" Mike Zawacki, Dagny Hanner, Jason Winkler and Dr. Amanda Eubanks-Winkler, Adele Smaill, Matt Messana, Eric Braun, Lindsay Braun (no relation), Dan and Karen Sugalski, Michael and Kathy Neufeld-Dunn, Alexis Palmer, David MacMillan, Rollande Krandall, Emily Peterson, Jennifer Schupska, William Cavnar, Gary Bratzel, and my second-printing German coach, Jürgen Pünter.

David MacMillan, who provided indispensible information and trivia on all matters Horological, down to the smallest minutae. Without David's expert help I would have said "Vögelein's just magic. I don't know how she works!" a lot more often.

Dan Sugalski, who keeps the website up and kicking, and provides me with email gadgetry even before I know I need it.

The Singing Lemur Foundation, for their inestimable help in the publication of the first issue of the comic book.

The scores of fans who preordered both the first issue and the trade paperback, sight unseen. Thanks for taking a risk, and helping my dream come true.

The staff and neighbors over at www.SequentialTart.com, who helped get *Vögelein* on the map with reviews, interviews and articles. There are too many Tartsvilleians to mention, but I would be remiss if I did not thank Barb Lien-Cooper, Tim O'Shea, Rich Watson, Jen Contino and Lisa Jonté.

My comic book mentors: Layla Lawlor, Pam Bliss, Carla Speed McNeil, Jim Ottaviani and Paul Sizer, who offered help and advice when I most needed it.

Matthew "Virus" Messana, for moral support, poetry donations, sushi, chai, chess, plane tickets, mama tiger hugs, Project Raskolnikov, sunshine-to-ass ratio management, and full-tilt boothmonkey services.

And last but definitely not least:
This new version of *Vögelein* wouldn't look anywhere near as good as it does without the tireless help and support of Paul Sizer, who logged many late nights with me getting the manuscript ready to go to press. Thanks, Paul.